P9-DXI-849

Kris Mohandie, Ph.D.

School Violence Threat Management

A PRACTICAL GUIDE FOR EDUCATORS, LAW ENFORCEMENT, AND MENTAL HEALTH PROFESSIONALS

*A Practical Guide Series
By Specialized Training Services*

L.C.C.C. LIBRARY

DISCARD

SPECIALIZED
Training Services

San Diego, California

Published by Specialized Training Services
(An imprint of Specialized Training Services, Inc.)
9606 Tierra Grande, Suite 105
San Diego, CA 92126

Copyright © 2000 by Specialized Training Services
Updated March, 2002. 2nd printing.

All Rights Reserved

Printed in the United States of America

No part of this book may be reproduced, stored in a retrieval system, or transmitted, in any form or by any means, either electronic, mechanical, photocopying, microfilming, recording, or otherwise, without written permission from the publisher.

Editing of this book was done by Reid Meloy and Drew Leavens.

Library of Congress Cataloging-in-Publication Data

Mohandie, Kris
    School Violence Threat Management / Kris Mohandie.
      p. 230
    Includes bibliographical references (p. 223-227)
    ISBN 0-9703189-1-X

                00-109816
                CIP

For my mother and father, humble servants of humanity...
teachers who have dedicated their lives to making a
difference in the lives of others.

The Specialized Training Services Practical Guide Series:

School Violence Threat Management
    Kris Mohandie, Ph.D.

Violence Risk and Threat Assessment
    J. Reid Meloy, Ph.D.

Children Who Witness Homicide and Other Violent Crimes
    Tascha Boychuk-Spears, Ph.D., R.N.

For information on these and other books, tapes, and videos offered by
Specialized Training Services, contact us at:
Specialized Training Services, Inc.
9606 Tierra Grande, Suite 105
San Diego, CA 92126
(858) 695-1313, (858) 695-6599 (fax)
or visit our website at: www.specializedtraining.com

TABLE OF CONTENTS

Disclaimer vi

Preface vii

Acknowledgments ix

Special Dedication...x

Section One: SCHOOL VIOLENCE OVERVIEW
Chapter One: Introduction to School Violence...........................p. 1

Section Two: SCHOOL VIOLENCE THREAT ASSESSMENT
Chapter Two: Threat Assessment: Warning Signs ....p. 29

Chapter Three: Threat Assessment: Risk and Stability Factors ......p. 53

Chapter Four: Threat Assessment: Applying the Concepts ....p. 81

Section Three: SCHOOL VIOLENCE INTERVENTION
Chapter Five: General Intervention Considerations ....p. 111

Chapter Six: High Risk Case Intervention Considerations ....p. 145

Chapter Seven: Moderate/Lower Risk Case Intervention
 Considerations ....p. 167

Section Four: SCHOOL VIOLENCE AFTERMATH
Chapter Eight: Aftermath Crisis Management ....p. 197

References ....p. 223

Recommended Resources ....p. 229

Disclaimer

A short disclaimer is in order. The information in this book is not intended as a rigid set of directives, but rather as an array of ideas, guidelines, considerations, and suggestions. Each and every situation is different, and all require unique solutions. This book is not meant to be a substitute for competent and appropriate multidisciplinary consultation.

PREFACE

This book is the culmination of the work of many in the field of threat assessment, modified and adapted to the issue and problem of managing and responding to school violence risk. It was written with the explicit goal of offering an approach to managing certain types of cases and situations, particularly those in which we may have the opportunity to intervene and interrupt the progression of behavior into extreme violence. It offers a conceptual model that addresses the continuum of potential risk levels, and response options commensurate with the apparent risk, so that we are not under or overreacting.

The past is our best teacher. Whether systematic research into past events of violence and factors that relate to increased violence potential, or anecdotal case study accounts, there are lessons to be learned. The results of both types of endeavors will be presented throughout the text.

Well-known cases that fall within public purview will be presented without any fictionalizing of identities or locations. Other school cases presented throughout the text will have names, locations, and other identifying details modified to protect privacy. As readers may already be aware, confidentiality is an important issue.

A Word About Prevention

Any violence prevention efforts that target the known risk factors for violence, and school violence in particular, would be helpful. There are many good programs that are being piloted and implemented throughout the United States and abroad. Some address societal issues at large, such as the prevalence of violence in the media. Other programs focus upon the local community, like creating after-school programs; some address family issues, such as the impact of violence and abuse that occurs in families; while others address individual coping skills, helping at-risk individuals with psychotherapy.

Some of these programs have been subjected to research and program evaluation studies to determine if they really work. Many of them do work, while for other programs, the results are equivocal. The core ingredient in many of these programs is to facilitate improved coping and healthy relationships. For at-risk individuals, simply having one healthy trusting relationship, with somebody the person can turn to when the chips are down, hope is lost, and options are perceived as extinguished, can make all the difference in the world. These programs create multiple opportunities for these healthy attachments to grow. The more quality programs, the more opportunities for such bonding. In addition, just because one program in program evaluation studies is shown across the grouped data to be of questionable utility, there may be individual cases where that benefit has been realized. We seek to create parachutes for those who are falling.

There are several recommendations for prevention that are related to the threat assessment theme of this book. Schools need to have clear anti-violence policies–so-called zero tolerance polices around a host of related issues–and clearly define acceptable and unacceptable behavior. These types of policies communicate norm expectations to students, staff members, and parents alike, and begin the process of setting the tone that violence has no place in our schools, and that threats will be dealt with swiftly and effectively.

Schools should assess their security, highlighting areas of vulnerability for improvement. Local or school police and other security professionals conduct these kinds of assessments. It is up to the district to act upon their recommendations, many times establishing priorities for improvement. At a minimum, it is imperative to control access to the physical premises, and have some way of recognizing those who belong versus those who do not. At a minimum, the school needs some way of locking down the premises during high-risk situations.

Programs that teach alternatives to violence for solving social problems are also important. Many of our social institutions, especially some families, are failing to adequately teach our next generations to cope with life, and all of its disappointments and frustrations. We may decry the need to compensate for these deficiencies by offering classes beyond "reading, writing, and arithmetic." However, if schools do not teach values and skills, this critical task may not get accomplished. "Life 101" might be an appropriate and important addition to many curriculums.

It is imperative to find ways that all stakeholders might become involved in taking responsibility for making a difference. Educators, parents, students, mental health professionals, law enforcement, and the community at large all contribute to redefining our violent culture and world. Leaving any major group or entity out of the solution generating process will lessen our overall effectiveness.

Acknowledgments

I am grateful to the many people who helped to make this book a reality. Drew Leavens at Specialized Training Services supported this project and provided encouragement and criticism where needed. Dr. Reid Meloy spent many tedious hours rendering this manuscript readable and conceptually sound. Bill Modzeleski, Director of the U.S. Department of Education's Safe and Drug Free Schools Program provided detailed, thought-provoking feedback on important issues, and guided me to accurate reference material. Greg Boles suggested the need to develop school-based threat assessment approaches. Rick Massa provided expertise in the security realm. I am grateful to my attorneys and friends, Doug Stuart and Ron Takehara, for their generous legal advice. Dr. Phil Trompetter kept me informed of current cases. Dan Isaacs, Dr. Michael Pines, Marleen Wong, and Bill Ybarra, troops in the trenches dealing with the real world, helped me better understand the practical needs of educators and mental health professionals managing cases. Manuscript reviewers Dr. Megan Scannell, Dr. Angela Donahue, Dr. Charles Ewing, and Chief Wesley Mitchell were immensely helpful and encouraging in their comments. A special thanks goes to Susan Isaacs, Shawn Reaves, and Don Blue from the Kentucky Center for School Safety for their innovative ideas and support. Gene Wilkins provided information about the Bath, Michigan tragedy. Thanks to the many investigators and detectives who provided information about the cases included throughout the book. Chris Hatcher, during all the years of mentoring, generously provided me with more than I can ever repay, and left before I could thank him. And I am grateful to my wife, for her tireless patience and support with this endeavor, not to mention her wonderful charts and tables.

Special Dedication

This book is dedicated to the families and friends of both victims and perpetrators of school violence. They have been profoundly afflicted. In many cases, they are left to ponder the question of "why." We owe it to you to make a difference. Your pain and loss should not be without meaning, nor should it be endured alone.

CHAPTER ONE

Introduction to School Violence

Myth One: It won't happen here.

On a sunny May morning, as students were finishing up their exams on the day before school was to be recessed for the summer, a massive explosion ripped through the campus of Bath Consolidated School (student population 250) in Bath, Michigan, a small town ten miles northeast of Lansing. Thirty-eight children, two teachers, a retired farmer, the town postmaster, and the superintendent were killed by the explosions. Fifty-eight people, many of whom were children, were injured. The date was May 18th, 1927. This event was the world's most lethal act of school violence, and the third largest mass murder in the history of the United States, surpassed only by the tragic terrorist events of September 11, 2001 and the Oklahoma City Alfred P. Murrah Federal Building bombing in 1995.

After the initial explosion, as parents and residents rushed to the site of the blast, Andrew Kehoe drove his car back into the schoolyard. He motioned the school superintendent over to his car and then fired his gun into the back seat setting off more dynamite, killing the superintendent and himself instantly. A malfunction kept an additional 500 pounds of dynamite from detonating. The next day Kehoe's wife was found dead at their farm, apparently killed the morning of the blast. Kehoe's house and six outbuildings were burned, having been set afire by explosions rigged to go off around the time of the school blast. Forty-five people, including Kehoe and his wife, were dead. Kehoe had painted a fence on his farm that same day with the following message: "Criminals are made, not born."

Fifty-five-year-old Andrew Kehoe was a local farmer who served as treasurer of the local school board. He had spent the better part of the spring rigging the school basement with wiring and dynamite. School administrators, well aware of Kehoe's penny-pinching ways, believed that he was doing odd jobs to save the school the expense of having to hire an electrician. Kehoe, angry and bitter, was outraged about new taxes that were levied to pay for the five-year-old school, and was fearful that he would lose his farm to foreclosure. He sought to punish the citizens of Bath (Ellsworth, 1927).

Today, this town still remembers 1927, as this event has become a permanent aspect of this small community's identity. A new school stands nearby, a project that was an integral part of the healing process more than seventy years ago. Students today still mourn and grieve those they never knew. In 1927, the members of the Bath community had no reason to believe that an act of such devastating violence could occur in their community. In the 21st century, quite unfortunately, the reality is that school violence can potentially occur on any campus anywhere in the world.

This horrific case demonstrates that school violence is nothing new. However, it is painful to acknowledge that the second most devastating act of mass murder in the United States took place at a school in a small, seemingly safe community. Violence devastates communities. Our challenge for the future is to develop strategies to prevent violence to the 53 million students, three million teachers, and other staff members who attend and work for the 109,000 public and private elementary, middle, high school, and other schools in the United States (U.S. Department of Education, 1999). We are also obligated to share these lessons with other countries that are beginning to experience their own school violence concerns. This book is about understanding the violence that occurs in our public and private elementary, middle, and high schools, and introducing approaches to help make our schools safer, particularly from extreme lethal violence. Whether one's relationship to schools is administrator, educator, law enforcement or campus security, mental health, legal counsel, or other, it is essential to understand school violence and how it may be prevented.

At the same time, a thorough understanding of school violence threat management strategies will help to prevent hysteria and overreaction. A recent case exemplifies this important point. On March 15, 2000, four six-year-old kindergartners from Wilson School in Sayreville, New Jersey were playing "cops and robbers." They were pretending their fingers were guns and said they wanted to shoot one another. Classmates reported them, and the district superintendent reiterated the district's commitment to zero-tolerance around weapons and threats, suspending each of these children for three days. However, the district agreed to review the policy due to complaints that they had overreacted. The assistant superintendent later acknowledged that officials were overly cautious in the wake of other school shootings ("Kindergartners suspended," 2000). The shooting two weeks earlier of a six-year-old girl by a six-year-old boy in a Flint, Michigan elementary school (described later in this chapter) likely played a role in sensitizing students and staff to this behavior. Perhaps there was a need for intervention with these young boys around violence oriented play, but most would agree their behavior was not unusual. Realistic awareness and thoughtfulness, not paranoia and overreaction, are the goals in responding to these situations.

This book is divided into several parts. Section One outlines the grim realities of the problem of school violence by presenting an overview of violence and violence-related behaviors on our school campuses, describing the different types of perpetrators, discussing research relevant to this problem, identifying contributing conditions, and reviewing the psychodynamics of youthful offenders. Relevant summaries of extreme school violence events from the past are presented throughout this text to illustrate key learning points and educate readers about case dynamics. Section Two begins the journey into threat assessment and intervention by outlining the process, describing the warning signs, risk factors, stability factors, and precipitants associated with school violence, and discussing dynamic ways of arriving at categorical descriptions of risk. In Section Three, the process of intervention is presented, and specific legal, criminal, mental health, and social support system strategies for threat management are discussed in detail. Finally, in Section Four, aftermath crisis management issues are reviewed.

Grim Realities

Myth Two: The school violence problem is all about homicide.

Fatal Violence
School violence encompasses a broad range of violent behaviors

3

that may be acted out on school campuses and during school related functions held off campus. At the most extreme end of the continuum are the multiple victim homicide events, *mass murders*, which have recently captured our attention. Evidence indicates that school-associated *mass murder* events have increased from two in the 1992-93 school year to six in 1997-98, or from an average of one per year to five per year when comparing the three-year interval of August 1995 thru June 1998, to the previous three-year period of August 1992 thru July 1995 (U.S. Department of Education, 1999; Kaufman, Chen, Choy et al., 1999). However, despite this increase in mass murders, since the 1992-93 school year there has been a steady decrease in overall school-associated violent deaths. Between July 1992 and October 1999, there have been at least 257 school-associated violent deaths (Stephens, 1999). These numbers are possibly an underestimate, given reporting difficulties and the relative newness of efforts to accurately record such homicides. Deaths by year are noted in Table 1.

TABLE 1

School Associated Deaths by Year
and School Year 1992 through 1999

Calendar Year	Total Deaths	School Year	Total Deaths
1992	17	1992-93	54
1993	62	1993-94	51
1994	35	1994-95	20
1995	28	1995-96	35
1996	26	1996-97	25
1997	34	1997-1998	43
1998	31	1998-1999	26

The Centers for Disease Control and Prevention (CDC) reports that less than 1% of all homicides among school-aged children (5-19 years of age) occur on or around school grounds or on the way to and from school (U.S. Department of Education, 1999). These data indicate that tragic and extreme multiple homicide events are rare but increasing, while single homicide events are decreasing. School-associated homicides are an extremely rare event, and most youth homicide takes place outside of schools. In fact, it is estimated that there exists a less than one in a million chance of suffering a school-associated violent death. These events violate expectations regarding the safety of our children, making them more newsworthy and contributing to inflated perceptions of risk. However, any homicides at our schools are unacceptable. The fact that this is a less prevalent arena for homicide among our youth does not preclude us from developing more effective prevention and early intervention efforts.

Weapons used in these homicides are primarily firearms (75%), of which most are easily concealed handguns. Fifteen percent of the weapons used are piercing instruments such as knives, and the "other" category accounts for the remainder of weapons that are lethally deployed. The "other" category includes weapons such as blunt instruments, and instruments of strangulation, not to mention bombs, arson, and poisons.

One study examined school violence victimology and found that 72 percent of the victims of school-associated homicides were students; the rest were teachers and other nonstudents. Eighty-three percent of the victims were male. Thirty percent took place within the school building, 35 percent outdoors on school property, and 35 percent off campus at a school-related function (Kachur et al., 1996).

Suicide

Suicide is another form of violent behavior that may be categorized as a school-associated violent death if it takes place in a school. A significant proportion of adult mass murder perpetrators will commit suicide at the end of their murderous rampage, and most will have considered suicide at some point prior to the event, as the logical culmination of their violent behavior (Hempel, Meloy, & Richards, 1999). A recent U.S. Secret Service study (Vossekuil, Reddy, Fein, Borum & Modzeleski, 2000) examined 37 school shootings involving 41 attackers who were current or former students. Prior to the incident, nearly 75 percent of these attackers threatened suicide, made suicidal gestures, or tried to kill themselves. Some people, quite mistakenly, fail to view suicide for what it is, an act of violence directed towards oneself. Experience dictates that consideration of harming one's self violently may also correlate with a lessening of inhibitions towards harming others first. Stated simply, the person has gotten "over the hump" in terms of the acceptability of violence directed towards a human being.

It is estimated that nearly 50 people, primarily students, have committed suicide at schools since 1992. Countless others have made attempts, and even more have communicated suicidal intentions and thoughts to their classmates while at school. Statistics regarding youth suicide indicate that in 1996, 2,119 youth aged 19 or younger committed suicide and for every completed suicide there are 10 times as many suicide attempts (Snyder & Sickmund, 1999). In fact, the suicide rate for teenagers has tripled over the last twenty years. Suicide is the third leading cause of death for persons aged 15 to 24 years, and the fourth leading cause of death for children aged 10 to 14 years (Tomes, 1999). Schools, for some children and adult staff members, can become a forum for suicidal acting out behavior.

Nonfatal Victimization

Assaults are another manifestation of school-associated violence. There were an estimated 2.7 million episodes of crime on school campuses in 1997. One million of these crimes were nonfatal violent crimes (serious violent crime and simple assault). This same study (Kaufman et al., 1999) reported that students aged 12 through 18 were victims of approximately 202,000 serious violent crimes at school (rape, sexual assault, robbery, and aggravated assault) and a total of 800,000 assaults.

Fights

Nearly 15 percent of students polled in another survey reported that they had been in one or more physical fights on school property during the preceding 12 months (CDC, 1999). Males were more than two times more likely than females to have been in a fight on school property, and students in lower grades reported having been in more fights on school property than students in higher grades (for example 21 percent of ninth graders versus 10 percent of 12 graders).

Threats/Injury with Weapon

In 1993, 1995, and 1997, seven to eight percent of the high school students surveyed reported that they had been threatened or injured by someone with a weapon on school property during the previous 12 months (Kaufman et al., 1999). Weapons were defined as a gun, knife, or club. Females were less likely than males to have been so threatened or injured. Assaults and the threat of assault are quite common on our school campuses and represent the most frequent form of school-associated violence.

Other forms of violent behavior noted on campuses include

threats, intimidation, stalking, and bullying. Unfortunately, for many of these behaviors, there are only rough statistical approximations of their incidence on our school campuses. The National Center for Education Statistics (NCES) conducted a random survey of 1,234 principals from public schools throughout all 50 states. Overall, they learned that there are about 1000 crimes per 100,000 students and 50 serious violent crimes (murder, rape, assault with a deadly weapon, suicide) per 100,000 students yielding incidence rates of one percent and .05 percent respectively (NCES, 1998). Broken down by grade, elementary schools reported 13 serious violent crimes per 100,000, while middle schools had 93 per 100,000, and high schools 103 per 100,000. This pattern of greater frequency associated with higher grades is not surprising, and consistent with what one would intuitively expect. Size of school seemed to matter as well, with smaller sized schools (less than 500) reporting 61 serious violent crimes per 100,000, and larger sized schools (more than 1000) reporting 90 per 100,000. One would expect more violence in larger, urban schools.

Bullying

Bullying was defined in one study (Kaufman et al., 1999) as when a student frequently picks on others or makes other students do things such as give them money. "Bullying" as a term is deceptive since it minimizes, trivializes, and softens the impact of behavior that is often violent, threatening, or harassing. It contributes to a climate of fear and intimidation in schools, reducing perceptions of safety. Eight percent of all students in grades 6 through 12 reported that they had been victims of bullying at school during the 1992-93 school year. It is a phenomenon which apparently decreases in prevalence as grade in school increases, from a high of 13 percent in the sixth grade to a low of three percent in the 12th grade (Kaufman et al., 1999).

Nonfatal Teacher Victimization

As with fatal injuries, students are not the only victims of nonfatal assaults on our school campuses. Over the five-year period from 1993 to 1997, teachers were the victims of 657,000 violent crimes (rape or sexual assault, robbery, and aggravated and simple assault). During this same period, middle/junior high school teachers were more likely to be victims of violent crimes than senior high school teachers, who in turn were more likely to be victims than elementary school teachers. The rates were 60, versus 37, versus 18 crimes per 1,000 teachers, respectively (Kaufman et al.,1999).

7

During the 1993-94 school year, 12 percent of all elementary and secondary school teachers were threatened with injury by a student, and four percent were physically attacked by a student. According to Kaufman et al. (1999), this amounted to 341,000 teachers who were victims of threats, and 119,000 teachers who were victims of attacks by students during that school year.

Group Differences

The fact that there are significant gender differences in terms of victimology across fatal and nonfatal school situations prompts the question of "why." There is likely interaction between male socialization and gender role expectations leading to macho oriented problem-solving. Males are brought up to be competitive and aggressive in our society, and those with limited coping skills will dysfunctionally attempt to assert their need for dominance and power through aggression. Others have noted (Meloy, 2000) the role of biological differences contributing to male aggression.

It was noted that younger children were more likely to report having been a victim of a violent crime, to report that they were threatened or injured with a weapon on school property, to have been in a fight, and to report having been bullied. Why? Skills building and coping strategies become more developed with age and experience, enabling kids to more adeptly avoid these situations as they grow older. Older kids may also be less likely to report these events.

Statistics also reflect less lethal and nonlethal violence on the campuses of private schools (Kaufman et al., 1999). This is likely a function of a variety of factors including socioeconomic status, greater involvement of parents in the lives of their children, more value placed upon education and achievement, more resources, increased individual attention, lower student-teacher ratios, smaller schools, and less tolerance for misbehavior by these institutions allied with parents and guardians who support stricter boundaries. In addition, many of these private schools have a religious affiliation, attracting children from families who actively practice religion–mainstream spirituality being a deterrent to violence.

Violence is reported more frequently in urban than rural schools. These schools are larger, with greater anonymity, social disruption, and poverty. Smaller communities tend to have greater involvement and awareness about what is going on with its members, and exert substantial informal group and social control mechanisms to deter deviance.

Perceptions of Safety

Between 1989 and 1995, the percentage of students who felt unsafe while they were at school and while they were going to and from school increased from six to nine percent and four to seven percent, respectively. These perceptions of increased vulnerability translate into avoidance of one or more places by students, with an estimated 2.1 million students in 1995 changing their established routines to avoid becoming a victim of violence. There are schools where many students do not feel safe, and these perceptions result in barriers without walls within the school (Kaufman et al., 1999).

All of these statistics are likely to underestimate the true prevalence of violence in our elementary, middle, and high schools. Most episodes of sub-lethal violence go unreported, and only recently (1997, 1998, 1999) have some states established demands upon their educational institutions for the accounting of such behavior. There are many private educational institutions excluded from such reporting requirements because they do not depend upon public funding. Organizations may also withhold or minimize their reports because of negative consequences such as bad publicity, perceptions of safety, and fears about the impact upon staff careers.

Summary

School-associated violent deaths have declined in number, but multiple victim events have increased. Further, the occurrence of reported serious violent crime is actually a statistically rare event, an aberration, while less lethal forms of violence such as assaults without a deadly weapon and fighting are somewhat common. Student perceptions of safety at school have decreased, lowering attendance. While lethal violence is a statistical aberration, our institutions and social systems are obligated to develop prevention and intervention strategies. There are numerous examples of "close calls" interrupted, thanks to the astute observations and good judgement of those in positions of responsibility. Attending to the prevention of the "worst case scenario" reassures, interrupts those who were evolving towards extreme violence, and quite possibly derails the precipitating events that set those wheels in motion.

Types of Violence

*Myth Three: School violence perpetrators
are always disgruntled students.*

Who perpetrates these acts of violence: where does the violence come from? It comes from several sources, and no threat management program is adequate unless it addresses each potential threat source. *Type I* events of violence are perpetrated by someone with no legitimate relationship with the school. *Type II* acts of violence are perpetrated by someone who is a service recipient or customer of the school, a category which in addition to students, may also include parents or guardians of students and those who are currently or formerly in relationships with students. *Type III* episodes of violence are those which are perpetrated by someone who has an employment-related relationship with the school such as a current or former employee, or someone who is currently or formerly in a relationship with an employee of the institution.

Type I Events

Brenda Spencer, a 16-year-old girl, lived across the street from Cleveland Elementary school in San Diego, California. On Monday, January 29, 1979, she opened fire upon the elementary school, wounding eight children and a police officer, before killing the principal and custodian who were attempting to protect the children. A chronic drug abuser and poorly supervised by her father who had custody, she lived across the street from the school, and had told a friend two days earlier "I am going to do something big." Spencer had been caught burglarizing the school about one year prior, was sent to probationary diversion, and received counseling. Her counselor opined at the time that there were indicators of suicidality in Spencer. She had received a .22 rifle and several hundred rounds of ammunition as a gift from her father several days prior, and made her final decision to do the shooting the night before the event, as she was watching *Battlestar Gallactica* on television. As she was taken into custody after several hours of dialogue with police negotiators, she commented, "I don't like Mondays" (Lieutenant R. Sigwald, personal communication, December 28, 1999).

Another example of the *Type I* event is the case of Buford Furrow, who in the summer of 1999, stormed the Jewish Community Center in Los Angeles, California, shooting and wounding several

10

children and several adults, including the receptionist. Motivated by racial hatred, Furrow had traveled from Washington State to Los Angeles, to kill some Jews and send a message. He had cased at least two other locations, the Museum of Tolerance and the University of Judaism, before settling upon the Jewish Community Center because security was too stringent at the other locations. While making his escape, he shot and killed a Phillipino U.S. Postal worker. His statement to the police after he turned himself in was, "This is a wake-up call for America."

A third example of the *Type I* event is the case of 43-year-old Thomas Hamilton. An avid gun collector and disgraced scoutmaster, Hamilton was known as "Mr. Creepy" by the boys in Dunblane, Scotland, a village (population 7,300) 40 miles from Edinburg. Disliked by all his neighbors, Hamilton enjoyed filming young boys with their shirts off. His fixation with young boys eventually got him dropped by the Boy Scouts. Nearly twenty years later, he was still seething with anger over having been banned from the Boy Scouts. In the weeks before the massacre, he had been turned down as a volunteer at the Dunblane Primary School. A week before his deadly rampage Hamilton wrote a letter to the media and Queen Elizabeth II complaining about a campaign by the police and Dunblane teachers to ruin his reputation (Douglas & Olshaker, 1999).

On March 13, 1996, Hamilton walked to the Dunblane Primary School armed with four guns, and burst into the gymnasium where 29 children were attending class. He systematically killed 16 children, their teacher, and then shot himself. Another teacher and a dozen other students were wounded during the rampage. Five- and six-year old children were sitting in circles on the floor playing when Hamilton started firing. Hamilton had timed his assault to when he believed a major school assembly was to be held in the gymnasium. Fortunately, his timing was incorrect and there were far fewer children than he had anticipated.

Type I events are fairly rare on school campuses. However, they can be devastating, such as in the Brenda Spencer and Dunblane, Scotland case. In some of these cases there may be less possibility to "see it coming" and detect early warning signs, while in others, there may be threatening communications or a history of problems between the perpetrator and members of the school. Nearly every school has chronic complainers who live nearby, and various unstable community members that require monitoring to determine whether

11

their issue of grievance may escalate into something deadly. However, the best way to address these events, is to tighten the physical security of the premises thereby making the location unattractive to would-be perpetrators. This insures their detection and denies easy access for an episode of targeted or impulsive violence.

Type II Events

An obvious example of a *Type II* event is the April 20, 1999, Columbine High School shooting in Littleton, Colorado, in which Eric Harris and Dylan Klebold killed twelve students and a teacher before committing suicide. Obsessed with weapons, Hitler, the music of the German metal band *Rammstein*, and the video game *Doom*, for nearly a year they plotted their crime and communicated veiled and direct threats of their intentions towards others. Interventions were attempted, but failed to quiet their simmering resentment and desire for notoriety. This tragic event unleashed a level of school violence unseen in modern times, and stimulated a wave of copycat threat cases, close calls, and actual violence throughout the United States and abroad. Later, it would be discovered that they left five videotaped diaries chronicling their motivation, planning, and thought processes pertaining to this heinous crime, as well as sad and empty apologies for their grieving parents (Gibbs & Roche, 1999).

Another *Type II* event occurred May 1, 1992, in Yuba County, California at Lyndhurst High School. Twenty-one-year-old Eric Houston, a former student, shot and killed three students and his former high school civics teacher, and wounded ten others. After the murders, he initially took 86 students hostage before surrendering to police negotiators several hours later. During the negotiation process, one of Houston's friends called police saying he knew the identity of the gunman, because Houston had talked about his plans and fantasies beforehand. His friends never thought he would actually carry it out.

Houston had recently been laid off from his contractual employment at Hewlett Packard. They were converting all part-time and temporary contractual employees to full-time regular employees provided they met certain minimum requirements, specifically in Houston's case, a high school diploma. He blamed his employment failure upon his high school civics teacher whom he believed had prevented him from graduating high school, and sought revenge against an institution that he perceived favored others, such as athletes. Today, he is awaiting execution in San Quentin State Prison

(Sheriff V. Black, personal communication, October 26, 1999).

Not all *Type II* events involve students or former students. On November 23, 1998, in Orange County, California, Michael P. Generakos, a father who was angry over the special schooling for his disabled son, was shot to death by a police sniper after taking several school officials hostage at gunpoint and claiming to have explosive devices. He had recently lost custody of his children and was embroiled in court battles with his estranged wife and the school district over the care of his disabled child. Generakos told one of his hostages, "I came here today to get myself killed, because I don't have the guts to kill myself." Throughout hours of negotiation, he ranted and raved about the inadequate education that the school district was providing for his 16-year-old deaf son. At the end of the ordeal, he paraded a hostage at gunpoint in front of police, who shot him. During the months that had preceded this incident, Generakos had escalated his negative contacts with school board officials from multiple complaints and disrupting school board meetings to threats of harm (Reza & Willon, 1998).

Type II events may involve a student's current or former significant other who utilizes school property as the arena for violent acting out against the love object and/or themselves. On October 22, 1997, at John Glenn High School in Norwalk, California, 16-year-old Catherine Tran was shot and killed by her estranged boyfriend 21-year-old Robert Drang, who then committed suicide. ("Parents of slain student," 2000; Stephens, 1999). While Tran may have taken precautions to insure her safety outside of school, the campus provided a known location for Tran's whereabouts. The girl's parents filed a wrongful-death suit against the school alleging the campus was not properly secured, and the school agreed to a $125,000 settlement.

The Type II event is the most frequent type of lethal and non-lethal event that occurs at school, and since it most often involves students, offers significant opportunity to observe early warning signs of a developing problem. Carefully crafted interventions may therefore provide some interruption of an evolving violent thought process.

Type III Events

The Bath, Michigan mass murder, described in the introduction to this book, is a prime example of a *Type III* event. As treasurer of the local school board, Kehoe was affiliated with the school in an administrative capacity and acted out against children and school personnel before killing himself.

A *Type III* event may also involve someone currently or formerly in a relationship with a past or present employee. On February 12, 1998, 61-year-old Geraisimov Metaxas, described as the delusional husband of former substitute teacher Linda Metaxas, shot and killed 48-year-old teacher John Sacci on the campus of Hoboken High School in New Jersey and then committed suicide. Metaxas believed that Sacci, a 23-year veteran of the school district, had had an affair with his wife. In reality, no such affair had ever occurred (Stephens, 1999).

A more common manifestation of the *Type III* event is the so-called disgruntled current or former employee. For example, on February 7, 1994, superintendent James Adams was gunned down on school property by former district special education teacher Larry Ray Shelton in Fort Meyers, Florida (Stephens, 1999). These events, like most employee-related workplace violence events, typically evolve out of deep grudges, perceived poor treatment by administrators and/or coworkers, and adverse personnel actions.

Type III events are the second most frequent types of school-associated violence. As with *Type II* events, the participants usually have some history and are known to those within the school. These events provide opportunity for prevention and early intervention because warning signs of escalation may be observed or become known through various channels. Thoughtful intervention may interrupt would-be perpetrators from violent action plans.

Why Now

Proliferation of Firearms

Firearms are readily accessible within the homes of many citizens within the United States. The right to bear arms, a constitutional issue, has important implications. The United States has the highest rate of firearm deaths out of all of the 26 industrialized nations combined. In fact, U.S. children are 12 times more likely to die of a firearm related death than children of all those 26 nations combined (CDC, 1997). In California for example, firearm deaths are the number one cause of death for children aged 1 to 19. Weapon availability in the home has been identified as a strong risk factor for suicide and homicide (Kellerman et al., 1993; Kellerman et al., 1992). To make matters worse, these weapons are finding their way onto the campuses of our educational institutions. During the 1996-97 school year, 5,724 students were expelled for bringing a gun onto the school campus, and 3,930 students were expelled the following school year for the same reason (U.S. Department of Education, 1999). These statistics reflect only the students who are caught, and while there appears to be an overall trend towards a reduction in the numbers of students caught with a gun, the FBI reports that 100,000 students carry a gun to school each day (FBI, 1999). The FBI report is likely an overestimate, but most experts would agree that there are many more guns on school campuses than are detected (B. Moczeleski, personal communication, September 27, 2000; U.S. Department of Education, 1999).

In the heat of passion, the presence of a firearm can turn a fight into a killing, a fact observed by other violence researchers in other contexts (Wright & Davis, 1994). Seventy-five percent of the school-associated violent deaths are committed with guns, primarily handguns. Ready accessibility in the homes of at-risk individuals or their close affiliates is an important contributing factor to school-associated violence. In particular, access to weapons in conjunction with the idea to attack another person elevates risk (Vossekuil et al., 2000). Other countries that traditionally have had no problem in this arena have recently had episodes of firearms use during school violence. For example, on December 7, 1999, the Netherlands experienced their first school violence episode when a 17-year-old student wounded a teacher and three other students. He was upset over a relationship between his sister and another student and may have been avenging her honor. In the Netherlands, there is tight gun control, but weapons may still be accessed through the black market, adding another dimension to the weapon accessibility issue.

Any country or region with relaxed or tolerant views regarding firearm ownership will have an elevated risk for lethal interpersonal violence. In the worst case scenario described below, we see the tragic outcome of weapon availability and improper accessibility upon a recent school violence incident. There are more firearms than ever in certain cultures, particularly the United States, drastically elevating potential risk.

Case Example: Buell Elementary School, Michigan

On February 29, 2000, a six-year-old first grade boy killed a six-year-old classmate. A teacher was standing in the doorway when the boy retrieved the gun from where it was hidden in his pants, pointed it at the little girl and fired once, striking her in the neck. He then ran down the hall and dropped the gun into a trash bin. A records check indicated that the gun, a .32 caliber semiautomatic, had been stolen during the previous December and had recently been seen in the boy's home. During a search of the boy's home, investigators also found crack cocaine and another stolen firearm, which was a loaded 12-gauge shotgun.

The day before the violent act, the dead girl, Kayla, had allegedly scuffled with the boy, because he had spat on her desk. The victim was described as a kind, smiling girl who was "fearless" and the best reader in her class. In fact, he had attacked Kayla before, and the day before had tried to kiss her but she had rebuffed his advances. The boy told investigators that he had only been trying to get even with her by scaring her. He went home and searched for the gun, which he had seen his uncle's friend twirling around on his finger. The night before the shooting, the boy found the loaded weapon under a pile of blankets and took it.

That morning, he arrived at school with the semi-automatic handgun and a knife. The particular handgun, a .32 caliber Davis, is marketed as the "original pocket pistol" because of its small compact size that makes it easy to conceal. Unfortunately, its small size means that it can also be operated by a small hand, in this case the hand of a six-year-old boy. Another child reported the knife to a teacher, and the teacher took the knife away but the boy managed to hold on to the gun. As classes were changing, he pointed the gun at other classmates, and then at Kayla as she walked up the stairs to the second floor. He called out, "I don't like you" and as she turned around and said, "So," he fired one round of three in the gun, striking her. As she lay on the ground, she said, "I'm dying," then her eyes closed and she spoke no more.

Immediately after the shooting, the principal came on the intercom and imposed a lockdown of all classrooms. The boy was identified, taken to the principal's office, and then the police station.

The boy's 29-year-old father, jailed since February for a parole violation on a burglary charge, told police authorities that his son had been suspended three times, once for stabbing another student with a pencil and twice for fighting. His father also stated that he had asked his son why he fought other kids, to which he responded, "Because I hate them." He added that his son spent his time watching violent movies and TV. Other witnesses reported that he was made to stay after school nearly every day for saying the "F" word, flipping people off, pinching and hitting. Reportedly, the boy was scheduled to begin anger management counseling the following week (Naughton & Thomas, 2000; Rosenblatt, 2000).

This six-year-old child, the perpetrator, was living with his eight-year-old brother and an uncle in conditions described as a "drug-infested flophouse," where police had found the stolen guns and a cache of drugs. He did not even have a bed to sleep on, and his mother was living elsewhere for the last week after the family was evicted from a home nearby. More than 80 percent of the children in this working-class neighborhood qualify for a reduced-cost school lunch program, an area hard hit by layoffs from the local General Motors plants.

Buell has security guards but no metal detectors. School administrators canceled classes for one day, but provided counselors to defuse grief and fear among students and parents.

This case generated a considerable amount of media attention, and the event was decried by President Clinton, "The suspect was six-years-old, how did that child get a gun? Why could the child fire the gun? If we had the technology today to put in these child safety locks, why don't we do it?" As with the aftermath of most school shootings, a heated debate and public discussion ensued among leaders, special interest groups, and politicians about gun control, criminal prosecution of juvenile offenders, and sanctions against adults allowing a child to have access to a weapon (Braun & Cart, 2000; Cart, 2000).

In the aftermath of this event, the uncle and mother of this boy were both arrested and charged with crimes. The mother was charged with neglect for allowing her son to be in a destructive environment, while a 19-year-old man living in the house was charged with involuntary manslaughter for allowing access to the weapon. The charges are pending.

Multiple Media Factors

The media also plays an important role in school-associated violence. There are several important ways in which the media contributes to the problem. Sensationalistic "journalism" glamorizes violence in reports of other incidents, and focuses extensive attention upon the perpetrators. This serves to stimulate other individuals who may have fantasized about perpetrating similar acts, creating an anti-hero identification. The fantasy then enters the world of possibility.

Somebody else has done it and they are getting notoriety. These other incidents perform a permission-giving function, setting a goal to which one may strive.

Extensive information is also provided to angry dissatisfied people about violent ways to cope with their angst. Movies, books, television, and the Internet bombard individuals with information in a way that might increase the attraction of violent problem-solving, particularly if there are no parents or other responsible persons helping the at-risk individual to appropriately "filter" this information. Subconsciously, this erodes the development of other, more healthy coping strategies for dealing with life. Consciously, violent, realistic video games emphasize the value of high body counts, improved killing efficiency, and serve as yet another bridge between fantasy and reality. As we will see later, in the individual who may already have decided to act out, such information can be used to deliberately increase motivation to act out violently.

The way in which violence has weaved itself into the very fabric of culture, particularly American culture, subtly shapes expectations, attitudes, coping strategies, and serves the stimulation and permission-giving function. Freedom to express ideas of all sorts in a variety of mediums comes with a price tag. This free expression results in books, television, cartoons, comics, movies, music, games, and Internet sites which are graphically violent. The following case from West Paducah, Kentucky exemplifies the contribution of several forms of media to a school violence incident.

Case Example: West Paducah, Kentucky

On December 1, 1997, 14-year-old eighth grade student Michael Carneal shot to death three female students and injured five additional students attending a prayer meeting held at Heath High School in West Paducah, Kentucky. He was armed with a .22-caliber Luger Mark II handgun, two .22-caliber semi-automatic rifles, one double barreled shotgun, and one single barreled shotgun. Each of the weapons was fully loaded, and he brought extra clips for his handgun and an estimated 600 rounds of ammunition. He had stolen the weapons from a neighbor several days before the shooting.

Reportedly, he had written angry essays about wanting to strike out at others, felt weak and picked on, and evidenced longstanding suicidal ideation. Michael Carneal wrote an essay for his class titled *The Halloween Surprise* that describes how a boy named Michael, picked on by the preps, was saved by a brother with a gun, at which point Michael gives the corpses to his mother as a gift. Several months prior to the shooting, Carneal complained that the student newspaper suggested he might be gay, and was called "faggot" on many occasions after the publication. Witnesses report that he "had a crush on" one of the girls in the prayer group and felt his advances had been rebuffed. He was described as physically small and immature, and the day before had warned another boy not to show up to the prayer meeting. When he finished shooting, he begged another student to shoot him. While in juvenile hall awaiting trial, he commented, "People respect me now." Carneal pled guilty but mentally ill, and was sentenced to life in prison without the possibility of parole for 25 years (Belkin, 1999).

Carneal was depressed and indicated that he heard voices calling his name, and evidenced paranoia, believing that people were always talking about him and that he was being watched by criminal type people. He had brought his father's handgun to school on one occasion about two months before the shooting and showed it off. Another boy threatened to turn him in, and extorted Carneal to sell it to him for a hundred dollars. In fact, Carneal stated he had stolen the gun from his father so that he might commit suicide with it. On another occasion several days before the shooting, Carneal stole one of several guns from the same friend's house he would later steal the additional weapons from, took it to school, and pointed and waved it at other students. No one reported this to school authorities until after the tragedy. In fact, he had pulled it out in response to two students saying they were going to beat him up and they had asked him questions about it, then said, "You couldn't hurt anybody with that."

After he surrendered to the authorities, Carneal disclosed to investigators that he had seen the 1995 movie *Basketball Diaries*, starring Leonardo DiCaprio, the autobiographical account of the life of writer/poet/musician Jim Carroll. During questioning he acknowledged that he had seen the movie "over and over."

The central character portrayed by DiCaprio is described as a "high school basketball hero headed for trouble" who "finds solace in all the wrong places, and the dark streets of New York tear him up." DiCaprio is a student in a Catholic high school at war with the secular and religious authorities at the school, his mother, and rival students. DiCaprio in real life is small in stature, a demeanor he carries in the majority of the movie. After his coach attempts to molest him, the

19

scene of this weak and drug addicted victim of others suddenly shifts. He is shown lapsing into unconsciousness in a bathtub, while writing his thoughts and feelings, and a dream/fantasy sequence follows, prefaced by the narrative, "dreams move in crazy pieces, anyway they want to, and suddenly you're capable of anything." The scene transitions to the "hero," DiCaprio, dressed in a black leather trenchcoat and boots, walking in a purposeful fashion down the school hallway, looking powerful as a slight breeze blows into his hair. He appears bigger than life, camera angles magnifying his power and strength. DiCaprio kicks down the door to the classroom, and the picture of the Virgin Mary hung on the classroom side of the door disappears from view as the door collapses. He trounces effortlessly upon this door as he enters the room, produces a sawed-off shotgun from under his trenchcoat, and begins shooting his classmates, who are dressed in Catholic school uniforms. At one point, he racks a round in the shotgun with one hand, in one coordinated, fluid movement, demonstrating his control of his chosen method over life and death. His friends are cheering him on and "high-fiving," while the targets are screaming in terror.

Each kill is preceded by slow motion and eye contact with the victim, who each must perceive their own imminent death. DiCaprio screams unintelligibly as he approaches the terrified Christian Brother teacher cowering in the corner. DiCaprio turns the desk over, and as he points the shotgun and pulls the trigger, he awakens from this dream/fantasy to find himself in the classroom being told to "wake up," by this same man. Educators, mental health professionals, and police who have viewed this segment have commented: "The essence of what school violence is about is captured in this clip; the move from weakness to power, violent fantasies to compensate for feelings of inferiority and to re-instill control, identification with the victim role, and externalization of blame. And to make matters worse, it is acted out by someone most kids these days look up to...Dicaprio."

Investigators found a number of important items in Carneal's room including a magazine picture of Dustin Hoffman and John Travolta from the movie *Mad City*, with the headline *Gunning for the Story*. *Mad City* is a film about a disgruntled terminated employee who takes hostages in a museum. It was also learned that Carneal had an affinity for Stephen King books and violent video games, including *Doom* (Belkin, 1999).

One cannot blame these movies, books, and video games as the sole cause of Carneal's violence. However, in the next chapter, the concept of aggression immersion, the process whereby offenders use these media to stimulate their aggressive impulses, will be described in detail.

Copycat Contagion

While media stimulation may be a subtle contributing factor that influences and shapes attitudes and behaviors across a lifetime, the most immediate impact of this variable is the cluster effect so often observed after high profile suicides, as well as school-associated violence. Media guidelines for reporting suicides and other violence underscore the significance of this problem, but we are inundated with examples. For example, subsequent to the Columbine incident, literally hundreds of threats and close calls occurred across the country, and abroad. One week after the incident, four 14-year-old boys from Danforth Junior High School in Wimberley, Texas were arrested and accused of plotting a deadly attack at the campus. Other students tipped off law enforcement officers after hearing discussion of plans for an attack similar to Columbine. A search of the suspects' homes turned up crude explosive devices, gunpowder, and computer disks and Internet documents about bomb-making.

Less than two weeks after Columbine, a 14-year-old boy dressed in a blue trenchcoat showed up on an Alberta, Canada high school campus armed with a sawed-off rifle. He killed one classmate and seriously wounded another, before being tackled and taken into custody by the unarmed school resource officer. The boy, described as "unpopular" and as a "real loser type" by his classmates, was a troubled student who had recently dropped out of school and was being taught at home. One month after Columbine, a 15-year-old student in Conyers, Georgia, despondent over a failed relationship, brought a .22 rifle and a handgun to school, then shot and wounded six people before surrendering to the principal who intervened while he was threatening to commit suicide. The perpetrators of the Columbine incident were clearly influenced by other incidents as portrayed in the media, despite claims to the contrary by Harris in his suicide tape. "Do not think we're trying to copy anyone," he said, referring to school shootings in Oregon and Kentucky, "we had the idea a long time ago before the first one ever happened" (Gibbs & Roche, 1999). Harris' statement makes apparent that their actions were influenced by those of others, and suggests that the two perceived their violence as a competition, a macabre game of one-upsmanship,

21

with previous incidents serving as the playing field for earning success, superiority, and notoriety.

Warrior Culture

We live in a violent culture that reveres the mythical lone warrior: one man standing alone fighting against his oppressor. Gibson (1994) makes a compelling argument for how this myth has become more pronounced in the aftermath of the Vietnam War. In particular, he observes that the impact of the U.S. defeat in Vietnam has had a profound effect upon the collective psyche of American society, creating a world of shared disappointment and a need to restore faith in failed institutions. Movies and popular culture reflect the hunger for tales of the lone warrior, unsupported, even betrayed by others, yet undaunted, using violent power for restoration of some undefined order. This myth is not lost upon those with their own individualized causes and conditions, and most people in America accept some violence as a means to solve some social problems. Studies of male adult mass murderers indicate that they do in fact demonstrate a "warrior mentality" (Hempel, et al., 1999).

Related to the lone warrior theory is the issue of what it means to be a boy and a man in many industrialized societies. Most of the incidents of extreme violence involve male perpetrators. American men and boys are encouraged to be strong and aggressive, and discouraged from showing any signs of weakness or vulnerability. The myth of the aggressive loner serves as a ready stereotype that may be adopted in extreme form by those without adequate prosocial role models who are desperate to "come of age" and earn respect.

Social Institution Problems

Social institutions have also contributed to the development of our school-associated violence problems. Breakdowns and failure in the nuclear family, lack of meaningful extended families to compensate for deficiencies, and lack of teaching and modeling basic values to our children are contributory factors. Our schools and their staff members are often underpaid and devalued relative to the critical role they play in determining the development of the next generation. It is ludicrous and shameful the amount of money that teachers are paid, particularly if we compare their salaries and degree of recognition say, to popular sports figures. How do we as a society justify this discrepancy? These educational institutions, and the people that work in them, have committed their lives to making a difference, and are often the safety net in which children fall into when the other institutions have failed.

Poverty may also be a contributing condition in certain cases. The Buell Elementary shooting presented earlier is a prime example of many of these important contributing factors. Social breakdown, poverty, dysfunctional families, and weapons availability create the essential elements for tragedy.

The legal system and constitutional safeguards evident in many democratic societies, a true gift of freedom and by far the best system in existence, is a double edged sword. These freedoms often create obstacles for administrators, law enforcement, attorneys, mental health professionals, and others who are trying to avert violence in at-risk situations. These professionals, trying to manage situations, are sometimes punished with litigation as they try to do the right thing. Lawsuits have been initiated in the aftermath of risk intervention for alleged civil rights, privacy, and Americans with Disabilities Act (ADA) violations. One case example, that surprisingly went in the favor of those responsible for managing school safety issues, involved a teenage girl who was suspected of dealing drugs on campus. Campus administrators authorized a search of her purse, and while they turned up no drugs, a ledger with monetary amounts owed by various students, clear evidence of drug dealing on campus, was located. Her parents, unhappy about this search, sued the school for unreasonable search. Perhaps they should have been more concerned about their daughter's drug dealing activity. Instead they turned on the messenger, the institution, for intervening. Fortunately, they lost their suit and now the New Jersey v. TLO ruling allows that school officials do not have to conform to the same stringent search standards that law enforcement does (probable cause); rather, they must have "reasonable grounds" to suspect that a search of a student will turn up evidence that the student has violated the law or the school rules (New Jersey v. TLO, 1985). Cases like these certainly evoke a "you've got to be kidding" response and fuel frustration and hopelessness about taking proactive action to deal with developing problems. Professionals sometimes may conclude that they are better off doing nothing. However, we owe it to our schools to work with the existing laws and strategies to manage risk in a reasonable fashion. At the same time, these rules, so necessary for living in a free society, may create inadvertent windows of opportunity for violence to occur in schools.

Dynamics of Youthful Offenders

Developmental Issues

It has already been noted that most perpetrators of lethal and nonlethal school violence are teenagers. There are some unique characteristics of this developmental phase that contribute to this kind of acting out.

Teenagers are frequently impulsive; in that they act without regard for consequences. The Nike motto, "just do it" is an apt descriptor for this characteristic. Probably a fair number of nonlethal and lethal acts are exacerbated by this developmental feature. However, reviews of most multiple event homicides indicate that most, if not all, involve a significant degree of planning. The impulsive dynamic applies differently in these cases. Impulsivity is evident in the decision-making process that precedes selection of the violent problem-solving option, and failure to consider the significance of long-term consequences upon self and others. Impulsivity refers not only to short-term "snap" reactions, but also to a decision-making style related to consequential reasoning.

Teens are addressing a stage in their life in which they are trying to find their place in the world with respect to others. They are trying to fit in and be accepted. While on the surface they may articulate rebellion and disdain for convention and certain segments of their peer world, their peers, stated or unstated, are everything, and what their peers think matters very much. This manifests itself in a hypersensitivity to rejection, and the resulting shame and embarrassment are experienced as intolerable. Whether denied access or acceptance to the "in-group" of the hour, or jilted by that special person or first love, the emotional injury is particularly intense, with that intensity occurring prior to the development of coping skills to handle it. Add to this mix pre-existing attachment issues generated by flaws in their family dynamics, and it is a wonder that there have not been more violent episodes.

Related to this conflict around conformity, particularly as it relates to their peer group, is the fact that in a significant number of extreme cases, there are accomplices and co-conspirators involved in the planning and implementation of violent attacks on our school campuses. The Columbine, Jonesboro, Arkansas, and Pearl, Mississippi tragedies all involved more than one person. In one research study (Meloy, Hemphill, Mohandie, Shiva & Grey, 2001), it

24

was noted that this phenomenon is a sharp contrast to adult cases of mass homicide, which rarely involve accomplices, co-conspirators, or a second perpetrator. This seems to be a function of developmental dynamics around peer involvement and acceptance.

Another phenomenon of this life stage is the emergence of higher order conceptual thinking, specifically, the idealism that so often characterizes "coming of age." The teenager adamantly knows what is right and wrong, best and worst. Many of us may recall the often heated conversations we may have had with parents and other authority figures, as we challenged status quo and the way it "settles for the unacceptable." The initial ability to conceive of an ideal, may also be the fertile breeding ground for judgment of those world realities that one finds lacking. Judgment and intolerance are by-products of this particular dynamic, and in extreme cases form the basis for justifications of violence.

Fantasy life also becomes more highly developed during this stage of life. While violent fantasies may develop prior to adolescence, it is during this particular life phase that they become more highly detailed and consciously used to compensate for perceived life inadequacies, and in particular, feelings of powerlessness. Such fantasies may have detailed plot lines, extensive character development, and incorporate adult-like weaponry such as guns and explosives as props to add realism, a factor which may distinguish them from the somewhat limited characteristics of earlier fantasy life. "Leakage" or break-through behaviors suggestive of these kinds of fantasies may be indicated by participation in role playing games, various fantasy games such as *Dungeons and Dragons*, extensive playing of video games such as *Doom*, and detailed statements, writings, or other communications which indicate a multi-layered and violent private internal theater.

Many teenagers also suffer from a deficient understanding of the finality of death. In fact, they may romanticize death and violence rather than exhibiting a true realization of the significance of death as a concept with all of its varied implications. One young murderer in a school shooting commented as he was being taken into custody, "How come they're not getting back up." Suicide counselors often hear the excuse, "They'll just get over me." Perhaps these thoughts of death had become only a game, the expression of a fantasy. Many kids, raised on a steady diet of video games and violent movie fare have failed to develop a realistic concept of death, are repetitively

25

desensitized to violence, and measure success by kill ratios. Each time they renew the game, it begins anew, the characters are there once more, and the stars they so love in movies are magically resurrected to appear in yet another production.

The teenage world has always had certain developmental tasks and issues. It can be a confusing time when a young person is struggling to find his or her way and a place to fit in. It has always been a time when there is excitement over a first love experience, and depression or disappointment over losses and rejections. Teenagers have always been somewhat reticent about bringing information forward about the misdeeds or potential misdeeds of others for fear of being branded a "snitch." What is new is the availability of violent role models, the available access in so many homes to guns and the technology of violence, and the gauntlet of high profile violent events that invite others who are angry, lost, and misguided. What is also new is the overt and covert breakdown of many families through divorce, abuse and neglect, and the loss of the extended family. Many of our next generation are learning violence in their own homes, or have parents so preoccupied with the battle of survival, or the chase of the almighty dollar, that they throw money instead of time at their kids. Other parents are simply ineffective: well-intentioned but ill-informed. What is also new is the proliferation of violent sources of information, in the news, media, and music. These information sources help to define the violent fantasy life of those craving power over others to compensate for feelings of inadequacy.

There are at-risk people out there right now. How do we notice them and what can we do about it? Most importantly, how can we determine who is likely to present a real risk to the safety of themselves and others in schools? In the next several chapters the topic of school violence threat assessment will be examined.

Chapter Summary

School violence events can happen anywhere. Single event homicides are decreasing on school campuses, but there has been a noted increase in multiple event homicides. Nonlethal events such as assaults and threats are quite common on our campuses. This has resulted in many students experiencing fear of violence at school and avoiding school on specific days or certain campus locations. There are three types of school violence events that can pose a risk to our campuses. *Type I* events involve perpetrators who have no relationship to the school and choose to attack the school for their own idiosyncratic reasons. *Type II* events involve perpetrators who are customers of the school, including students, former students, and family members of students. *Type III* events involve perpetrators who have an employment-related relationship with the school. *Type II* and *III* events are the most common types of school violence, respectively, but offer the greatest opportunity for early detection and intervention. There are many contributing factors to the school violence problem including weapons availability, the media, cultural issues, and breakdowns in social systems. Adolescent developmental dynamics such as impulsivity, judgment and intolerance, and susceptibility to peer influence elevate their risk for acting out.

CHAPTER TWO

Threat Assessment: Warning Signs

Myth Four: Potentially violent individuals just snap.

Overview

Threat or risk assessment is the process of assessing risks to a particular target, individual, or group of individuals, and designing and implementing intervention and management strategies to reduce that risk or threat (Mohandie & Hatcher, 1999). The term "threat" is used to describe situations where an individual poses or actually has made a threat. Researchers and practitioners in this arena have noted that a person may make a threat but not pose a threat, that an individual may pose a threat without having made a threat, and that some individuals who have made a threat will actually pose a threat (Fein & Vossekuil, 1998).

Consider the situation where middle school students are involved in a team sport, for example, and they call out to their opponents "We're gonna kill you!" Clearly, a threat has been made. In the absence of other important information, one can easily look at the context and arrive at the conclusion that there is no threat posed. This situation is quite similar to the case described in the beginning of Chapter One, in which school officials overreacted to six-year-old kids playing "cops and robbers." In another situation, a high school student playing baseball perceives, perhaps even accurately, that he has been wronged by an opponent, lets out a blood-curdling yell and rushes this other student, fists clenched. No threat has been *made*, but obviously, a threat is *posed*, and rapid intervention in the moment to safely separate the two is indicated. In both of these examples, a rough and unrefined applied threat assessment guides our decision-making.

The formal discipline of threat assessment originated in the work of the U.S. Secret Service, who needed an approach to proactively maintain the safety of their protectees. While their pioneering work represents the beginning of a technology for managing threats and risks, safety and dangerousness assessments have long fallen within the purview of psychology and psychiatry. In everyday life in a variety of contexts, people often conduct their own informal risk assessments.

Within municipal law enforcement, threat assessment technologies were applied to the management of stalking cases. In 1991, the LAPD developed the first dedicated municipal threat management unit, tasked with managing stalking and threat cases. As with many new developments relative to managing violence risk, this innovation was in response to several tragedies, in particular the killing of actress Rebecca Shaeffer by her obsessed fan, Robert Bardo.

Other similar units have been founded since that time. Special entities have been developed for the prosecution of threat and stalking cases, such as the San Diego County Stalking Strike Force. The Association for Threat Assessment Professionals (ATAP), a unique multidisciplinary association for those involved in addressing various types of threats within their span of control, was founded in 1992. It offers recurring training and networking opportunities, and has a growing association of chapters throughout the United States, and members from around the world.

The technology and practice of threat assessment has been applied to the tasks of protecting the safety of public figures and private citizens, reducing the risk of workplace violence, and, most recently, school violence threat management. With recent concerns about high profile incidents on our school campuses, particularly multiple victim events, there is a need to apply and modify this technology to school safety.

Threat assessment utilizes available information about warning signs, risk factors, stabilizing influences, and potential precipitating events to arrive at a categorical description of risk for a particular point in time (Mohandie & Hatcher, 1999). Risk investigation is only as good as the data collection to support it. Use of collateral data sources such as teachers, treating mental health professionals, and classmates, is essential.

It is also critical to define and distinguish the terms *warning signs or clues, risk factors, stabilizing influences, and precipitating events.* Detailed examples of each will be provided, derived from actual and "near miss" past school violence events.

Warning Signs

Research indicates that potentially violent individuals do not just snap; rather, they exhibit important warning signs prior to acting out. The Secret Service found that in more than 75 percent of the incidents they studied, other kids knew about the attack before it occurred, and an adult had expressed concerns about the student. In more than half of the cases, more than one person had expressed concern. Over half of the attackers developed the idea to harm the target at least two weeks prior to the incident. In well over 75 percent of the incidents the attacker planned the attack, some the same day, but more than half developed a plan at least two days prior (Vossekuil et al., 2000).

The terms *warning signs* or *clues* are used interchangeably to describe four broad categories of behaviors which a teacher, student, or other person may notice in an individual, thereby triggering concern that there *might* be a developing problem. Notice that the term *dangerous* is avoided. At this level of review, we are simply wanting other people to serve as eyes and ears for potentially problematic behavior. The behaviors described below may indicate violence potential or simply be evidence of difficult or problematic

TABLE 2

Warning Signs–Verbal Clues
• Direct and indirect threats
• Verbalizing a violent plan
• Recurrent suicide threats or statements
• Expresses a wish to kill, a wish to be killed, and a wish to die
• Threatens or brags about bringing a weapon to school
• Threatening/harassing phone calls or e-mails
• Hopeless statements
• Bragging of violent behavior or fantasies
• Excessive profanity (contextually inappropriate)
• Challenging or intimidating statements
• Name-calling or abusive language

behavior. The point is that we want people to be aware, and to know where to report this information. Then a deeper, informed level of review can occur which, in turn, may facilitate making more formal kinds of assessments and distinctions.

The four broad categories of warning signs are verbal behavior, bizarre thoughts, behaviors/physical clues, and obsessions. Stalking, a special subcategory of obsessive clue will also be discussed in this chapter. Summaries of these different warning signs are in Tables 2, 3, 4, and 5. There may be some overlap among the categories, which serve only to facilitate recall, recognition, and reporting.

Verbal Behavior

At the top of the chart (Table 2) are verbal threats. The Secret Service found that, in over 75 percent of the school shooting cases they studied, the attacker told someone beforehand of his interest in mounting the attack at the school (Vossekuil et al., 2000). Most of us intuitively realize that threats of harm should be taken seriously. At the same time, we are all aware of situations and contexts where people make threats and it is obvious that they are either joking or not meant to be taken seriously. Common sense should be our guide in evaluating these situations. However, there are other situations in which we might be tempted to say, "If he really wanted to kill somebody, do you think he'd say something about it?" One must realize that many times threats are indicators of the tremendous pressure these people feel to have somebody take notice and deal with them. The threats are a form of communication and serve an *expressive* or *instrumental* function. Violence in many school-associated circumstances represents a desire to express a feeling, or to influence some course of events. The talk of violence represents the individual's attempts to "get their point across" or influence accordingly. Another way of looking at this is to identify this behavior as *break-through behavior* or *leakage*. The at-risk person may be viewed as a bubbling cauldron of simmering resentment, or a container for some other building emotional pressure (fear, anger, jealousy, injured pride and the like) which has a way of escaping periodically in the form of statements and behaviors. Early warning recognition is awareness of the significance of this *leakage* and/or these *expressive* or *instrumental* gestures. Therefore, any threats of violence and/or verbalization of a violent plan should be taken seriously and reported, evaluated, and addressed.

Adolescent mass homicide perpetrators who act out on school campuses nearly always communicate their intentions to someone–but usually not the target–beforehand (Meloy et al., 2001). These findings parallel the results of other researchers indicating that adult workplace violence perpetrators communicated their intentions beforehand about 86 percent of the time (Feldmann & Johnson, 1996). Commonly these statements will be communicated to friends and acquaintances, less frequently to the intended victims.

Studies conducted by Shneidman (1996) indicate that in 90 percent of actual suicide cases, individuals had given verbal or behavioral clues within the week or so before they committed suicide (p. 55). He notes, however, that most individuals who threaten suicide do not attempt or commit suicide, a finding that parallels those of researchers of other types of violent behavior (Fein & Vossekuil, 1998). Schneidman recognizes the *prospective* view of violence threats: very few people who make threats or generate behavioral clues actually do something violent. He believes, however, that common sense dictates the adoption of a conservative or *retrospective* view, taking any talk or indicators of violence potential seriously (Schneidman, 1996, p. 56). Episodes of violence, particularly lethal violence, are irreversible. Therefore, we should err on the side of caution.

Another verbal warning sign is the individual who articulates or boasts about their violent fantasies or plans. While it may not necessarily indicate that s/he plans to make good on it, this clue certainly suggests that their anger or other issue is more than just a passing thought. They have considered a dangerous approach for handling their problem. In most school shootings, the attacker told one or more friends about his idea or plan, but told their intended victim in fewer than 25 percent of the cases (Vossekuil et al., 2000). Eric Houston, discussed in Chapter One, communicated his violent plan to his friends, as have many school violence perpetrators, yet those friends did not take him seriously. Eric Harris allegedly posted some of his violent plans on the Internet ("Dylan & Eric's refuge," 2000):

Philosophy:
My belief is that if I say something, it goes. I am the law, if you don't like it, you die. If I don't like you or I don't like what you want me to do, you die. If I do something

33

incorrect, oh fucking well, you die. Dead people can't do many things, like argue, whine, bitch, complain, narc, rat out, criticize, or even fucking talk. So that's the only way to solve arguments with all you fuckheads out there, I just kill! God I can't wait till I can kill you people. I'll just go to some downtown area in some big ass city and blow up and shoot everything I can. Feel no remorse, no sense of shame. I will rig up explosives all over a town and detonate each one of them at will after I mow down a whole fucking area of you snotty ass rich mother fucking high strung worthless pieces of shit whores. I don't care if I live or die in the shootout, all I want is to kill and injure as many of you pricks as I can, especially a few people like Brooks Brown.

Wie Gehts.
Well all you people out there can just kiss my ass and die. From now on, I don't give a fuck what almost any of you mutha fuckas have to say, unless I respect you which is highly unlikely, but for those of you who happen to know me and know that I respect you, may peace be with you and don't be in my line of fire, for the rest of you, you all better hide in your houses because I'm coming for EVERYONE soon, and I WILL be armed to the fuckin teeth and I WILL shoot to kill and I WILL fucking KILL EVERYTHING! No I am not crazy, crazy is just a word, to me it has no meaning, everyone is different, but most of you fuckheads out there in society, going to your everyday fucking jobs and doing your everyday routine shitty things, I say fuck you and die. If you got a problem with my thoughts, come tell me and I'll kill you, because...god dammit, DEAD PEOPLE DON'T ARGUE!

God DAMMIT I AM PISSED!

The reader will note that in these violent threats, Harris indicates an intention to arm himself, another important verbal indicator of a potential problem. His communication is replete with angry profanity, another indicator. The important issue is that this profanity is contextually inappropriate, possibly indicative of a loss of emotional control and an inability to channel his impulses into appropriate activities. There is a challenging, provocative quality to these statements. These verbal behaviors are important warning signs that should precipitate prompt reporting and thoughtful intervention.

Violent threats also include suicidal statements: an individual expresses a wish to die, a wish to kill, or a wish to be killed. These are indicators of a highly destructive mindset. Related to suicidal statements are statements of a hopeless nature–hopelessness being the most common emotional state of those who attempt suicide, and a strong indicator of intense emotional pain.

These communications may be made in-person, through third parties, by letter, telephone, fax, and e-mail. While in-person communications are usually of greater concern, any verbal warning signs communicated through these various modalities should heighten concern and trigger appropriate notifications.

Bizarre Thoughts

Bizarre thoughts are delusions, hallucinations, paranoia, other expressed distorted perceptual experiences, and generally deteriorated mental processes (See Table 3). A *delusion* is a fixed and false belief, which may present itself as bizarre or non-bizarre, grandiose, persecutory (victimization based), somatic (pertaining to the body), erotomanic (love based), or a host of other qualities. Sixty-one-year-old Geraisimov Metaxas, husband of former substitute teacher Linda Metaxas, shot and killed 48-year-old teacher John Sacci on the campus of Hoboken High School in New Jersey and committed suicide. Metaxas had the non-delusional belief that Sacci, a 23-year veteran of the school district, had had an affair with his wife. No such affair had ever occurred (Stephens, 1999).

A bizarre delusion is a belief in events not typically viewed as possible by most people. Examples include alien abduction, the

TABLE 3

Warning Signs–Bizarre Thoughts
• Persecutory delusions with self as victim
• Paranoid
• Delusions in general
• Command hallucinations
• Grandiose delusions that involve power, control, destruction
• Significantly deteriorated thought processes

perception that individuals in caregiver positions have been taken over by imposters with evil intentions, or the belief that some disaster or Armageddon is imminent. In these cases, concern arises in anticipation of the pre-emptive strike or other evasive efforts that some delusional persons will initiate to avert the outcome.

In 1993, convinced that Armageddon was going to occur Mother's day, Mark Hilbun, a terminated postal employee, came to the belief that he had been chosen to become the new Adam. He believed that Kim Springer, the former coworker he had been stalking, was destined to become *his* new Eve. Hilbun determined that he was supposed to abduct her, and take her to Baja, California, where they would live out the nuclear holocaust. In this tragic situation, Hilbun stabbed his mother and his pet cocker spaniel to death, then went to the post office searching for her. Hilbun then shot and killed his best friend while searching for Springer. Thwarted in his efforts, he went on the run for several days prior to being taken into custody. He admitted that when he heard music, there were special messages there for him, and that signs of impending Armageddon were present in certain events such as the Waco tragedy and the fact that the swallows had not flown to San Juan Capistrano. This case is a prime example of the dangerous delusion, with an obvious grandiose component. The delusion designated a dangerous role for Hilbun in relationship to other persons, and an erotomanic component. He also evidenced another serious warning sign of mental disturbance: *ideas of reference*. Hilbun believed that there were special messages meant just for him present in outside life events. He had been treated in the past for manic-depressive illness, now known as bipolar mood disorder, and decided upon his own, several months prior to the tragedy, to discontinue his medications in order to purify and prepare himself for a love relationship. Incarcerated and serving multiple life terms, today his symptoms are controlled by medication and he is sadly aware of the consequences of his mental illness.

A *hallucination* is a false sensation. The person senses something that is not there. Such false sensations may occur in any sensory modality. Most frequent, however, are auditory hallucinations. The individual hears voices, sometimes critical, demeaning, or threatening that are perceived by the subject as distinct from his/her own thoughts. For example, Michael Carneal, the school shooter from Kentucky discussed in Chapter One, reported that at times he heard voices calling his name in empty rooms. When the voices are telling the recipient to do something, they are called *command hallucinations.*

Between October 1972 and January 1973, Herbert Mullin killed thirteen people in Santa Cruz, California. He believed that San Francisco would fall into the ocean during a cataclysmic earthquake if he did not intervene as the voices were telling him. The "voices" told him that in order to avert the potential crisis, he needed to make random human sacrifices. Feeling the pressure and the weight of the world upon him as a consequence of the delusion, coupled with the voices encouraging violence and bloodshed, Mullin complied with the voices: thirteen persons died prior to his capture. His delusions and hallucinations were the result of paranoid schizophrenia which may have been induced by LSD usage, a pre-existing biological propensity for mental illness, and reading about the Mayans' human sacrifices. Obviously mentally ill, Mullin was sentenced to life without the possibility of parole because jurors were afraid that he would somehow be released by the mental health system. Mullin had been released from a mental health facility prior to the murders (Lunde & Morgan, 1980).

Paranoia is the general term for believing that other people or entities are conspiring to do you harm. Those who evidence such symptoms may be willing to do violent things in order to protect themselves from such real or imagined persecution. Carneal, referred to in Chapter One, thought he was being watched by criminal type people and that people were looking in his windows at night or under his bed (Belkin, 1999).

Bizarre thoughts are an important category of warning signs. Such thoughts, if expressed and somehow observed in written or spoken word, are likely indicative of a serious problem, such as schizophrenia, manic depression, acute drug intoxication, or some other imminent medical problem. These thoughts are usually indicative of a serious mental problem, referred to as a "psychotic break" or in everyday nomenclature, the so-called "nervous breakdown." Serious mental disorders often first manifest themselves in the late adolescent years, probably due to the rapid physiological and hormonal shifts that are taking place during this developmental phase, and in response to the serious life stressors which may be peaking at this stage of life. Therefore, we may see for the first time unexpected evidence of problems in a student who previously seemed to have it together.

37

These phenomena are also important to us, because individuals actively experiencing active psychotic symptoms, particularly command hallucinations and persecutory or grandiose delusions, have seriously impaired judgement and an increased risk of violence directed towards others or themselves (Monahan, 1992; Meloy, 2000). Students are not the only individuals who may demonstrate bizarre thoughts. Staff members and parents of students can have these problems. They may have taken medication to control their symptoms. Denial of an existing mental disorder, stress, side effects, or oversight may cause the person to discontinue their medication. Two weeks later, the person may become increasingly bizarre in their

TABLE 4

Warning Signs–Behavioral/Physical Clues
• Physical altercation/assault upon another person- frequent fighting
• Inappropriate weapons possession or use
• Drawings and other creative outlets with persistent or intense violent themes
• Violent attire (camouflage fatigues, violent message shirts)
• Physically intimidates peers/younger children
• Following/surveilling targeted individuals
• Short-fused, loss of emotional control
• Destruction of property
• Bullying or victim of bullying
• Deteriorating physical appearance and self-care
• Inappropriate possession of violent literature and information pertaining to known or suspected hate groups
• Inappropriate displays of emotion, particularly anger, depression, or rage
• Isolating and withdrawn
• Signs or history of substance use/abuse/dependence
• Signs of depression/severe mood swings
• Rebellion against school authority
• Identifiably violent tattoos

behaviors and statements. Other times, body chemistry changes and they are no longer responsive to the medication, leading to deterioration. These various circumstances precipitate the emergence of important clues, clues that require responsible and compassionate review with the input of experts, so that safe referral and assessment decisions can be made. While some of the case examples in this section are not specifically school examples, these events can happen in any institutional setting.

Behaviors/Physical Clues

While all of the warning signs, to one degree or another, represent behaviors which may be observed, *behaviors/physical clues* are those signs we may observe in the at-risk person which are not typically verbal or spoken, but rather demonstrated. This is the more general category of warning sign, and a catch-all for what does not fit into the other categories. Examples of these types of clues are included in Table 4. Several will be specifically discussed in this section: violent/intimidating behavior, weapons possession, victim of bullying or threats, creative outlets with violent themes, and behavioral observations of emotional distress and difficulties.

If a person is exhibiting violent behavior, we should be highly concerned and immediate intervention should occur. A student, staff member, or parent who has assaulted others, or is physically intimidating in their non-verbal behavior when interacting with others, is giving off a critical warning sign. They are out of control already. Within the mental health profession, it is well documented that the best predictor of future violence is past violence. Physical intimidation suggests immediate intervention to re-instill safety and control. Additionally, the need for serious evaluation of future risk potential is indicated. Rapid escalation is also indicated for the person who regularly violates the body space of others, is provocative in their interactions with others, and exhibits aggressive body language such as clenched fists, jaw tightening, or glaring ("evil eye"). People demonstrating these particular warning signs are out there provoking and inviting conflict, and will likely end up as a future perpetrator or victim through their actions.

In the heat of passion, the presence of a firearm can turn a fight into a killing (Wright & Davis, 1994). Contrary to viewing student weapon possession as an indicator of a defensive strategy, a more accurate viewpoint is to consider the armed student having a more aggressive and antagonistic posture or mindset. Arming oneself is indicative of a person who has made a decision that there are circumstances in which it might be okay to use the gun (Snyder & Sickmund, 1999). Another layer of control, another barrier of restraint has been eroded. Therefore, a student or other at-risk person in possession of a weapon, particularly a lethal one, is giving off a very important warning sign. The recent Secret Service study confirms that when an at-risk individual has the idea of an attack, any efforts to acquire, prepare, or use a weapon may represent progression from that idea to carrying it out (Vossekuil et al., 2000).

Carneal, as discussed earlier, had taken a gun to school on prior occasions and had even pointed it at other students days prior to his shooting. Kip Kinkel, from Springfield, Oregon, was caught and suspended for possession of a handgun on campus. Fifteen-year-old Nathaniel Deeter, the copycat shooter in the Conyers, Georgia school violence incident, had had his gun (a gift from his parents) taken away from him when his parents learned he was carrying it around.

In somewhat of a different vein, consider the student who is an observed or known victim of bullying. Now this fact may not be indicative of anything other than the need to intervene. However, a certain percentage of the more extreme school violence incidents involved students who perceived themselves as a victim of other students, and sometimes blamed teachers for joining in the fray (through omission or commission). This warning sign is significant, because here we are observing what may later become the precipitating event for violence by the student (Vossekuil et al., 2000). The perpetrator feels like he had to take matters into his own hands as a result of the following thought process: "Nobody was going to help me, they just stood by, so I had no choice or it never would have stopped."

Creative outlets may also provide us the opportunity to observe critical warning signs of an increasingly violent thought process. Consider Harris, from the Columbine shooting, who wrote an essay about what it would feel like to be a shotgun shell in a weapon. He also drew violent pictures, and posted violent ideas on his Internet website (See Figure 1 for drawing attributed to Harris). These types of writings indicate that they are either very creative or that there is a very important and potentially dangerous thought process occurring. Similarly, Luke Woodham, who killed his mother and two fellow students in Pearl, Mississippi, had made a number of strange drawings with violent themes and content. Such information does not

FIGURE 1

conclusively indicate violence potential, but it certainly should capture our attention so that we conduct follow-up investigations and inquiries into the meaning of such behavior.

We should also be keen to observe behavioral signs consistent with emotional distress or difficulties. The student who is losing control of his/her temper, lashing out in frustration, or withdrawing and isolating from others, is exhibiting noteworthy behavioral clues of a potential problem. These signs should prompt us to notice, report, and orchestrate appropriate additional assessment and intervention. It is critical that we attend to these signs of anger or depression. In the worst case scenario they may indicate a growing menace, while more commonly it may simply be indicative of a student or staff member in deep emotional pain, needing our thoughtful intervention and assistance.

Obsessions

An *obsession* is the repetitive or persistent preoccupation with a particular idea. It becomes an individual's focus, filling their mind so that no other information is effectively processed. As a warning sign, people should be alert to the following kinds of evident obsessions: resentments and grudges against particular individuals; romantic obsessions; themes of violence; and the perception that there are no solutions to life's problems other than violence (See Table 5).

TABLE 5

Warning Signs–Obsessions
• Self as victim of a particular individual
• Grudges and deep resentments
• Particular object of desire
• Perceived injustices, humiliations, disrespect
• Thoughts of death or other incidents of violence
• Narrow focus- "sees no way out"- tunnel vision
• Publicized acts of violence
• Historically violent figures
• Violent music and other media
• Weapons and destruction
• Stalking

Resentments and grudges are nearly always present in extreme school violence scenarios, and often present in situations that erupt into less-lethal violence. The fact that a person has a particular obsession is usually not a surprise to his or her circle of friends, other students, or coworkers, as the at-risk individual focuses and talks about little else other than how so-and-so has done them wrong or ruined their life. Such unresolved anger, bubbling about on the surface and communicated to or observed by others, is important to note.

Romantic obsessions are similarly problematic. Unrequited love may rapidly turn to hate, shame, rage, and occasionally violence directed towards the love object. The student who can't let go of how some love object abandoned them, continuously pursues that person, and generally centers their life around what that person is doing, is out of control and an accident waiting to happen.

Individuals may also become preoccupied with violence, destruction, hatred, intolerance, and a host of other morbid ideas. Perhaps they repetitively listen to a particular song with violent lyrics and melody, watch movies, or play video games with intensely violent themes. Everything they seem to be interested in involves death or killing. Such warning signs, when present, suggest the need for deeper understanding of the unfolding morbid preoccupation. Is it a cry for help, passing rebellion "for shock value," or something more sinister? Our concerns should magnify exponentially when an individual is having problems and indicates that "death is the only solution."

Aggression immersion is the deliberate seeking of multiple form, high intensity, or repetitive exposure to aggression information sources by an aggressively inclined individual. This activity primes and prepares the individual for violence, helping to induce the right "mindset," provide technical know-how, and establish behavioral norms for the violent conduct. While it is not necessarily causative, it certainly is contributory, analogous to the concept of a chemical accelerant, which enhances an already flammable device into a more lethal, volatile mixture. *Theme consistent* and *sequence specific stimulation* are two important underlying dynamics of *aggression immersion.* That is, the behaviors of the heroes, villains, and violence in particular movies, books, and music video, are thematically similar to the crimes, and discrete portions of behavior are clearly imitated during the murders (Meloy & Mohandie, 2001). Activities indicative of *aggression immersion* were present in Columbine, Springfield, Oregon, West Paducah, Kentucky, and several other school violence cases. A case example will serve to introduce this important warning sign.

Case Example: Moses Lake, Washington Incident

On February 2, 1996, at 1:50 pm in the afternoon, 14-year-old Barry Loukaitis entered his eighth grade algebra classroom, and calmly shot and killed two male classmates, his teacher, and critically wounded a female classmate, before taking the remaining students hostage. The first student killed was a Hispanic student who had reportedly called Barry a "faggot" approximately six months earlier. While attempting to force his gun into the mouth of another teacher who had tried to intervene, Loukaitis was overpowered and taken safely into custody.

Loukaitis arrived at the event dressed head to toe in black, from his Stetson hat to his recently purchased Drover's outback coat, jeans, and cowboy boots. Prior to the murders, the honors student would typically dress in jeans and a pullover shirt. He was armed with a Western-style Winchester 94 lever action 30-30 rifle, a .25 caliber semi-automatic pistol, a .22 caliber revolver, and 81 rounds of ammunition for the rifle and his revolver.

For approximately six months to a year prior to his crimes, other students noted a marked change in Loukaitis' behavior. He became more withdrawn and "darker," with his poetry and personality reflecting a preoccupation with themes of death. He was overheard to mutter under his breath statements such as, "I wonder what I'd do if I had a gun right now," and "Do you treasure your life?" Barry's home life was in turmoil. His father was having an affair, and his depressed mother was confiding her suicidal plans to Loukaitis. Barry took responsibility for intervening in his mother's plans.

Described as an odd, immature loner, Loukaitis had a closet filled with the complete Stephen King book collection. One well-worn, obviously well-read book in his collection was *Rage*, which was written early in King's career (1977) under the pseudonym Richard Bachman, about a high school student who goes into his algebra class, killing two teachers, before taking the remaining students hostage and making a mockery of the authorities. The student considers suicide during the ordeal, is shot by officers when he pretends to be reaching for a weapon during the surrender, and is ultimately found not guilty by reason of insanity and committed to a hospital.

Loukaitis' favorite movies were *Natural Born Killers*, *Tombstone*, Clint Eastwood's so-called spaghetti western series, especially the 1964 classic *Fistful of Dollars*, and the rock group *Pearl Jam's* music

44

video titled, *Jeremy* (Pearl Jam, 1991). *Natural Born Killers,* a 1994 movie starring Woody Harrelson and Juliette Lewis, is a sensationalized modern day Bonnie and Clyde story about a couple of traveling serial killers on a murderous spree across the United States. Their exploits are chronicled by a tag-along sleazy newscaster portrayed by Robert Downey, Jr. This movie could best be described as presenting serial murder as "sport." The 1993 modern western *Tombstone,* starring Kurt Russell and Val Kilmer as Wyatt Earp and Doc Holliday, presents the story of the Shootout at the OK Corral. This movie glorifies the American macho cultural archetype of gunslingers shooting it out in the old West, with primary characters wearing traditional Western wear (cowboy hats, Drover coats, jeans, and cowboy boots) and armed with lever action rifles and handguns. *Fistful of Dollars* and the other spaghetti westerns similarly glorify the lone stranger assassin/gunslinger who strolls into the lawless town, persecuted by others, emerging superior over his enemies through his violent skills. In *Fistful of Dollars,* a bartender tells Clint Eastwood, "Here you can only get respect by killing other men..." And the 1991 music video *Jeremy* is about a lonely and isolated high school boy who eventually succumbs to his rageful fantasies against other people. This song was actually loosely based upon the 1990 suicide of student Jeremy Wade Delle, who committed suicide in front of 30 fellow students at Richardson High School in Texas.

At the time of Loukaitis' arrest, a compilation of Clint Eastwood movies titled *Fistful of Dollars* was cued up in his VCR to a scene where Eastwood was standing over some people he had killed with a rifle. Loukaitis was able to quote to investigators numerous lines from the movie *Natural Born Killers,* and had been overheard to say to his school acquaintances (he had no true friends), "Killing is natural, it's a basic animal instinct, and people are just like animals," as well as, "It would be neat to go across country on a killing spree–I would like to do something like that before I die..." (Sergeant D. Ruffen, personal communication, November 4, 1999)

Loukaitis deliberately sought books, movies, and music with high intensity violence. He repeatedly exposed himself to this material, accelerating whatever unfolding aggressive response was within him. The behaviors of the heroes, villains, and violence in these movies, books, and music video are thematically similar to his crimes, and discrete portions of behavior are clearly imitated during his murders. *Theme consistent stimulation* is evident in his emulation of the "get even" mentality espoused across these different media sources. *Sequence specific stimulation* is illustrated by Loukaitis' choice of weapon, clothing, and other discrete portions of behavior which were directly culled from the book *Rage*. He relied upon multiple movies, music videos, and literature for his information and stimulation, a common observation in studies of adolescent mass murderers (Meloy et al., 2000).

Other warning signs were present in this case. Loukaitis exhibited verbal clues such as threats and violent fantasies, an obsessive grudge against the student who called him a "faggot" six months prior, and noteworthy behavior such as his withdrawal and morbid poetry.

Be alert for signs of *aggression immersion*. Evidence of voluntary exposure to high intensity violent media, repeatedly seeking such stimulation from a single source, and/or seeking multiple sources of violent media information are important warning signs, particularly in conjunction with the various risk factors discussed in the next chapter. Reviews of past school violence incidents indicate that this type of behavior is a late step in the sequence of moving from violent thought to action. It should be taken very seriously when observed.

Stalking

Legal Definition

Stalking is the willful, malicious, and repeated following and harassing of another person that threatens his or her safety (Meloy & Gothard, 1995). This behavior was criminalized 10 years ago in California, and is now a crime in all 50 states in the U.S., and a federal offense in the U.S., Canada, Australia, and Great Britain. *Repeated* simply means more than once, so if a person has pursued another person on two occasions across distinct time periods (for example, morning and then afternoon), that would typically fulfill the definition. Fortunately, or unfortunately for the victim, most cases of stalking do not involve such hair splitting; rather, pursuit and harassment behaviors are far more frequent than the bare minimum to qualify under the criminal statute. And threat in many jurisdictions now enjoys a fairly liberal and realistic definition, as inferred by a *pattern of conduct* that would create reasonable fear in the individual and may or may not include actual verbal threats.

Stalking Behavior

Stalking behavior runs the gamut and includes a range of behavior which has at its core an obsession with the victim: telephone calls, showing up at locations (residence, school, work, health club), letters, packages, gifts, faxes, e-mail, and the Internet (cyberstalking), third party contacts and involvement, vandalism and property damage, assaults, surveilling, abduction, and, in extreme cases, murder.

Types of Stalkers

There are several patterns of stalking which may be categorized by the relationship history between the victim and the stalker. The first and most common pattern is that of the previous relationship gone sour, referred to by some researchers as the *simple obsessional stalker* (Zona, Sharma, & Lane, 1993). The stalker obsesses about, and pursues the victim for a variety of reasons. He or she may hope to rekindle the relationship through persistence, attempt to disrupt the establishment of another love relationship, or wish to "teach the person a lesson" for dumping them. Sometimes the relationship was an employment relationship gone sour, in which case the stalker may be trying to convince the targets to do something, or punish them for perceived mistreatment. Whichever "previous relationship gone sour" type, the reality is that most stalking cases are of this variety, and these are the most dangerous in the shortest interval (30-90 days) after the relationship disruption or trigger. These cases are so "hot," because of the previous intimacies or social contracts that existed before the disruption—there was frequently an intense level of previous attachment. Most of these cases involve individuals who manifest attachment and abandonment issues, exhibit extreme self-centeredness, have a tendency to misread and distort social cues, and possess a strong sense of entitlement, characteristics often associated with the various personality disorders described in the next chapter. Luke Woodham, the school shooter from Pearl, Mississippi (see Chapter Three), exhibited this pattern of obsession after being rejected by his first love, Christina Menafee. He killed her and several others one year after their breakup, and several weeks after she had again rejected his attempt to reconcile.

The second pattern of stalking involves a pattern of obsession and pursuit where there has been no or limited previous relationship. These are cases where there is no basis for the stalker's perceptions except their distorted thinking processes, which in turn are usually a function of major mental illness (often paranoid schizophrenia, bipolar mood disorder, and delusional disorders) and/or long-term use of mind-altering chemicals. One subgroup, referred to by some researchers as the *love obsessional* stalker, does not actually believe that they have a relationship with their victim; rather, they believe if they pursue hard enough, they might be able to convince the person to have a relationship with them. They are involved in a campaign to get noticed. Suzie's case, presented in Chapters Four and Six, represents this stalking pattern. She pursued another student by sending threatening e-mails and letters, and reported feelings of anger and rejection when her attempts to communicate with Jennifer went ignored. The third subgroup, known as the *erotomanic*, genuinely believes that they are loved by or in a relationship with the victim, and they communicate and pursue based upon that gross misperception. There have been several cases in Southern California involving mentally ill workers who have become obsessed with teachers and students as a function of their delusions and distorted perceptions. In one aggravated erotomanic case, a female janitor was terminated from her employment with the district after she harassed and stalked a married teacher. She claimed to be married to him, refused to get necessary medical help, and continued to stalk after her termination. Ultimately, she was arrested and convicted of stalking. Upon release after serving a short sentence, she again stalked the teacher, resulting in re-arrest and incarceration.

Research indicates that this group is overall not as dangerous in the short-term as the previous relationship gone sour group. However, common sense and anecdotal experience indicates that these are very serious warning signs which could lead to lethal behavior towards the victim based upon rage in response to rejection, or directed towards some third party who intrudes upon the stalker's perceived entitlement. Prudence suggests taking these warning signs very seriously.

Stalker Dynamics

Most experts agree that irrespective of the type of stalker, there are a number of issues that they tend to have in common. There are obsessions, persistent thoughts, and actions that stalkers believe they have to take to address their thoughts and concerns. Meloy (1998) quite accurately refers to the phenomenon as obsessional following, since these cases involve obsessional thoughts and pursuit behavior. Frequently there are disrupted early relationships and attachment failures, and stalking behavior emerges as a consequence of a distorted pattern of attachment designed to stave off feelings of loneliness, abandonment, and inadequacy. While the distinguishing feature between the two broad categories of stalkers is whether there has been a previous relationship, the potential results of rejection by the victim are the same. Whether real or perceived, rejection may precipitate rage and acting out behavior.

Victim Dynamics

Victim dynamics in stalking cases requires special mention. It is not uncommon for the situation to be quite out of hand and entrenched by the time it gets to the attention of responsible parties or law enforcement. The victim, particularly if it is a relationship gone sour situation, often will try to deal rationally with their pursuer. They may have tried "normal" strategies to fix it, such as calling or meeting the person, trying to explain the logic of why things can't work out. With a "normal" relationship breakup, that may eventually work to create a successful separation. The problem is that the stalker does not perceive these cues as indicative of the need to move on; rather, they may interpret them as "a sign of hope, maybe I have a chance, after all she's still willing to talk to me!" Or the stalker may get further enraged and justify additional pursuit behavior based upon not getting the answer he believes he was entitled to. Further, on other occasions, the stalking may be a component of a domestic violence cycle and relationship, with the victim feeling responsible for having caused it. The victim may feel the need to take care of the stalker so that a sense of control in a terrifying situation may be incurred. Victims often feel responsible for having caused the stalking and self-blame is common, a factor which fits nicely with the fact that a core theme with many stalkers is the externalization of responsibility and blame. Complicating matters, it seems that many stalkers have the rather uncanny ability to select victims who are "nice" people who prefer to avoid confrontation and hurting the feelings of others. Perhaps that is what attracted them to victim in the first place. The net result is the same: the attachment is reinforced, as any attention is better than no attention.

School personnel confronted with a student or staff member demonstrating these victim dynamics may be tempted to blame the victim in these situations for what appears to be bad judgment. It needs to be recognized that normal people "get the hint" and understand that "no means no." Stalkers, on the other hand, do not, and are adept at manipulating their victims and others.

The impact upon victims is profound. Depression, anxiety, panic attacks, and feelings of helplessness are common. In some cases, victims will suffer from suicidal thoughts as they feel trapped in an unworkable, inescapable situation. The stalking experience may be described as one involving the creation of a prison without walls, the victim's autonomy crushed by the various behaviors of the stalker. As a consequence, it is critical that mental health referrals be considered for victims, and that professionals be sensitive, knowledgeable, and conversant with these dynamics.

Cyberviolence

With each new technological development, people adapt their behaviors to make use of it, good or bad, and various forms of violence are no exception. The computer has been used by a number of students and others within our schools, as an instrument of threat, stalking, terror, and foreshadowing of violence.

Case Example: Cyberviolence

On December 15, 1999, 18-year-old Michael Campbell (an aspiring actor and community college student from Cape Coral, Florida) was arrested by federal authorities for using an interstate communications facility to make a threat of injury to another person. He allegedly sent an instant Internet message to a 16-year-old Columbine High School sophomore warning her not to go to school the next day as, "I need to finish what was begun and if you do I don't want your blood on my hands." The e-mail threat was conveyed by the victim to authorities prompting classes to be canceled on Thursday and Friday. The mother of the suspect claimed that her son wrote the letter because he "was bored to death," while his public defender indicated that his father had died approximately one month prior to the threat. If convicted, he faces a penalty of up to five years in prison and a $250,000 fine, and the U.S. attorney prosecuting the case stated, "Today's arrest should send a strong message that threats, especially against our schools, will not be tolerated." His mother added, "He didn't mean to do anything. This was a stupid, stupid mistake, and he knows it and they know it too," referring to the FBI agents who made the arrest ("18-year-old jailed," 1999). Ultimately, Campbell pled guilty to one felony count of communicating a threat across state lines, and at the time of this writing, prosecutors were recommending a lenient sentence ("Teen pleads guilty," 2000).

Early Warning Recognition in Practice

Early recognition is essential to preventing school violence. Early intervention begins with recognizing the warning signs of a developing problem and intervening appropriately. Training students, parents, and school personnel such as teachers, administrators, security and campus police, and campus-based mental health about the early warning signs is an important first step (Mohandie & Hatcher, 1999; IACP, 1999). Training should be supported with suggested action steps, beginning with mandatory reporting by students, school personnel, and others. Threat assessment and intervention resources in the form of campus-based law enforcement or security, mental health, and legal expertise should be available for immediate consultation (Mohandie & Hatcher, 1999; IACP, 1999).

Once a situation has been recognized and reported, then a deeper level of review by appropriate professionals available within and to the school district should occur. At this level of review, information described as *risk factors, stabilizing influences, and potential precipitating events* needs to be integrated with the behavioral clues that have been identified. *Risk factors* are individual, situational, familial, and contextual issues in the person's background or situation that have a known relationship to increased violence risk. If these issues have a known relationship to decreased violence risk, then they are referred to as *stabilizing influences. Precipitating events* are events that have happened or are anticipated to happen in the person's life, which may be the catalyst, the so-called "last straw" that disinhibits the person and triggers their violence.

Chapter Summary

Threat assessment is a process that utilizes available information about warning signs, risk factors, stability factors, and potential precipitating events to arrive at an assessment of risk. Warning signs suggest that there might be a problem with an individual and that there is a need to review the situation further to determine if there is an increased risk for school violence. These are the clues that we want individuals to notice and report, beginning the process of threat assessment. In most past school violence cases, there were warning signs that were ignored or not reported. There are four broad categories of warning signs in school violence risk situations: verbal behavior such as direct and veiled threats; bizarre thoughts including delusions and hallucinations; behavioral/physical clues such as emotional outbursts and social withdrawal; and, obsessions, including grudges and preoccupations with death or violence. Stalking behavior is another clue from the obsession category. There are two patterns of stalking behavior: one type of stalking behavior emerges out of a previous relationship gone bad; and the second type can occur where there has been no relationship at all.

CHAPTER THREE

Threat Assessment: Risk and Stability Factors

General Violence Risk Factors

Violence risk factors have been identified by mental health researchers. Meloy (2000) has identified a biopsychosocial model of risk factors that suggest increased violence potential. Individual/psychological domain factors include past crime or violence, aged 15-24, male gender, lower intelligence, paranoia, anger/fear problems, and psychopathy and other attachment problems. Social/environmental factors include family of origin violence, adolescent peer group violence, economic instability or poverty, victim availability, weapon availability, and alcohol or psychostimulant use. Biological domain factors include history or evidence of head injuries or seizure disorder, central nervous system symptoms such as blackouts, recurrent dizziness, or severe headaches, and major mental disorders. Monahan (1992) nicely summarizes the research pertaining to major mental disorders. He reported that a) the prevalence of violence is more than five times higher among people with a diagnosable mental disorder than those who are not diagnosable; b) the prevalence of violence among people who meet criteria for a diagnosis of schizophrenia, major depression, or mania/bipolar disorder are remarkably similar; and, c) the prevalence of violence among persons who meet criteria for a diagnosis of alcoholism is 12 times that of persons who receive no diagnosis, and the prevalence of violence among persons who meet criteria for being diagnosed as abusing drugs is 16 times that of persons who receive no diagnosis (p. 516).

Risk Factors Unique to School Violence Risk

Peers

Peers relationships are an important factor that can influence school violence risk in a variety of ways. Peers may challenge and provoke an at-risk individual, leading to a *victim precipitated* violence event. They may also encourage or conspire to participate in a violent action plan.

Victim precipitation refers to behaviors on the part of victims that may give the unstable person or at-risk student the excuse or rationalization to erupt in an episode of violence. In the Columbine case, for example, Harris and Klebold were very vocal about their disdain for jocks and others who were perceived to have tormented and teased them. They had "hit lists" and were hell bent on revenge against those whom they believed had treated them badly. Public commentary from school officials and other official representatives downplayed the role of such bullying in this event; however, a quotation from Evan Todd, 255-pound defensive lineman for Columbine, wounded in the library shooting, is very telling:

> "Columbine is a clean good place except for those rejects," Todd says of Klebold and Harris and their friends. "Most kids didn't want them there. They were into witchcraft. They were into voodoo dolls. Sure we teased them. But what do you expect with kids who come to school with weird hairdoos and horns on their hats? It's not just the jocks; the whole school's disgusted with them. They're a bunch of homos, grabbing each other's private parts. If you want to get rid of someone, you usually tease 'em. So the whole school would call them homos, and when they did something sick, we'd tell them, 'You're sick and that's wrong'" (Gibbs & Roche, 1999).

This quotation indicates some validation for the notion that these kids were being hassled by others with intolerant attitudes and beliefs. At the same time, their violence would never be justified. With certain at-risk students, events like these serve as potential catalysts–justifications for violence.

This quotation invokes a related risk factor, social dynamics around in-groups versus out-groups. When groups are extremely polarized on campuses, and even within communities, the meting out of rewards and punishments by those in authority can sometimes reinforce perceived disparities. This may serve to elevate the risk for violence. Why? Certain at-risk individuals may already have a chip on their shoulders about favoritism issues, perhaps going back to family dynamics they have experienced or perceived their whole lives. The ready supply of resentment and rage gets displaced to yet another target. Perhaps it is easier to act out against classmates or perceived favoritism at school represents the "last straw." It is also important to view violence as a choice. Some people who feel they have no legitimate avenues for solving their dilemma will "step outside the box." Homicide and/or suicide may be viewed as their last course of action. The thought process may go like this: "After all, teachers look the other way when I am bullied and there is no sense in going to them. Besides, when the jocks don't do well they still get a passing grade. No, if you are having a problem, you have to deal with it yourself–with violence!"

Peers may also encourage the violence, blatantly challenging the at-risk individual to "go ahead and do it," provoking him with statements such as, "You don't have the balls!" In these types of cases, peers serve as a private cheering committee, reinforcing the notion that it is okay to use violence to solve the problem, and suggesting that to do otherwise is a sign of cowardice. In nearly half of the school shooting cases from the Secret Service study, for example, attacks were influenced or encouraged by peers (Vossekuil et al., 2000). The Pearl, Mississippi case, presented later in this chapter, is a prime example of this risk factor.

Peers may occasionally co-conspire in the violent action plan, joining up to become an accomplice. In studies of adolescent mass murderer events (Meloy et al., 2001), there is a noted prevalence of pairing among school violence perpetrators. Columbine is a good example. Harris and Klebold met each other in the eighth grade, rapidly gravitating towards one another in a relationship centered around hatred, violence, and vengeful fantasies. Chance brought together two individuals who were strikingly similar, and who, when together, acted as one, synergistically escalating rather than dampening violent impulses. Both were youngest children in the shadows of older, well-adapted brothers in an achievement-oriented household. Both experienced considerable anger.

School

The school environment itself may serve to elevate violence risk. Some schools may be inconsistent in their implementation of policies and/or discipline, reinforcing the notion that certain groups are favored and can do no wrong, while others are to be persecuted or abandoned in their time of need. Columbine again is a recent example of these perceptions. One year prior to the shooting, Harris and Klebold had gotten into minor trouble for a burglary. They became enraged because they believed they were treated unfairly compared to some athletes who had been involved in a similar low grade criminal matter. The Eric Houston case, discussed in Chapter One, involved a former student who showed up and shot four people, including the Civics teacher who had flunked him. Houston's perception was that jocks had gotten a break when it came to their grades, but when it came to him, a "nobody," no allowance was given. As a result his life was harmed, so "they" had to pay.

Some institutions have teachers and other staff members who engage in demeaning and oppressive treatment of students or other employees. Related to this is the organization that "looks the other way" when students or others are being mistreated by their peers or staff members. Such institutionalized "bullying" is particularly destructive, as it creates the belief that no one will intervene. This leads some to simply resign themselves to powerlessness, but a small minority perceive that acting out is their last opportunity for defending their ego and earning self-respect.

A school may also elevate its risk by failing to have in place mechanisms to insure its physical safety and security. In California and other states in the United States, there are now requirements that schools assess and address certain threats to safety by having a safe schools plan. These plans typically mandate assessment and improvement of existing security measures and procedures to reduce areas of identified risk (See Table 6).

Not all procedures are ideal for every school, but examples include: control of access to school property, on-site police or security presence and/or patrols, metal detectors, surveillance devices, visitor sign-ins, zero tolerance policies around violence and violence-related issues (i.e., weapon possession), violence prevention or reduction programs, school uniform policies, and closed campuses. Failure to address the important basics of safety that might apply to a particular institution in a particular setting will serve to elevate risk. *At a bare minimum, schools that fail to control campus access and prevent intruders who don't belong, lack zero tolerance policies, and have no early warning and reporting system for identifying potential problems, are evidencing denial and likely elevating their risk for violence.*

TABLE 6
California School Safety Plan

THE FACTS ON SENATE BILL 187
COMPREHENSIVE SCHOOL SAFETY PLAN

On October 6, 1997, Senate Bill 187, chapter 736, was signed into law by Governor Wilson. This bill, referred to as the Comprehensive School Safety Plan, provides that each school district and county office of education is responsible for the overall writing and development of comprehensive school safety plans for its schools operating kindergarten and any of grades 1 to 12.

Required Elements
Each school safety plan shall include the following elements:
(1) An assessment of the current status of school or school-related crime for each site;
(2) Identification of appropriate strategies and programs designed to maintain a high level of school safety and development of the following procedures for compliance with existing laws related to school safety:
- Child abuse reporting procedures.
- Disaster procedures, routine and emergency.
- Policies related to suspension, expulsion or mandatory expulsion and other school-designated serious acts which would lead to suspension or expulsion.
- Procedures regarding teacher notification of dangerous students pursuant to EC § 49079.
- Sexual harassment policy pursuant to Education Code, § 212.6(b).
- Provisions of any schoolwide dress code, established pursuant to EC § 35183, that prohibits pupils from wearing "gang-related apparel," if the school has adopted such a dress code. *Note: "Gang related apparel" must be defined and shall not be considered a protected form of speech.*
- Procedures for safe ingress and egress to and from school. *Applies to pupils, parents, and school employees.*
- A safe and orderly environment conducive to learning.
- Rules and procedures on school discipline adopted pursuant to EC §§ 35291 and 35291.5.

Compliance Issues
In order to ensure compliance, each school shall forward its completed plan to its respective school district office or county office of education for approval. In addition, each school shall meet all of the following requirements:
- Comprehensive school safety plans shall be written and developed by each schoolsite council established pursuant to EC §§ 52012 or 52852, unless delegated to a school safety planning committee.

- If delegated, the school safety committee shall be made up of the following members: principal or designee; teacher representative of the recognized certificated employee organization; parent of an attending student; classified employee of the recognized classified employee organization; and other members, if desired.
- The schoolsite council or, if delegated, the school safety committee shall consult with representative from a law enforcement agency regarding the writing and development of the comprehensive school safety plan.
- Each final adoption of the plan, a public meeting shall be held by the schoolsite council or school safety planning committee at the schoolsite to allow for public input.
- Each school district or county office of education shall notify the State Department of Education by October 15, 1998, of any school that fails to develop a comprehensive school safety plan.

Note: If a small district (less than 2501 ADA) develops a districtwide comprehensive school safety plan that is applicable to each schoolsite, that district shall not be required to utilize a schoolsite council or school safety planning committee in the development of the plan.

Available Resources
It is the intent of the Legislature that schools utilize existing resources in the development of comprehensive safe school plans. The following resources, although not all inclusive, may be of value in the development of individual school safety plans:
- Materials and services of the School Safety Partnership, California Department of Education.
- "Safe Schools: A Planning Guide for Action," developed and distributed by the School/Law Enforcement Partnership Program, California of Education.
- Grants available through the School Safety Partnership as authorized by EC § 32262.
- Consultation, cooperation and coordination, when practical, with other schoolsite councils or school safety planning committees.
- Safe School Center of the Los Angeles County Office of Education.

The comprehensive school safety plan shall be evaluated and amended, as needed, no less than once a year to ensure that the plan is properly implemented. An updated file of all safety-related plans and materials shall be maintained and readily available for inspection by the public.

A related issue is the need to have in place an effective liaison with local law enforcement. Whether that is done through on-site school police in larger school districts or through the building of bridges and relationships in smaller districts, there must be mutual trust and exchanges of information to reduce risk in specific situations. To the extent that this state of conditions does not exist, the level of risk is enhanced. Why? Cases requiring law enforcement intervention will not be responded to in the thorough and efficient manner necessary for stabilization. Unfortunately, there are some educational institutions who simply refuse to work with their local law enforcement. Perhaps it is due to the different cultures of the two professions, disappointment related to the handling of past cases, mutual distrust, or other factors. The bottom line is that this creates circumstances where the high-risk case can slip between the cracks. Intervention relies on a multidisciplinary approach.

A final school risk factor is the situation where faculty and staff refuse to respond and intervene due to apathy, ignorance, burnout, or fear. Teachers and educators are grossly underpaid relative to the important socialization task with which they are involved. Now teachers are tasked with yet another role: early warning recognition and intervention. Some may not care any more, burned out by ceaseless demands and a lack of appreciation. Some may be downright afraid to get involved. If these factors exist in any school, then school violence risk is enhanced.

Case Example: Pearl High School, Pearl, Mississippi

At 8:00 am on October 1, 1997, 16-year-old sophomore Luke Woodham walked onto the school grounds, approached two students near where he entered, gave them several articles, some literature and notebooks, with instructions to give the items to another boy, and exited the location. He re-entered a short time later, walked straight into the commons area armed with a 30-30 lever action rifle which he kept hidden under a long dark coat. Woodham approached two girls, 16-year-old ex-girlfriend Christina Menafee and 17-year-old Lydia Drew, and fired his weapon, killing them both. He continued randomly shooting into the commons area as hundreds of students frantically tried to escape, wounding seven more students.

Luke walked out of the building, and as he was driving his mother's car out of the parking lot, he lost control on a wet grassy area, and crashed into a tree. Woodham was then taken safely into custody by assistant principal Joe Myrick, who had armed himself with a handgun he had procured from the trunk of his car during the initial assault by Woodham. Woodham commented as he surrendered, "Mr. Myrick, you remember me, I'm the one that gave you a discount on your pizza the other night?"

Immediately, Woodham was handed over to responding police personnel. During his interview and interrogation, Woodham admitted that he had killed his mother with a butcher knife and an aluminum baseball bat several hours prior to assaulting the school. Investigators rapidly deployed to their house and found her body. Later it would be determined that she suffered multiple stab and blunt force trauma wounds; evidence of overkill often present in intimate homicides. Woodham tearfully explained, "She never loved me, always said I was stupid and told me I would never amount to anything."

He also talked about the significance of his former relationship with Menafee, "A friend of ours set us up...I finally had somebody to love and somebody to love me, the first time in my life...And then she broke up with me." The killings took place one year to the date that Woodham considered the anniversary of their breakup.

After his confession, the investigation revealed that Woodham belonged to a group of individuals led by 18-year-old Grant Boyette known as "the group," who adhered to a home grown belief system they called "Kroth," based upon Satanism and the philosophy of Hitler and Nietzsche. "The group" of approximately six students allegedly had planned for nearly a year to assault the school. Several days before their established date, Woodham decided to act on his own. He allegedly called Boyette after he killed his mother, and reported that Boyette told him to "finish the job," implying that he should continue on to the school to kill Menafee and others. For months prior to the killings, Boyette had reportedly told Woodham that he should just kill her and be done with it so he won't have to see her again. Boyette was charged with three counts of accessory to murder, and at the time of this writing had pleaded guilty to a lesser charge of conspiracy in Brandon, Mississippi (Brown, 2000). He was sentenced to up to six months in a boot camp-style rehabilitation program and placed on five years probation (Payne, 2000; "Shooter's friend," 2000).

Woodham told investigators that Boyette claimed he could summon demons to protect Luke. Woodham confessed that, prior to the shootings, he got on his knees, placed his thumbs on his forehead, and prayed to Satan. Woodham had numerous writings, a so-called manifesto, and a suicide note. Excerpts of these writings given to another student prior to the shootings include: "Throughout my life I was ridiculed. Always beaten, always hated. Can you society, truly blame me for what I do? I am not insane! I am angry... I am not spoiled or lazy for murder is not weak or slow-witted, murder is gutsy and daring. I killed because people like me are mistreated everyday. I am malicious because I am miserable."

Woodham was one of two sons whose brother was ten years older than he. Both boys lived in the home. Woodham used his brother's rifle in the assault. His parents had divorced approximately five years earlier, he had limited contact with his father, and reportedly blamed himself for their breakup. Members of the group referred to Boyette as "father."

Woodham claimed that he was always bullied, called "fat" and "queer" by others, and had a particularly strong hatred for jocks and athletes. In recent years, his grades were low Cs and upper Ds, in contrast to higher grades he had received years earlier. He enjoyed reading philosophy, particularly the writings of Nietzsche, played in the school band, and role-played day-long fantasy games such as "Star Wars" with his friends. Several months prior to the killings, Woodham described in his journal, in gruesome detail his "first kill": he had tested out his resolve for murder through the torture death of his "beloved" pet dog, "Sparkle." Woodham and his friends placed the dog in a plastic bag, and set the bag on fire while the dog "screamed."

Two to three days prior to the shootings he had called a friend expressing suicidal thoughts, reportedly despondent over the anniversary of his breakup with Menafee. Friends and family noted he had seemed depressed during the days before. He had made general threats to his group of close associates, intimating that he was very disgruntled over the situation with Menafee, felt jilted, and was "gonna get back at her in the worst way." Both defense and state experts characterized Woodham's personality structure as "narcissistic," a personality feature characterized by extreme egocentricity, feelings of entitlement, extreme sensitivity to rejection and criticism, and a propensity for rage when needs and demands for entitlements are thwarted (APA, 1994; Investigator Ecklund, personal communication, February 4, 2000).

The Woodham case is a sobering example of a number of risk factors, precipitating events, missing stability factors, and how these issues interact to elevate violence risk. In the next sections, each of

61

these factors will be discussed, using the Pearl High School tragedy to demonstrate the learning points.

Family

Certain family history and background issues may function as risk factors if they interfere with the development of healthy attachments and self-concept, disrupt social support, impair self-control, provide poor modeling for coping strategies, and limit overall resiliency. Examples of family background risk factors include: disruptions in the family unit caused by separation, divorce, marital affairs, and difficult child custody situations; violence in the home, such as domestic violence, emotional, physical and sexual abuse, and excessively harsh or severe discipline; substance abuse and dependency; neglectful and/or ineffective parenting, such as when parents are not emotionally or physically available to their children or are unable to set appropriate limits for their kids; homes characterized by high conflict; and, a weak or absent same-sex parent. Any of these family characteristics may elevate a person's risk of violence under the right conditions. In other situations, with the appropriate buffer or stabilizer, negative effects may be countered. These factors may also represent changing events as they unfold in the family, at which time they can also serve as potential precipitating events. If the family has violent, ineffective, anti-social or toxic role models, risk is increased.

Several examples of these issues can be seen in the Woodham case. His parents had been divorced five years, a situation for which he reportedly blamed himself. Primary custody was awarded to his mother, a woman described by Woodham as demeaning and degrading. His father was uninvolved with him. A connection between the father and son, if present, may have served as a safety net and mitigated the void filled by destructive peer and conspirator Boyette.

The disruption in Woodham's family had a significant impact upon him. Left by his father, mistreated by his mother, he suffered from deep feelings of inadequacy and abandonment. A flaw created from his past family life primed him to react severely to perceived rejection by others, and in particular to any love interest in his life. Feeling worthless, it is no surprise that he would gravitate towards other misfits who have similarly jaded views of the world. Thus begins a downward and violent spiral. Even hungrier for acceptance than most teenagers, he was particularly susceptible to the influence of malevolent others.

62

Psychological Issues

Various psychological issues, mental disorders, or symptoms of mental disorders may increase the risk for acting out behaviors and lethal violence. Mental disorders, as identified in the DSM-IV (APA, 1994) are simply agreed upon names for behaviors and symptoms that often cluster together. For an already at-risk person, the presence of a diagnosable mental disorder or behaviors consistent with one, may indicate increased risk for violence under the right set of conditions. *While the presence of any disorder elevates risk for violence potential, most people with a mental disorder do not become violent.* The important issue noted in some recent studies, for example, is the interplay between mental disorder and drug or alcohol use, and active psychosis (Meloy, 2000).

Mood Disorders

Mood disorders, in particular depression and bipolar disorder, represent one major category of problems, the presence of which may elevate risk. Depression is characterized by feelings of worthlessness, helplessness, and hopelessness, and is occasionally accompanied by suicidal thoughts and feelings. Bipolar disorder, also known as manic-depression, is characterized by an elevated, expansive, or irritable mood, which may become so pronounced that it leads to racing thoughts, distractibility, a diminished need for sleep (three hours or less per night), delusions, excessive goal directed activity, and involvement in pleasurable excesses without regard for their consequences. The reason they call it bipolar or manic-depression, is that the period of elation or expansive mood typically lasts a week or longer, at which point the person may swing to a profoundly depressed mood state (sometimes exacerbated by the experience of consequences incurred while manic). Both depression and bipolar mood disorders are often treated with a combination of psychotherapy and psychotropic medications, and it is generally believed that bipolar mood disorder is caused by a chemical imbalance; depression may be a reaction to life events and/or a chemical imbalance (APA, 1994). More than half the attackers in the Secret Service study had a history of feeling extremely depressed or suicidal (Vossekuil et al., 2000). There are other disorders with a depressive component. To the extent that coping skills and perceptions are impaired, any particular disorder can increase a person's risk for violence. Woodham's misery, suicidal thoughts, feelings of worthlessness, and despondency were consistent with a mood disorder.

Substance Use/Dependence

Substance abuse or dependence has been shown to increase risk potential significantly in research studies, although it is conspicuously absent in workplace and school violence situations, at least during the more predatory assaults. Interview and other data indicate that perpetrators do not want to reduce their control during the event, but there may be a prior history of substance use or abuse. Chemical abuse and dependency is both a symptom of poor coping, as well as a factor that can contribute to constriction of problem-solving skills. Secondarily, these problems may elevate risk because the at-risk individual may experience decreased frustration tolerance, as well as become involved in criminal activities and cultures that encourage violence in order to maintain drug connections.

Any mental disorder not mentioned specifically here may have the impact of increasing a person's risk, depending upon how it complicates their life or distorts their perceptions (Feldman & Johnson, 1996; Monahan, 1992).

Personality Disorders/Traits

Personality disorders are chronic, maladaptive ways of interacting with the world, viewing oneself, and interacting with others, and represent a relatively stable personal style. There are a number of personality disorders defined by the DSM-IV (APA, 1994). There are several which are commonly encountered in adult workplace violence situations. By analogy and experience, many of the same dynamics apply to the school setting (O'Toole, 2000). The narcissistic personality disorder is found in the person who feels morally superior to others, entitled to special treatment, sensitive to criticism, and is prone to rageful resentments and reactions when denied perceived entitlements. The antisocial personality has little regard for rules and the truth, a history of law breaking and lying, manifests significant egocentricity, may appear superficially glib and charming, and is extremely manipulative, often using people and telling them what they want to hear. The paranoid personality is touchy, unforgiving, suspicious of the motives of others, distrustful, and often hostile and accusatory. The schizotypal personality is odd, eccentric, and often isolative, displaying peculiarities of thought and reasoning which are readily noticed by others. The borderline personality is characterized by unstable and intense relationships with others, chronic feelings of emptiness or boredom, mood swings, intense fear of abandonment, and may engage in self-mutilative and suicidal behavior. Technically, a diagnosis of one of these disorders may not be made until a person is 18-years or older; however, one does not turn 18 and suffer from these issues "all of a sudden." Rather, these patterns have already begun to manifest themselves before the person turned 18.

Woodham evidenced narcissistic personality traits. His perception that he was mistreated by others and that his mother was "always against me" may reflect paranoid personality tendencies. His willingness to strike back violently against the system is evidence of antisocial traits. Woodham's intense neediness, desire for acceptance, and warped reaction to abandonment by Menafee could be a function of borderline personality traits as well. His adherence to a strange belief system might originate from some schizotypal tendencies.

Self-Esteem

Low self-esteem and feelings of inadequacy are common characteristics of at-risk individuals noted in a number of worst case scenarios. The person suffers from the pervasive feelings of not "fitting in," not being "good enough," and worthlessness. These characteristics may be defended through a compensatory process that involves denigrating those with whom the person feels inadequate. Woodham suffered from low self-esteem and developed a sense of moral superiority, a false self, to make his life bearable. In this world view, one is either better than or less than, which in turn can contribute to consideration of violent action plans and fantasies to counteract feelings of impotence and personal powerlessness. "You can make fun of me, but I can and will kill you." Similarly, other personality traits may have developed to serve a protective function for a fragile and scared, and now dangerous teenager.

Locus of Responsibility

Life outlook can be an important risk factor, particularly a pattern of blaming others and externalizing responsibility. This raises risk because if it is somebody else's fault, then there is already justification for directing anger, rage, and retaliation outward. It also elevates risk, because it prevents the person from making adjustments and changes in their life that will prevent further problems, and leads to the creation of new precipitating events, such as rejection or interpersonal failures. This perceptual process is common in the personality disorders. Woodham clearly blamed others for his problems, and came to believe that they must be punished accordingly. Just as personality traits may help the person defend against unbearable attacks on their self-esteem, externalization of blame protects from intolerable, internalized pain. If it's "their fault," the attention is shifted outward.

Attachment Issues

Many of the individuals who have gone on to commit major acts of violence, and even lesser forms of violence such as stalking or assaults, have had attachment problems and failures in their backgrounds. Difficulties derive from intense or absent attachments. In the former situation, emotional "stickiness" and an unwillingness to let go of relationships when it is time to do so creates the type of "perseverance" that may evolve into harassment, and aggressive pursuit behavior such as stalking, property destruction, assaults, and even murder. Luke Woodham had never had a significant positive attachment until he fell in love with Christina Menafee, whom he would later kill. The disruption was overwhelming to him. At the other extreme, absent attachment may lead to the same violence. There may be such estrangement from others that the person does not reach out for help, or lacks the level of empathy required to serve as a restraint when they begin to have violent impulses and a wish to retaliate for perceived wrongs.

Learning Disabilities

Some perpetrators of extreme school violence have suffered from learning disabilities. Again, most people with learning disabilities, with or without assistance, will go on to live fairly normal, nonviolent lives. Problems arise when the disability creates intense and unbearable feelings of powerlessness, shame, isolation, and inadequacy. In conjunction with other life issues, it contributes to a downward spiral and a vicious cycle of anger, rejection, failure, and constriction of pro-social problem solving options.

A similar dynamic may evolve from attention-deficit hyperactivity disorder (ADHD). Impulsivity as a symptom of that disorder, or attribute by itself, may elevate risk by contributing to social failure, lower inhibitions to violent acting out, or constrict problem-solving and decision-making activities. Impulsive people fail, then they seek ways to cope with their failures, some of which may be maladaptive and in extreme cases, dangerous.

Fantasy Life

Many of the individual factors contribute to the development of an active fantasy life. In higher risk cases, fantasies are usually violent, with strong themes of power and control as a way of coping and compensating for life difficulties. An alternate identity as a "force to

66

be reckoned with," or as someone "they'll be sorry they messed with" is developed. It is important to assess such fantasy development since it is a risk enhancing coping tool. Fantasies may be directly and indirectly measured by remaining alert to verbalizations, activities, and written and creative narratives or stories.

This kind of fantasy life may be indicated by an extensive interest in real or fictionalized violence, participation in violent role-playing games, and writing violent short stories and poetry. Woodham exhibited this risk factor in several forms.

Spiritual Issues

Few people have systematically studied the impact spiritual issues have upon risk, specifically the absence of or hostility towards a positive spiritual belief system. Deviance in this arena has been noted in many adolescent mass murder and school violence cases. In Woodham's case, there was the invocation of an anti-God, pro-occult belief system. Similarly in Columbine, the pair were vehemently anti-God and anti-religion. For many people, spirituality serves to create meaning, bridging the gap between what we as people can realistically control and that which we must let go. It offers a very powerful coping tool and sense of connectedness to others and the world at large. The renouncing of a benevolent God is often indicative of anger over some serious disappointment or perceived abandonment in time of need. One violent young murderer addressed his adherence to Satanism in a recent interview: "I prayed to God that he get me out of going to juvenile hall. It was the only thing I had ever turned to God for. When I had to go anyway, I decided to start praying to Satan, since it didn't make any difference, God abandoned me." The spiritual difficulty then may be indicative of broken relationships, violated trust, intense unresolved anger, and extreme self-centeredness. Or it may simply be a logical choice for a person. In a situation of some apparent risk and observed warning signs, it may indicate a lessening of coping skills and explicit dismissal of restraint.

Birth Order

Birth order is a static risk factor present in some cases of school violence. There is a seemingly higher proportion of perpetrators with older, successful siblings. Harris, Klebold, and Woodham all had older brothers who fit in well with their peers, and Kinkel and Carneal had older sisters who were very successful. Some comments from Carneal are enlightening: "I have an overachieving sister whom is a senior. I hate being even compared to her. Thus explains my reasoning behind being odd and strange and dressing the same way I act...Everybody asks why I am not like her... teacher tells me 'your sister never got in trouble'" (Belkin, 1999). While this dynamic may reflect another contribution to low self-esteem, the sibling rivalry aspect is noteworthy. As teenagers jockey for position in their families, and as they succeed or fail in that endeavor, they draw their own conclusions about themselves and others. Broken self-esteem, in conjunction with other factors, may fan the flames of rage towards others who are similar to their hated sibling.

Background Issues

Geographic Mobility

In some cases of adult and adolescent mass murder, the perpetrator's background was marked by several or multiple relocations. These moves disrupted their living arrangements, took them out of a community where they were beginning to establish roots, and forced them to adapt to an entirely new environment. Several of the individuals were "military brats" whose fathers were on active duty, staying for a couple of years in one location before moving again. Multiple relocations might cause several problems depending on the stage of life. It interrupts long-term attachments to people, thus lessening the presence of an important inhibitor of violent acting out. The person may, as a consequence of a diminished ability to attach, learn to treat people as objects for their entertainment while passing through, instead of developing a deeper connection to them. Disruptions in peer relationships and constant introductions to new social environments can result in the perception *and reality* of starting over at the bottom, a sentiment expressed quite candidly by Eric Harris in one of his pre-Columbine videotapes.

Early Initiation of Problem Behaviors

Cruelty to animals correlates with later violence (Meloy, 2000). It represents desensitization to the notion of harming living creatures, sadism, and an abnormal enjoyment for power over other beings, and may indicate underlying anger or rage. It also indicates lack of empathy.

Early initiation of problem behaviors (K-3rd grade) is an important risk factor for at least two different reasons. At a young age, if the child is failing, struggling academically, or having problems socially, it may be the beginning of an eroding self-concept, creating the need for ways of experiencing mastery and control over the world. In extreme cases, this may express itself in the development of a violent fantasy life to cope with feelings of powerlessness in relation to traditional school and social tasks. "I'm not good at anything, but if push comes to shove I can hurt you," might characterize conscious thought. These early problems may indicate that the child already has significant anger or other troubling emotions, suggesting a more pervasive and rigid dysfunctional adaptation to life circumstances. It can also represent the early onset of a serious mental disorder.

Criminal

The youth or at-risk individual's criminal background can be an important risk factor. The best predictor of future violence is past violence, and a criminal history that includes violent crimes indicates that the person has less inhibitions when it comes to acting out. One should not restrict their review to violent crimes, however, since property crimes, vandalism, and other offenses may suggest a general theme of disregard for the feelings of others. There may also be contacts with members of law enforcement that do not result in arrest, but rather some other "contact documentation." Communication with a law enforcement representative who may have encountered and documented these "sub-arrest" events might be productive to learn more about an at-risk individual.

The at-risk individual may have been convicted and incarcerated at some point, perhaps being placed on probation or parole. In these cases, contact with their probation or parole officer is likely to be productive and may shed some light on the behavioral tendencies of the individual. When it comes to intervention, it may prove critical, as these individuals offer another potential outside control mechanism.

Poverty

Poverty is another background factor. Research has demonstrated that those with a lower socioeconomic background have increased risk for violence (Meloy, 2000). Hopelessness, neglect, anger and frustration may readily breed in impoverished conditions. A single parent who is struggling to make ends meet may not have the time necessary to buffer against these stressors, and the child may turn to violent remedies as an escape from the futility. Fortunately, most people growing up in poverty do not succumb to this, but in some of the cases, such as in the Buell Elementary school shooting described in Chapter One, this was one of the pathways to violent acting out.

Cautionary Note

An important note is that these factors should not be used to "jacket" a child or teen as a static entity, incapable of transformation. Such an attitude directed towards these risk factors could impair the willingness of educators and others to invest time and energy into making a difference in the at-risk individual's life. Research has identified the phenomenon of the *self-fulfilling prophecy*, whereby a person with a label is perceived and treated by others consistent with their expectations. If the label is positive, such as, "This child is smart," they will put more energy into the child's education, because they anticipate and expect their efforts to be fruitful. The child will often achieve as a partial consequence of these extra efforts. If the child is labeled "dull" or "a trouble-maker," the temptation is to not put as much effort into their development, and to write them off. This will then contribute to their decline. We should avoid "writing off" any person, particularly the at-risk for violence individual. If anything, more effort, intervention, and thoughtful case management is demanded.

Educators and others should use their understanding of these risk factors to develop and provide effective remedial programs.

Case Example: Thurston High School

On May 21st, 1998, 15-year-old ninth grade student Kipland Kinkel, walked into the cafeteria of Thurston High School in Springfield, Oregon, and opened fire upon other students, killing two and wounding 25. He was armed with a .22 Ruger semiautomatic rifle, a .22 Ruger semiautomatic pistol, a nine millimeter Glock model 19, a Tanto fixed blade knife taped to his leg, and over a thousand rounds of ammunition. He was dressed in a trenchcoat, with a NIN (Nine Inch Nails) hat, and had taped two bullets to his chest under his shirt. As he ran out of ammunition in the .22 rifle and was attempting to use his Glock handgun, another student tackled and subdued Kinkel, who was taken safely into custody as he screamed, "Just kill me, just kill me now!" Later at the police station, he unfastened the knife taped to his leg and attacked a police officer while yelling, "Just kill me, just kill me." When investigators initially approached the Kinkel home for follow-up investigation, they heard loud music coming from inside. Kinkel had turned his stereo CD player on to a deafening roar which kept replaying the haunting musical soundtrack from the contemporary film version of *Romeo and Juliet*, a movie he loved. Kinkel's parents, Bill and Faith, were murdered. He had killed them

70

the night before. Ammunition from his weapons was piled high in the living room. He tearfully told the story of the murder of his parents to investigators, "I had to do it, I had no other choice! I said 'I love you mom' and then I shot her... I had to! I had to!" He truly believed he had no choice; his coping skills were faulty, limited, and compromised. Death and mayhem had become his answer.

The day before the school shooting, Kinkel had been caught with a handgun stolen from the parent of a friend, a gun he had purchased that very day and stored in his locker. Investigators were told that Kinkel was one of the individuals who had been at the house. When he was interviewed, he immediately confessed to the gun purchase, and was suspended and arrested. His father was called and arrived to pick up Kinkel at the police station. It was the culmination of a long history of difficulties for Kinkel and his family, especially as it related to his fascination with firearms and explosives.

Kinkel's parents were both educators, his mother a well-thought-of teacher at nearby Springfield High School, and his father a dynamic, recently retired teacher from Thurston High. Kinkel was the youngest of two; an older sister Kristen was a successful student and cheerleader who had graduated from Thurston and left in 1997 with a scholarship to a college in Hawaii. She was athletic, social, and academic, as were the other Kinkels. Kip was awkward and early in school had severe learning difficulties; math and sentence structure were very problematic for him. Kinkel's parents, being educators, spent much time attempting to help him, to no avail. Kip was held back in third grade, an event which left him behind his friends and made him feel angry and more inadequate.

Kinkel developed an obsession with firearms and explosives to cope with these deep feelings of inadequacy. He surfed the Internet, learning as much as he could about guns, knives, and explosives. He sent for books on bomb making and experimented with explosives. He began to pester his frustrated parents to purchase him weapons of his very own. They never had been supportive of weapons or violence, in fact, restricting his viewing of certain kinds of television programs. However, they could not sway his interest in weapons. He got in trouble for stealing CDs at the local Target and throwing rocks at cars off an overpass, events that resulted in arrests and negative attention (Kirk, Navasky, & O'Connor, 2000).

Desperately seeing the signs of a deeply troubled son, Kinkel's mother took Kip to see a psychologist in January of 1997. Kip and his mother saw the psychologist for a total of nine sessions and followed through on a Prozac prescription for depression. Kinkel admitted to the psychologist that he would make explosives from gasoline and other household items and detonate them at a nearby quarry to vent feelings of anger. He reported to this psychologist that if he had a bad day at school, he felt better after detonating an explosive. Therapy was concluded July 30, 1997 with the note, "Kip continues to do well. He is taking Prozac 20 mg. A.M. daily with no side-effects. He does not appear depressed and denies depression symptoms. His mother reports his moods have generally been quite good... Kip continues to function well with no evidence of depression. Kip, his mother, and I agree he is doing well enough to discontinue treatment." There was no reported further mention of explosives in the psychologist's notes after January 27, 1997. In the January 20, 1997 session note the psychologist observed that, "Kip often lies to his parents about his interests in explosives."

This case would be a nightmare for any mental health professional to treat, given his obsession with weapons and explosives and his propensity to lie. His case illustrates a number of the risk factors previously discussed. Kip's weapon possession arrest served as a precipitating event for his murderous rampage, and early intervention efforts, which could have served as stabilizing factors, were inadequate to reduce his risk.

Precipitating Events

When reviewing an at-risk person for purposes of threat assessment, we should consider whether there are any potential triggering events in the person's life. Such precipitants may already have occurred, may be an unavoidable outcome of the intervention process, or otherwise can be reasonably anticipated. Triggering events are the catalyst for violent acting out, the final straw, which the person perceives pushed them to do what they did or are going to do. Some examples of triggering events include: bullying or ridicule by a classmate, significant personal rejection, loss of a romantic or other important personal relationship, personal failure, administrative or disciplinary investigation or discipline, extreme jealousy, and psychotic or thought disordered perceptions. Many of these events have as their common underlying theme, a loss of face or humiliation, injured pride, and shame.

In the Kinkel situation, he had just been disciplined for his illegal possession of a firearm at school, and his father had picked him up from jail. The embarrassment and shame he experienced was too much to bear, a factor complicated by his father's and mother's affiliation with the school district. He anticipated greater punishment and consequences in his home life and these anticipated events served as a further trigger. In the Pearl, Mississippi shooting, Luke Woodham was triggered by the anniversary of the breakup of his relationship with Menafee. In the Columbine incident, several precipitating events appear to be operative: the end of the senior school year for Harris and Klebold was rapidly approaching; Harris had just been rejected from the Marines; April 19th was the anniversary of Ruby Ridge and Waco; and April 20th was Hitler's birthday.

Stabilizing Factors

Stabilizing factors are those strengths in the at-risk person's background that may contribute to restrain impulses and increase non-violent problem-solving options. Many of the identified stabilizers are simply "risk factors in reverse."

Individual Stabilizers

Coping Skills and Resources

Those persons who have good coping skills, often exhibited in the past under stressful circumstances, are less likely to perceive that they have run out of options and resort to violence. Such individuals will be capable of balancing a number of important issues in their life without apparent difficulty. Students with good coping skills may perform well in school, achieve consistently good grades, and experience interpersonal success while holding down a part-time job. Adult employees with positive coping skills will manage multiple life issues, including their family and financial responsibilities.

Those at less risk may have appropriate outlets for their anger, people to talk to, and a physical fitness regimen where they can work out their stressors in prosocial ways. They differ from those who "gunnysack" their anger or do things, like Harris and Klebold from the Columbine incident, to magnify, intensify, and feed their anger and rage. Does the person have a demonstrated pattern of responsibility, honoring and valuing commitments to others? This might be evidenced by student involvement in extra-curricular activities, and with adult employees, their responsible fulfillment of their job role across time. Espousing a moral philosophy incompatible with violence usually goes hand-in-hand with this pattern of responsibility. These factors will serve as stabilizing factors in many situations.

Interpersonal Skills

Interpersonal skills also may mitigate violence risk. Those with the ability to mix with others are likely to attract other people as potential friends and confidantes, and create relationships that buffer against violent acting out. Friendships provide a lifeline to a person at their wit's end. Those that have these skills may be more adept at reading interpersonal cues so that they engender fewer negative social consequences such as rejection and ridicule. For individuals that do experience rejection, interpersonal skills create the confidence to seek new relationships and the healthy belief that they are going to fit in somewhere.

Mental Health Resources

People who avail themselves of meaningful and productive therapeutic relationships with competent psychiatric and other mental health professionals may also be less at risk. Meaningful implies a trusting relationship in which the individual is willing to share his or her innermost thoughts. Productive means that s/he values the relationship and makes use of the therapeutic input and/or medication. Competent means that the clinician's actions are commensurate with the standard of practice for the profession. The student or individual is getting what s/he needs. Like healthy connections with friends and family, therapeutic relationships offer another important lifeline when the chips are down. Many people choose to disclose their innermost fantasies and the things that "really eat them up inside" only to a select few. Therapeutic relationships are explicitly meant to facilitate change, therefore offering some hope of helping at-risk individuals to alter negative, self-defeating, and dangerous perceptions.

Adjunct Treatment

Adjunct treatments such as attending 12-step or other self-help programs may also enhance resilience and mitigate risk. Many of these programs offer solutions to drug or alcohol addiction, a structured approach to complicated life problems, and a sense of belongingness. It is important to weigh the extent of the person's involvement in these programs. For example, with the 12-step programs there are levels of participation that range from, "I go to meetings once in a while" to "I go to meetings several times a week, work the 12 steps, have a sponsor who I call all the time, and volunteer to help others." Familiarizing oneself with the particular program the person is involved is helpful. In some cases, the person claims to be actively involved, but upon further inquiry their participation is scant and questionable. In that scenario, risk may actually be enhanced due to deceptiveness, poor treatment compliance, and the person's continued denial of serious issues.

Spirituality

The foundation of some adjunct approaches is a spiritual belief system that helps to mitigate the control and power issues that often create or exacerbate violent behavior. Spirituality also provides a value structure contrary to violence. Violence prone individuals are in a sense, "playing God" in meting out judgment and punishment of others. Many spiritual belief systems interrupt this destructive and grandiose human dynamic.

Spirituality warrants special attention. Risk is reduced to the extent that the person is involved in organized religion, or has a belief in some higher power that is a positive force (as opposed to an evil deity), and does prayer, meditation, and other spiritual practices. It is important to specify *positive* prayer because there may be situations where the teenager or adult prays for negative outcomes for their enemies, essentially strengthening their resentment and commitment to ill will. These behaviors only serve to prolong the resentment and increase the level of risk. It behooves us to try to understand the true level of this participation and involvement. Just because somebody identifies that they attend church on Sundays or go to midnight mass on special occasions does not mean they implement a nonviolent ideology in their lives. Involvement in an organized religion is not essential since there are many people that have a deeply personal relationship with a God of their choosing or other spiritual beliefs that solidly preclude them from violent acting out.

Peer Support

The presence of law-abiding peers, pro-social friendships, and healthy romantic relationships may buffer against violence. When a person is having difficulties, intervention from these sources may make all the difference in the world. Fortunately, there are examples occurring everyday, seen and unseen, in which these types of support networks effectively de-escalate many potentially problematic situations. Friends may insist that the at-risk person stay with them, deter them from acquiring weapons, tell parents or authorities when they appear out of control, or demand that they get help. While some of these behaviors may result in short-term disruption in the friendship, irreversible violent outcomes are averted.

Organizational Stabilizers

School Culture

We also need to assess the health of the school as an organization. Healthy organizations lower risk because there are less potential precipitating events, fewer situations that are allowed to fester unaddressed, and they make less enticing targets. Districts described as healthy will value education, take pride in the institution's identity, have motivated employees, and encourage excellence. The school cares for its students and employees and expects people to care for each other. Students and employees have a place to voice their concerns or to get help when they are feeling bad. When assessing this factor, it is important for team members to be honest and not just re-iterate the party line that "everything's great." In particular, attention should be paid to whether there are hostile or negative teachers or administrators who disrespect staff and students, or whether respect truly is the operative word. Two-way communication is a characteristic of the healthy organization, and within a school district this translates into communications between line and administrative staff, students, parents, and the various staff members at the school. There are forums in which a person may communicate their concerns, and people that genuinely listen. Perceived fairness within the organization should be assessed, and not just by those in positions of power. The perceptions of students and lower staff also count. The presence of legitimate due process options for those who feel unfairly treated is critical. The operative word across many of these modes of school operation is perception, not necessarily reality.

Resources

Access to resources such as funding for alternative schooling or mental health professionals is also an issue. Adequate staffing results in manageable teacher/student ratios, insuring plenty of attention for those who may need it. This may seem too idealistic, given the realities of funding in many districts. Despite funding issues, there are many districts that may be easily characterized as reasonably healthy, typically the result of extra efforts by dedicated staff members.

Physical Security

Another district stabilizing factor is adequate physical security. This means control over access to school premises, security or police assigned to the campus, or any other strategies employed to increase physical safety and decrease the attractiveness of the school for a violent act. At the same time, security should not be too intrusive, as this can be a disrupting influence.

Rules and Boundaries

A final organizational stabilizer is the school's boundaries, expectations, and rules. Are they clear to staff and students alike? When violated, discipline is implemented in a progressive and fair fashion with respect for due process. In situations where there is a need to address serious disciplinary or criminal misconduct, those in positions of authority will not shrink from the task. Development of rules and boundaries is enhanced by the input of students, families, and staff, a factor that may increase mutual understanding and compliance.

Family Stabilizers

Healthy family situations also serve to mitigate potential violence risk situations. It is critical for caregivers to be involved and take interest in what goes on in their child's life. These guardians need to care about their children's performance in school, respect for authority, exposure to drugs and violence, types of friends, and what kind of media they are interested in. With this level of interest and involvement, potential problems get noticed and corrected before they stray too far off the path. The mitigation of risk occurs in the healthy family: whether an intact "normal" nuclear family or a single parent with or without visitation by a non-custodial parent. There are plenty of examples of so-called intact families, mom and dad both present, which upon further exploration are really a thinly veiled façade of caring and normalcy. Behind the curtain there is abuse, neglect, and ineffective parenting.

Healthy families notice problems, model effective coping, and have corrective mechanisms for aberrant behavior, even if that means reaching outside the family unit for assistance. They set and support limits, and are open-minded to new approaches to managing their kids. Closed systems fester and allow problems to breed. If necessary, they will thoughtfully utilize mental health resources to address their difficulties. Healthy families will control and restrict access to weapons, and if weapons are part of their recreational activity, teach responsible handling of them.

Cookbooks?

How many warning signs and risk factors, and which precipitating events in the absence of which stabilizing factors, will precipitate an act of violence in the at-risk person? In a sense, the question begs, "Is there some magic formula we can input to a computer to generate a risk potential quotient." Unfortunately, the answer to that question is a resounding "no," and anybody who says otherwise is trying to sell you a bill of goods. That is the bad news. The truth of the matter is that human behavior is complex and there are multiple ways it may evolve into violence. There simply is no formula.

There have been attempts by some to create computerized programs to assist in the threat assessment process. The potential for misuse of these tools is immense. Some people, if allowed to simply punch in numbers or check boxes, may discard common sense and the need to treat each situation as unique with its own particular dynamics. Simply put, there are no checklists or computer programs which are complex enough to assess these dynamic and evolving cases. There is also no "profile" of the "school shooter." There are many pathways for a person to move from the idea of violence to action. Therefore, one must note behavior and communication indicative of an unfolding violent pathway. The critical issue is to investigate the potential development of this progression in a person demonstrating warning signs using subject interview data and collateral information, assessing carefully for risk factors, stabilizers, and potential precipitants which may anchor and guide our decisions and interventions.

Consider the following hypothetical case example. One high school student 1) recently assaulted by another student (precipitating event), 2) blinded by rage which erupts in highly emotional specific threats (multiple warning signs) communicated to school staff by other friends of the student, 3) whose parents have a weapon in the home (risk factor), 4) impulsive in past behavior (risk factor), 5) exhibits agitation (warning sign), and 6) has uninvolved or absent parents (risk factor/missing stabilizer) should probably be considered high-risk for acting out and addressed very carefully by responsible parties. On the other hand, altering some of the risk factors or adding certain stabilizers might cause us to revise our opinions. For example, the student has a caring and involved parent and friends who try to discourage acting out.

However, facts one, two, and three, *even with* the other factors not being present should probably trigger heightened concern and the need for immediate intervention. Now consider the same facts with

78

the additional wrinkle that the student is permanently bound to a wheelchair, has been teased instead of assaulted, and is communicating these threats by e-mail over the computer (facts extracted from an actual case). There would be less concern for violence, a concern about preventing subsequent victimization of the threatening student, and a different kind of mental health and disciplinary intervention than might occur with other case facts. These situations are dynamic and complex, like the human beings that are involved in them. In one situation a particular factor may weigh more heavily than another. Professional judgments and common sense should guide decision-making, underscoring the need for training and consultation for those involved.

False Positives/False Negatives

No discussion about threat assessment is complete without addressing the issue of false positives and false negatives. A *false positive* is the situation where we surmise that a person is going to be violent, when in fact they do not become violent. A *false negative* is the situation where we conclude that an at-risk individual is not going to be violent, and then they do become violent. *True positive* is the circumstance of accurate prediction of dangerousness, while *true negative* refers to the accurate prediction of no dangerousness.

These concepts are important because we strive to maximize true positives and true negatives in our threat and risk assessments. To inaccurately conclude that somebody might be a dangerousness risk, when in fact no such risk exists, might lead to negative academic, social, and legal complications for that person, as well as liability for those who are attempting to intervene. To mistakenly identify that somebody poses no risk and have the person do something violent or, worse yet, commit lethal violence, is even more problematic. Not only might innocent people be injured or killed, but the sense of safety and security necessary for a healthy school and learning environment will be shattered. The trauma will cause lasting harm to many survivors, not to mention the secondary concerns of liability.

While we strive to reduce the likelihood of a false positive, the far greater harm comes from the false negative case. Therefore, in the work of threat assessment professionals, it is acceptable to "err on the side of caution," consciously choosing to elevate our risk of false positives in the interest of reducing the likelihood of making the false negative error. At the same time, we consciously balance the potential consequences of the false positive, and to the best of our ability make choices in intervention that will lessen their negative impact. Our intervention selections should lean towards trying to help the at-risk person.

The threat assessment team (discussed in detail in the next chapter) and process is not about prediction; it is about assessment and risk management. We borrow the above concepts from the prediction realm of hard science to improve our ability to be more thoughtful in our procedures. We are dealing with human behavior, dynamic and rapidly changing. We assess to the best of our ability under often less than ideal circumstances. We behave reasonably, but there is no crystal ball, only the best available assessment for a given point in time.

Chapter Summary

Threat assessment in school violence risk situations means understanding the risk factors, stability factors, and precipitating events that elevate or diminish risk. There are many biopsychosocial risk factors gleaned from violence research studies (Meloy, 2000). Predisposing factors unique to school violence risk include the destructive influences of peer relationships, dysfunctional family issues, and negative school environments. Psychological factors such as mood disorders, a violent fantasy life, and low self-esteem may also elevate risk potential. Deviant spirituality can diminish restraint. Birth order that precipitates dysfunctional sibling rivalry can enhance risk. Other background factors such as geographic mobility and past criminality may also increase violence potential. Precipitating events are situations that have the potential to trigger acting out behavior. Events such as rejection and discipline may create feelings of shame and wounded pride. Stability factors reduce risk. Individual strengths such as coping skills, peer support, and interpersonal skills can diminish violence risk. Organizational factors at the school such as a healthy culture, physical security, and access to resources may serve a protective function. A healthy family support system may buffer against violent acting out. There are no cookbooks or computer based approaches that are valid for predicting school violence risk. Each situation must be reviewed on its own merit, using information about risk and stability factors and potential precipitating events.

CHAPTER FOUR

Threat Assessment: Applying the Concepts

Threat Assessment Teams

Threat assessment teams (TAT), also known as *incident management teams (IMT)*, have been used successfully to help school districts manage violence risk. *Threat assessment teams* are multidisciplinary teams usually consisting of an educator (principal or assistant principal), mental health consultant, campus-based security or law enforcement, and school legal counsel (internal or external).

During those intervals when they are not managing at-risk individuals exhibiting warning signs, TAT members train teachers, students, and others in the early warning signs of a potential problem and reporting procedures. They may also help the district to draft school violence prevention policies and procedures, and arrange for the team's own training and development (See Table 7).

TATs typically convene when there is an identified problem, and their task is to seek appropriate information and resources to manage a potential threat and bring it to a logical conclusion. Once a problem is reported, members of this team may review additional information, apply their varied specialized expertise, advise decision-makers, determine essential information, and evaluate and recommend options for reducing risk. Safety is the primary emphasis of the TAT, with the rights of at-risk individuals running a close second. Many school districts, without realizing it, have already been using this process in an ad hoc fashion. School based TATs are being formed, trained, and used in innovative districts throughout the nation and abroad. As a result, high-risk cases are being successfully addressed, and tragedies have been averted.

TABLE 7

Sample Zero Tolerance Policy

We at the District would like your help in keeping our schools safe for everybody, and would like to share some safety information with members of our staff. We ask your help to identify any situations where a student, staff member, or any other person might present a threat to school safety.

Just as our airports have zero tolerance for certain statements at the security checkpoint, our District has zero tolerance for any statements or behaviors of a threatening nature, any behaviors by individuals that might pose a threat to the well-being of students, staff, and others, and weapon possession. We have an obligation to keep our schools safe and take any of the above seriously. All potential safety concerns will be investigated thoroughly and actions appropriate to the situation will be taken, up to and including discipline, criminal justice intervention, and any other applicable measures. This is not an area for practical jokes or offhanded comments, as recent events demonstrate the importance of investigating thoroughly all potential concerns.

If you become aware of a threat situation, you must report it to one of the following places: 1) school police; 2) Dean of Student Discipline; or the District's anonymous hotline or e-mail/website.

Potential Role Conflicts

A few individuals are conspicuously absent from the description of potential TAT members: parents and guardians, union representatives, other students, the subject of the threat assessment team review, and treating mental health professionals. Teams should also consider excluding any member who might be traumatized by the particular situation under review. The justification for these exclusions primarily stems from conflict of interest issues and the preference for a substantial degree of objectivity in this process. This is a management decision-making tool for addressing a potentially critical situation. It is not a parent/administrator conference situation, although that may be one of the later recommendations of the team.

The presence of family members and their myriad of potential emotions might cloud the necessary objectivity of this process.

Similarly, union representatives, if in the role of representing the subject of the investigation, might also obscure the concern for safety. Safety concerns should be first and foremost, as opposed to the often exclusively individual interests of any client the union representative might be defending. There are appropriate times to involve union representatives in this process, but situations should be avoided where there is an obvious conflict of interest. Likewise, union representative involvement should be restricted if there is the potential to somehow lessen control and potentially escalate the situation by prematurely "tipping off" the individual being reviewed. For the same reasons, other students, and most obviously the subject of the review, should not be included in the team. The subject of the investigation will likely be interviewed by one or more members of the team, but that will come later and involve a more comfortable and conducive arena. Any interviews need to be structured and scripted to address particular agenda items.

Team members who have been harmed, threatened, or traumatized by the at-risk individual may not be able to participate objectively in the review process. They should consider excluding or restricting their involvement in the investigation and decision-making. Occasionally a prospective team member in a given situation, such as a principal, may be the target of serious threat. The principal should designate an alternate, such as the assistant principal, to serve on the TAT during that particular situation. There are times when bringing in an alternate may be impossible. If the luxury exists to designate alternate personnel to handle the situation, that would be preferred.

Another conflict sometimes arises with the mental health consultant to the TAT. It is imperative that this consultant not be involved in a therapeutic, that is, treatment relationship, with the subject of the review. This represents a "dual relationship," another term for conflict of interest. Therapists in most mental health disciplines are advised against such conflicts if they can avoid it. If a mental health professional is advising the team, the team is the client; if they are treating the subject of the review, s/he is their client. These situations often have the potential for organizational decisions that may have a negative impact upon the subject of the review through some adverse educational status or employment action. This puts a therapist who would sit on such a team at extraordinary risk for "harming" their client, or not providing the proper input to the team. It creates a very uncomfortable, divided loyalties situation.

On the other hand, the treating mental health professional will likely become involved by providing treatment information to TAT representatives. This occurs after securing an appropriate professional waiver of confidentiality to address relevant safety issues.

There are times when a mental health professional in a strictly evaluative role may serve as a consultant to the team without such a conflict. It is imperative in these circumstances that the professional clarify with all parties beforehand the nature of the professional relationship and the parameters related to information sharing.

Logistical Issues

Sub-groups of the threat assessment team may meet as necessary, depending upon the issue, such as a straightforward decision that only requires, for example, the principal, district counsel, and campus security. For practical reasons, these meetings are often held by conference call or some combination of on-site meeting and conference call, or by other communication modalities such as e-mail. There is great value in having district counsel present during critical decision-making, one of which is the aspect of legal privilege. Legal privilege means that the communication is protected from discovery in any potential legal proceeding.

How do we label these teams in a given district? School districts and other organizational settings will commonly refer to these teams as *Threat Assessment Teams*, an appropriate and descriptive label. However, there have been cases where simply the name and the fact that such a team was convened formed the partial basis for a plaintiff's action against an organization. An attorney might argue, "Convening the *Threat Assessment Team* implies that my client is dangerous, doesn't it, how could convening it not defame him!" Or they could concretely assert, "My client never made a threat, you had no basis to convene the team!" There are three issues from a practical standpoint. First and foremost, a TAT is the first level of review to determine if there might be a problem, given the presence of information that has generated enough concern for somebody to feel like they should report it. Second, districts may want to consider a different descriptor such as *Incident Management Team, Critical Incident Management Team,* or *Safety Management Team,* as a way of lessening potential misperceptions. Third, the term threat applies to situations in which a person has actually *made* a threat and/or to situations where the person's behavior and other clues indicate that they might *pose* a threat. Therefore, the term *threat* as it applies to the team name is an appropriate descriptor. The issue does not have to be a problem. Schools need to have a way to deal with potential problems around safety, to facilitate decision-making in uncertain situations, and to access specialized resources. School personnel strive to do their best in these situations without the benefit of a crystal ball. They should not be so worried about potential plaintiffs' attorneys that they ignore safety issues.

When to Convene the Team

Typically, the team will be convened in part or whole when a TAT member becomes aware of safety concerns related to a potential threat. It is not necessary to convene the team every time a potential threat situation is brought forward; rather, convening the team should be a judgment call of the team leader (usually the principal or vice principal) based upon level of apparent risk. If initial information suggests a high-risk for violence potential (evidence to support Category 1 or 2 level concerns defined later in this chapter), the TAT should convene. In these cases, it is imperative to bring together multiple approaches to increase school safety, and strategies to manage the risk. If the initial information suggests a moderate level of risk consistent with repetitive and/or intentional infliction of emotional distress (evidence to support Category 3 level concerns), there should be strong consideration of convening the TAT. The TAT mission in this situation is to: 1) understand the distress created in others, 2) ascertain whether that distress is reasonable or an overreaction, 3) identify the potential motivation of the subject and complainant, 4) assess whether this may be a prelude to physical acting out, 5) determine appropriate strategies for containing the behaviors, and 6) evaluate the repercussions of the emotional distress upon the well-being of others and the school's mission. If it appears to be less serious (evidence consistent with Category 4 or 5 level concerns), a threat assessment team process is probably not necessary, although getting input from some team members may provoke thoughtful dialogue about the management of the case and its implications.

After the initial decision to convene or not convene, subsequent information will likely lead to more informed decision-making, as collateral data sources and follow-up investigation confirms or disconfirms initial reports, raises new issues, or alleviates initial concerns. At this point, decisions will be made which are more reliable, with greater certainty of what the appropriate level of concern ought to be. If the information suggests greater risk, the full TAT will likely convene, while if a less concern, individual team members will likely be delegated appropriate follow-up tasks.

Decision-Making

Each TAT should have a designated leader, someone who takes ultimate responsibility to oversee the activities of the team and decide when it shall be convened. He or she legitimizes the team's decisions and is the final arbiter of any conflicts. It is important that the leader possess sufficient power and status within the organization so that they and the team are taken seriously. The decision-making model of the TAT is most typically that of consensus building, with each participant sharing their respective expertise, ideas, questions, concerns, and suggestions in an open exchange of information. The relationship of the TAT's consensus to what is actually implemented is affected by a variety of practical factors within the school, district, and administration. These decisions should be viewed as recommendations to the final decision-maker who may or may not be part of the team (for example, when the principal is not on the team or the superintendent is more "hands-on"). Some organizations are more decentralized and delegate significant authority to their local district school.

Even if the principal is a part of the team, the culture and practices within the organization may still necessitate an additional level of review and approval. There may be another request regarding legal opinions or questions about other issues that the TAT may not have considered. However, time may be of essence in some situations, requiring streamlined decision-making.

Contingencies should also be anticipated. For example, "What should we do if Johnny does not come to school on Monday when we plan to address this" or "How will we handle the suspension if Bobby's parents are cooperative and supportive versus defensive and antagonistic?" This is a human decision process, it evolves, and what actually gets implemented may vary from the initial recommendations.

Documentation

No intervention effort is complete without adequate documentation. Documentation is the proof that issues were considered, safety and privacy were valued, and personnel were being "reasonable" in their efforts. Each time the TAT meets or a team

86

member consults, there should be documentation of the date, who was present, how the meeting was conducted (telephone or in-person), and issues that were the focus of review. Issues that were considered important, concerns that were ruled out, and the thought processes that were employed to reach those decisions should be documented. Who was tasked with what follow-up should be included. As that information becomes available the file should be updated. The ultimate decisions and action items should be noted. The goal is to demonstrate reasonableness and thoroughness. Documentation should be treated as a confidential file and secured like other personnel or student records, consistent with laws and rules in the jurisdiction.

Warning Signs and Reporting Procedures Education

Intervention begins with recognition of a potential problem. A major task of districts is to disseminate information about the early warning signs of school violence risk so that prompt intervention might occur. TATs can facilitate this important task. Staff, students, parents, and community members are likely to observe indicators, which should precipitate prompt reporting, review, and appropriate intervention. The following case is an example of the tragedy of early warning recognition and reporting failure.

Case Example: Bethel Alaska

On February 19, 1997, 16-year-old sophomore Evan Ramsey entered his high school armed with a shotgun in Bethel, Alaska, a small town of 5,000. It was just before 8:00 am, and he hid the shotgun under a long coat as he entered the campus, fired shots into the air, and yelled "You better run, you're gonna die, I'm gonna kill you!" He then shot and killed classmate Josh Pillacio and principal Ron Edwards, and injured two other classmates before police arrived. Ramsey was holding the shotgun as police arrived, which he pointed and fired at police twice while they scrambled for cover. One of the officers returned fire. Ramsey, who had threatened suicide, screamed, "I don't want to die," threw the gun down, and was taken safely into custody.

Ramsey was the middle of three boys and his older brother was in jail. He was living with a foster family at the time, having had a rough early childhood. His father had gone to prison for a shooting rampage at the state's largest newspaper, briefly taking the publisher hostage, several years prior. Reportedly, Ramsey had suffered

87

emotional and possibly physical abuse by his father. Ten days before the murders, Ramsey received a call from his father, who told him he had just been released after 10 years in prison.

His mother was reported to be an alcoholic. Evan and his brothers were removed from the custody of their parents by Childrens' Services at the age of seven, starting an odyssey of foster homes to mother's home, to state custody once more when Ramsey's mother would appear drunk. Evan lived in more than 10 foster homes.

Ramsey had had minor disciplinary problems in school, and two years prior to the event had been investigated for vandalism of property. He was known as "Screech" to others, a nickname derived from the nerdy character on the television sitcom, *Saved by the Bell*. Ramsey alleged that he had been picked on by upper level students at the school. Two years earlier, depressed about his home life and problems at school, he had been talked out of suicide by his best friend. About one month prior to the shooting, he became quite upset when his headphones were taken from him by a teacher. Ramsey claimed the idea of bringing a gun to school popped into his head one day after being bullied.

About two weeks before the shooting, Ramsey began to talk with his friends about harming others. His simmering resentment–and perceptions of being picked on by others–became focused upon the school. He made statements about his perceived tormentors such as, "I'm going to shoot and kill them, if I see them at school." Referring to his headphones, he stated, "If they don't give it back to me, I'll shoot them... if I see 'em, I'm gonna shoot them." He had a list with five or six people on it, and shared these statements with at least two of his friends, classmates at school. He told these friends that he wanted to, "go out with a bang," by taking the shotgun to school and scaring everybody with it, and then committing suicide. These two friends talked him out of suicide, then suggested that he might kill other students and the principal. One allegedly said, "Don't kill yourself...you got to live the fame and the fortune."

Surprisingly, for a boy raised in an outdoor oriented environment, Ramsey did not know how to operate a weapon. One of the two boys showed him how to operate the shotgun that he had acquired from a friend's home. A third classmate offered to bring his camera to take pictures of the shooting, and at least 10 friends gathered in the library, as per Ramsey's request, the morning of the shooting. He told them, "Something big is gonna happen... an evil day." Not one student alerted an adult!

Ramsey was convicted and given two life sentences for his crimes. Two of the sixteen-year-old boys he had shared his plan with were charged with accessory to murder (Fainaru, 1998; Officers J. Evans & T. Stonesifer, personal communication, January 3, 2000).

Getting the Information to Staff

It is imperative to get the information to staff about warning signs. Staff are in an ideal position to observe the behavior of students, family members of students, coworkers, and outside parties. They may overhear students talking about violent action plans, and a student may confide in a trusted staff member. Teachers, administrators, support staff, and maintenance personnel should all receive orientation or in-service training about school violence early warning recognition and reporting procedures. The orientation presentation for new employees might consist of a short (30 to 60 minute) presentation about zero tolerance policies, school violence warning signs, risk factors, and reporting procedures. This oral presentation should be supplemented by a brief written section (several pages maximum) in the orientation manual for reference purposes (See Table 8 for example). Similar in-service training supplemented by handout material should be provided to insure that all staff members are knowledgeable.

Staff should be encouraged to report restraining orders in effect that might relate to the school campus, or potential threats from their home life that might spill into the workplace. Help resources for staff and students alike should be identified, emphasizing early intervention and positive coping. There are a growing number of videos that may supplement the presentations (See Resources). The primary issue is to communicate how these events can happen anywhere (dispense with the myth), how integral their eyes and ears are to increasing safety, what to look for, and where to report the information. This training can be augmented by a refresher on emergency and crisis procedures, or occur within the context of an early intervention with a problem student. The important point is to not give so much information that people tune out. Most employees are already overwhelmed with a myriad of other responsibilities that relate to the well-being of their campus and the success of the overall teaching mission.

TABLE 8

Sample Staff Handout for School Violence Early Warning Recognition

Introduction:

We at the District would like your help in keeping our schools safe for everybody, and would like to share some safety information with members of our staff. We ask your help to identify any situations where a student, staff member, or any other person might present a threat to school safety.

School Safety Zero Tolerance Definition

Just as our airports have zero tolerance for certain statements at the security checkpoint, our District has zero tolerance for any statements or behaviors of a threatening nature, any behaviors by individuals that might pose a threat to the well-being of students, staff, and others, and weapon possession. We have an obligation to keep our schools safe and take any of the above seriously. All potential safety concerns will be investigated thoroughly and actions appropriate to the situation will be taken, up to and including discipline, criminal justice intervention, and any other applicable measures. This is not an area for practical jokes or offhanded comments, as recent events demonstrate the importance of investigating thoroughly all potential concerns.

Early Warning Signs

- Verbal clues such as direct or indirect threats, assignments or writings with violent themes or fantasies expressed (including suicidal themes), statements indicating hopelessness or desperation
- Bizarre thoughts such as hallucinations, delusions, or paranoia
- Behavioral clues such as assaultive or intimidating behavior, weapon possession, angry and emotional outbursts, signs of depression
- Obsessions with weapons, violence, violent media and music, thoughts of death, grudges and resentments against particular individuals
- Any other warning sign that causes you concerns about safety within our District

Reporting Procedures:

Report concerns, ask questions if you are not sure about something to:
- School police
- Dean of Student Discipline
- District anonymous e-mail/website or telephone hotline

Crisis Procedures:

- Get to safety, and if you are able, help children to escape as per our procedures
- Call 911
- Stay calm
- Avoid confronting any assailant–don't be a hero
- List District-specific procedures

Getting the Information to Students

The Ramsey case, where nearly a dozen students were aware of his violent intentions, makes clear the importance of effectively disseminating information to students about what to do if they have safety concerns. It is better to talk with students in general terms about what they should look for and report. Students should be told, "If you become aware of any situations that might affect the safety of others, such as somebody thinking about hurting themselves or others, weapons, or threats, you have a shared responsibility to bring that information forward." The information should be kept brief, without long laundry lists of warning signs, to avoid sensationalizing, introducing ideas to the at-risk individual, or unnecessarily creating fear. This information may be included in student orientation handbooks, reinforced through the occasional or timely reminder (such as when a school or other highly publicized violence event occurs somewhere), which may then be disseminated during a matter-of-fact discussion during the course of other classroom or school activities. These discussions should also be age-appropriate, using language and terminology commensurate with the target audience. Concreteness, simplicity, and brevity for students in lower grades or those who are intellectually challenged is required.

Student awareness is only part of the solution. Classmates of at-risk individuals must feel that they will be taken seriously. Their concerns will not be ignored or dismissed. They must perceive that they can bring the information forward without fear of repercussions, and that something will be done to increase safety. These issues underscore the need to establish a school culture where students and others feel like there is two-way communication about important issues, and a valuing of opinions and concerns. In the Ramsey case, not only did the students not bring the information forward, but Ramsey himself acknowledged in subsequent interviews how he perceived that people ignored his concerns and well-being as he was being picked on and struggling with his life issues.

A hot-line or anonymous reporting outlet should be available so that students do not feel as vulnerable to the "snitch" label. Some districts will publish a special telephone number. One novel approach is to consider having a website or e-mail address where students and others can respond, particularly if there is free anonymous access available through the school library or another public location. In addition, teachers, security professionals, administrators, and other responsible adults need to stay in touch and approachable to students in order to earn their trust.

Students should also be told where they can seek mental health assistance. They should be offered concrete suggestions or referrals should they become aware of a "friend" in need of such assistance. The availability of mental health 24-hour hotlines should be part of the short student-oriented safety discussions.

Getting the Information to Parents/Guardians

It is fruitful to alert parents and guardians to zero tolerance policies, warning signs, and reporting procedures for school safety. This information should be communicated at the *beginning* of the relationship between the school and the family (i.e., beginning of school), and again reinforced through periodic and timely reminders. This process may occur during normal parent/guardian orientation activities where the issue can be brought up as one of many issues to be covered. Safety should be underscored. It is something that the district takes very seriously, requiring the assistance of all members of the community—police, staff, students, and parents alike. A short handout may be prepared to send home to those who are not able to attend a formal orientation, or for those districts that may not have this forum. The importance of parental involvement should be emphasized, and a nonjudgmental, non-blaming stance should be taken. Parents/guardians should be encouraged to share any concerns that may have a security impact on the school: for example, if their child tells them about a safety issue regarding a classmate, or a family member poses a threat to school personnel or a student of the school. Maybe there is an estranged non-custodial spouse who uses the child as a pawn and the school as a forum for acting out behavior against the custodial parent. Parents should also be encouraged to let the district know if there is a restraining order relating to their child in effect. The handout and discussions should be empathic and sympathetic to the difficulty of parenting in the 21st Century, and address the issue of how the Internet, social changes, peer influences, and just plain old teenage antics make it hard to know every possible situation to which their child is being exposed. Helpful suggestions and resources might be offered as part of any informational handout (See Table 9). A "partnership perspective" is most beneficial, one which opens up channels of communication, lowers potential defensiveness, and focuses upon the goal of safety and the well-being of all.

92

TABLE 9

Sample Parent/Guardian Handout for School Safety Awareness

Introductory Statement:
We at the District would like your help in keeping our schools safe for everybody, and would like to share some of our safety information with parents and guardians.

School Safety Zero Tolerance Definition:
Just as our airports have zero tolerance for certain statements at the security checkpoint, our District has zero tolerance for any statements or behaviors of a threatening nature, any behaviors that might pose a threat to the well-being of students, staff, and others, and weapon possession. We have an obligation to keep our schools safe and take any of the above seriously. All potential safety concerns will be investigated thoroughly and actions appropriate to the situation will be taken, up to and including discipline, criminal justice intervention, and any other applicable measures. This is not an area for practical jokes or offhanded comments, as recent events demonstrate the importance of investigating thoroughly all potential concerns.

Recognizing Potential Problems:
- Threats by your child or others
- Threats made against your child by others
- Suicidal thoughts or attempts by your child or another student
- Missing or stolen weapons
- Restraining orders that involve your child or where any District property is listed
- Any other situations that may affect the safety of your child or others at the District

Where to Report Concerns:
- Campus police
- Dean of Student Discipline
- Our anonymous hotline
- District e-mail/website

Sample Parent/Guardian Handout for School Safety Awareness

Parenting Tips:
- Be curious
- Be involved
- Be interested
- You do have a right to know
- Check out your child's friends
- Make contact with their parents
- Do not use corporal punishment, as it may increase aggression in aggression prone kids
- Do not keep any ammunition and weapons in home, particularly if child is prone to seething resentment, excessive interest in violence and weapons
- Check out their rooms periodically
- Become computer literate
- Place home computers in public area of house to allow easier supervision of its use
- Inquire about movies, music, and interests–moderate and discuss violent themed entertainment
- Get help if you need it

Getting Help:
- District counseling services
- County mental health
- Private mental health plan
- School Resource Officer
- Local PTA

Parents and guardians may also be given similar information during normal or problem-specific parent-teacher conferences, or at special parent-teacher open houses, as part of parent education around a variety of different problem areas. Information sharing, communication, and partnership cannot be understated.

The forum for parents and guardians to share information about their potential safety concerns should also include a designated point of contact, as well as more anonymous venues such as Internet e-mail. Barriers to such reporting should be removed and school personnel should take actions to increase the perception that the school is interested and accessible.

Accessing Collateral Information

Threat assessment team members and others involved in investigating and managing threats to school safety have an obligation to seek out collateral information to assist their decision-making. Many times this is the only way in which we learn information about risk factors, stabilizing influences, and potential triggering events. In these situations it is common for first-hand knowledge of the at-risk person's behavioral clues to be distributed across several information sources. Each piece of information, in and of itself, might appear insignificant. However, when pieced together, it may form a three-dimensional picture of a rapidly escalating individual. Considerable information was available about Harris and Klebold during the year before their attack on Columbine High. They had legal problems, made violent diary entries, experimented with explosives, acquired weapons through friends, and made a series of threatening statements in a variety of contexts. Reportedly, the information was never centrally reviewed or investigated.

When accessing collateral information, one should give particular attention to the order of any staff, classmate, family member, or other interviews. When conducting interviews and seeking information, the reviewer(s) should consider whether the person who is being interviewed is likely to approach the target of the inquiry and somehow inflame the situation by telling the subject about the nature of the investigation. If the person is likely to do so, the interview should be timed so that it coincides with any imminent interviews of the subject. In this manner, necessary security precautions can be implemented in case of a knee jerk reaction from the subject. In other cases, there may be the need to postpone or abandon such a collateral interview. Common sense and judgment should prevail.

Collateral information may ultimately lessen our concern about a particular at-risk student. For example, we may learn that a student is in treatment with a competent mental health professional, and that professional, with appropriate releases, confirms a recent course of medication with positive effects.

Other sources of information may include the threat report origin, students, teachers, coworkers, school counselors, treating mental health professionals, arresting officers, campus police, police and criminal records, probation officers, parole officers, surveillance, school records, parents/guardians, spouses/significant others, employers, and others as appropriate. Threat assessment of the at-risk student should include information from his/her friends and classmates. They usually have advance knowledge of a developing violent action plan, and may influence violent intent, planning, and preparations (Vossekuil et al., 2000). This inquiry needs to assess efforts by the individual to acquire, prepare, or use a weapon. The decision to access these collateral information sources involves consideration of one or more of the following: 1) the potential direct or indirect benefits of the information to the investigation; 2) the perceived seriousness of the safety issues at hand; 3) the privacy rights of the individual; 4) local, state, and federal laws governing the release or access of the information; 5) the extent to which accessing the information will potentially inflame or complicate the situation; 6) ease of access to the information; 7) likelihood that the information source will notify the at-risk person of the inquiry and the impact that might have upon the stability of the situation; 8) the availability and cooperation of the information source; 9) time pressures; and 10) cost factors.

Integrating the Information

One way of integrating this information is to examine how the at-risk individual is evolving along the following five dimensions, assessing the extent to which s/he is: 1) organized or disorganized; 2) fixed on a particular idea or set of ideas; 3) focused upon a specific target; 4) demonstrating a violent action imperative; and 5) evidencing a time imperative or sense of urgency. This model is also a useful screening method for reviewing inappropriate or threatening communications.

Organized

Organized refers to the extent to which the at-risk person is logical, coherent, and able to stick to topics or themes within their thought processes, often represented in written and verbal communications. If a person is organized, it is not hard to follow their thought processes. Reviewers do not necessarily have to agree with the subject's ideas. In fact, TAT members may conclude that the information is bizarre or frightening. Organized simply means that there is a logic within the communication that is consistent and easily followed. Generally speaking, the more a person at-risk is organized, the greater their ability to engage in a purposeful, planned act of *predatory* violence, should they choose to do so. On the other hand, if their typical pattern of communication is chaotic, fragmented, and hard to follow, then it is more likely that any behavioral manifestations of violence will be impulsive, unpredictable, and disorganized. It is more typical for school violence perpetrators to evidence organized thought processes, centering upon one or several discrete themes. Eric Houston, described in Chapter One, represented a high degree of organization. He was able to hold down a job and communicated to his friends specific, revenge-based fantasies against Lyndhurst High School.

Fixed

Fixed describes the situation where the following three conditions are present in the written and verbal communication: 1) there are one to several primary themes; 2) blame is expressed or implied; and, 3) the blame is for issues important to the individual within the context of his or her life. The more fixed the theme of blame and suffused into important areas of the person's life, the greater the risk for harm. Eric Houston was stuck on the idea that representatives of the school had done him wrong by flunking him and favoring jocks (fixed themes). He believed that the major disappointments and failures in his life were the fault of those at the school (fixed blame), and that this had ruined his hopes for life (importance).

There are individuals who are "mad at the world" but express no attribution of blame beyond themselves. They have not settled upon any themes or explanations for the difficulties in their life. Sometimes they blame themselves, sometimes their parents, and other times state, "Oh, it's just my lot in life." There may be diminished risk under these conditions; however, monitoring may be indicated to detect shifts in perspective.

Focused

A person may be considered *focused* when s/he: 1) identifies specific individuals; 2) perceives that these individuals have had a significant negative impact upon them; 3) attributes malevolence to their actions; and, 4) expresses the need for them to be punished. Generally, the more focused the person is upon a target or targets, the greater the risk. Eric Houston's fantasies–expressed to third parties beforehand–exhibited a highly specific focus on the Civics teacher who had flunked him, and a general focus upon athletes and others whom he believed were treated more favorably. These factors are consistent with his actions the day of the homicides. He targeted this teacher and killed him, and shot randomly at other students.

Violent Action Imperative

Two conditions define the presence of a *violent action imperative*: 1) the at-risk person perceives that legitimate avenues for coping with their life situations have been exhausted or are viewed as inaccessible or inadequate; and, 2) the person indicates or evidences a willingness to "step outside the box" for the solution to their life situation(s). The more indicators consistent with a developing violent action imperative, the greater the risk for violent acting out. In the Columbine shooting example, a violent action imperative was demonstrated by Harris and Klebold long before their homicidal behavior. It was evident in their communication of threats towards others, their detailed fantasy life that centered upon violent revenge (as noted in videotapes, website verbalizations, and personal diaries), their possession of guns and explosives, and their choices of anti-heroes.

Time Imperative

Time imperative is noted when: 1) the at-risk person indicates a short-term time frame for taking matters into his/her own hands; and/or, 2) expresses urgency or desperation for initiating any discussed or intimated violent action plans. The shorter the time imperative, the greater the risk of violence. Harris and Klebold made references to something big happening on or about the date of their mass homicide/suicide.

This method of interpreting information pertaining to an at-risk individual across time is helpful; however, it may also be used as a way of screening and filtering individual communications to ascertain whether concerns should be enhanced or diminished. It is a useful model for guiding our thinking as we approach letters, diary entries, and records of conversations or other communications.

Case Example: Threatening Communications Part I

In the fall, 1999, a mid-western high school was confronted with the following situation. A high school sophomore, Jennifer Sampson, reported to her parents that she had received a series of distressing communications from another sophomore, Suzie Jones. The communications involved e-mails, letters directly handed to Jennifer, and letters passed to Jennifer through third parties. Excerpts include the following:

98

From: Haldol.com
To: Bitchface
First off I hate your fucking guts...you probably didn't know I existed in fourth grade but I did. I spoke to you several times but as the bitch you are you fucking ignored me. You know what it's like to be hated by everybody in a room? Probably not, but I do. Now let's talk fifth and sixth grade. You ignored me then too. You and Linda became friends and I was just some piece of shit tag along. Then in seventh grade you dumped her like a piece of shit. And in eight and ninth grade you're just a rude ass bitch and I hate you with all my heart and soul. Go screw your dead fucking horse. (E-mail one, September 25, 1999)

Jennifer,
Am I getting to you? Good. You don't know why I hate you do you? Am I getting to you yet? Its time to see how I feel. Revenge.
Suzie (Letter one, September 26, 1999)

Jennifer,
I don't give a shit if you have time or not. You have had enough time to fuck with my head like you do. You don't know what you do to me do you? You have no fucking idea. Imagine someone strangling you, you just stop breathing, but aren't quite dead and then they bring you back to life again. Then they let you recover. Then they take out a knife and cut your liver out while you are awake. Then they let you eat all kinds of food and then let you die cause you can't filter out the poisons and shit and you die slowly. That's what you do to me. But it's worse. You slowly rip my heart and soul out. I hate you so much.
Suzie (Letter three, October 3, 1999)

Jennifer,
Don't you just fucking want to kill me? The next pages are a poem I wrote just for you. Guess what? You're a bitch. How many people are you going to fuck over today? Did you enjoy your childhood? I sure as hell didn't. Do you know what it's like to be the one that everybody picks on?

The one that everybody hates? No you probably don't. When you go through that you get a little hateful bitch who fucks with her own head. But do you give a shit? Hell no. Bye bitch bye,
Suzie (Letter four, October 7, 1999)

Poem (Untitled)
Seeing you in this world
Makes me want to die
I don't know what tomorrow holds
My hate grows everyday
See my eyes full of pleasure
While you cry and suffer
Hate
Watching the bullet
Enter your brain, ending my pain
So fuck you (poem with letter of October 10, 1999)

To: Bitchface
From: Haldol.com
Knife splitting
Blood dripping
Bones cracking
I'm going to fuck up your face
Murder
No no
You have to be human for that
Revenge–yes
Hate–pure
First off I'm not threatening to kill you. I'm just showing you my fantasy. Your death would make my life happy. So don't try to even say that, I am not like you.
Bye,
Suzie (E-mail dated October 12, 1999)

It is clear that Suzie's letters and e-mails are *organized.* They are coherent and have their own logic that is easy to follow, centering upon her perception of mistreatment by Jennifer, and what awful interpersonal characteristics befit Jennifer.

Suzie's letters are *fixed* on the idea that Jennifer has treated her badly, that she didn't deserve that bad treatment, and that Jennifer needs to be punished. On the next dimension, *focused*, Suzie states and implies that Jennifer is the source of all of her problems and that Jennifer has intentionally mistreated her.

Violent action imperative is the next issue to contemplate. While Suzie is quite descriptive in her discussions of violent ideation and fantasy, she does not tell Jennifer she is going to do these things to her. Rather, she says, "I'm not threatening to kill you. I'm just showing you my fantasy. Your death would make my life happy." The action imperative is defined as a willingness to use unacceptable, illegal, or immoral problem-solving strategies to solve the problem personally and by any means necessary. Suzie has already demonstrated this by inappropriately communicating these e-mails and letters, despite her denials of intent to do harm. The details of her violent fantasies are well outside of legitimate remedies, therefore, the action criteria has been met.

It is on the *time imperative* dimension that Suzie's communications fall short of some imminent or urgent indicator of violent acting out. None of the letters or e-mails indicate urgency, or any stated time frame for acting out on the verbalized violent action plans. Suzie is keenly aware of time in a longitudinal sense, but does not give us any of the verbal indicators that would meet criteria on this dimension.

We conclude that Suzie is organized, fixed, focused, starting to settle upon a violent action imperative, but lacking any evidence of a time imperative. Based solely on the letters and e-mails, this is a case where imminence of danger is not the concern, but the potential for violence may exist at some later point. The simple question, "Is she dangerous?" is not particularly helpful here. Rather, there are other questions and more assessment is required. It is critical to assess collateral information pertaining to risk factors, stability factors, and potential precipitating events. We have an initial sense about the case, and the reasons why we consider it serious. There is an approach to describing or categorizing the risk in this situation which will be presented later in this chapter. This approach will allow for a range of risk levels and offer a useful way to communicate the results of our risk assessments.

Multiple Pathways to Violence

Many people have the capacity to become violent under the right circumstances. The problem with some "threat assessment" models is that they are static and fail to take into account that contemporary violence risk assessment (Meloy, 2000) views human behavior as dynamic and fluid, subject to changing perceptions and unfolding, novel sets of circumstances. There are multiple pathways and speed zones an individual can follow to become violent. Awareness of this variability will prevent a narrow, overly restrictive view of violence origins. Such a restrictive view could lead to the "false negative" problem mentioned earlier: no "threat" yet violence occurs.

In the Bath, Michigan case, violence emerged from a highly responsible individual's preoccupation with financial insecurity. He was married and had much to lose by committing an act of violence. The man could not let go of his obsession, and this psychodynamic, coupled with his tendency to blame others and believe that he had the entitlement to punish them, evolved into large scale, premeditated violence. The pathway in this case was a highly idiosyncratic, obsessional process in an otherwise healthy (on the surface) social/community context.

In the tragic Buell elementary case, a six-year-old girl was murdered by a six-year-old boy. Violence evolved quickly in an entirely different context which contained substantial parental neglect, violent and anti-social role models, and the irresponsible availability of illegal firearms. A young boy was capable of forming significant resentment and targeted anger after being raised on a staple diet of violent television and movies. Yet the boy possessed no realistic understanding of "death" as a concept. The victim in this case had high self-esteem and stood up to his inappropriate advances, the apparent precipitant. The context was an urban backdrop of poverty and oppression. The elementary school had some security procedures in place, but failed to take appropriate actions when the child was seen earlier in the day with a knife. A highly dysfunctional life was the primary violence pathway for this young boy.

In another case, the delusional husband of a former substitute teacher, stuck on the idea that his wife had had an affair, could not let go of the idea that his life has been destroyed by this affair. He concluded that he must destroy the source of his shame and kill himself. A serious mental disorder with substantial violent content was the pathway in this case.

The Columbine tragedy involved two teenagers from well-to-do homes, who evidenced a violent fantasy life to combat feelings of inadequacy. They were profoundly judgmental and intolerant of other groups. These two individuals harbored intense resentment, deliberately feeding it to increase their commitment to violence, and used violent media and video games to stimulate themselves. Both boys were obsessed with weapons and historical anti-heroes, and their closed relationship fanned the flames of their simmering rage in a synergistic way. The primary pathway here was a homicidal dyad, a violent fantasy life shared between two like-minded, similarly inclined individuals.

The threat assessment should consider several other issues which may relate to violence potential (Borum, 2000). Does the person have the ability (access, means, capacity, and opportunity) to become violent? Is there evidence of intent (specificity of plan, action taken toward plan)? Have they crossed thresholds (engaged in attack-related behaviors, broken rules) which indicate elevated risk? Are others concerned by observed behaviors (subject discussed plan/threat with others, others are afraid)? Does the at-risk individual demonstrate noncompliance with risk-reduction (lack insight, lack interest in reducing risk)? In varying degrees, each of these tragic cases evidenced ability, intent, crossed thresholds, concerned others, and noncompliance with risk-reduction.

Each of these cases also demonstrates the fluidity of human behavior, and how risk factors, stability factors, and precipitating events uniquely combine to produce a given level of violence potential. Familiarity with how actual cases evolve and occur, and the use of logic to integrate these different types of information so that we may create a three-dimensional view of an at-risk individual, forms the basis of our threat assessments. However, once we develop some ideas and information about the at-risk individual, we need a consistent language to communicate our assessment results–one that allows for a range of possibilities.

A Categorical Approach to Describing Risk

Myth Five: Individuals are either dangerous or not dangerous.

Experts recommend categorical rather than probabilistic systems for communicating the results of violence risk assessments (Monahan and Steadman, 1996). The technology for understanding human behavior is not sufficiently precise to allow for probabilistic statements such as, "a 75 percent probability of violence." Rather, the variable and complex nature of human behavior lends itself to statements that fall into categories. One particular model (Hatcher, 1994, 1995, 1996) uses a five category system for describing violence risk potential which can guide the construction of action steps appropriate to the level of risk. The Risk Investigation Model (Hatcher, 1994, 1995, 1996) recognizes that risk behavior does not fall into two simple categories of violent versus non-violent, but rather extends across a continuum.

These categories are a useful way of describing and communicating–not diagnosing–the results of risk and threat assessments at different phases of the process. For example, as information is initially presented to team members, it may be helpful to hypothesize what the level of risk may be, so that initial precautions may be taken. This is done with the knowledge that information may be lacking. Information will be sought to reduce that uncertainty at a later point. However, a preliminary assessment forces team members to be thoughtful about their initial game plan. As the process continues, new data are accessed which either confirm or disconfirm the initial level of concern. Then the situation is either upgraded or downgraded, and interventions modified accordingly. Subsequently, similar modifications in level of assessed risk may need to be made, so that intervention is at a level commensurate with risk, without a false sense of security nor overkill. Having an easy to use, easy to understand category system, a common language for descriptions, facilitates the assessment and intervention process. (See Table 10 for a summary.)

Category 1

In the Category 1 situation, the individual is imminently dangerous to self or others and qualifies for immediate hospitalization or arrest. In a composite case example, three high school students are locked into a high drama love triangle. Sheryl, the female, is pregnant by her ex-boyfriend Billy who attends the continuing education school down the street. She recently broke off her relationship with him due to his abuse, and struck up a relationship with Robert. One day Sheryl didn't show up to her afternoon classes. Just prior to disappearing she handed a note to her friend Tina to give to her parents. Tina opened it out of curiosity and found a detailed suicide

TABLE 10
(Adapted from Hatcher, 1994, 1995, 1996; Mohandie & Hatcher, 1999)

Risk Investigation Model	
Category 1:	High Violence Potential, Qualifies for Immediate Arrest or Hospitalization
Category 2:	High Violence Potential, Does Not Qualify for Arrest or Hospitalization
Category 3:	Insufficient Evidence for Violence Potential, Sufficient Evidence for Repetitive and/or Intentional Infliction of Emotional Distress Upon Students, Co-Workers, Supervisors, or Others
Category 4:	Insufficient Evidence for Violence Potential, Sufficient Evidence for Unintentional Infliction of Emotional Distress Upon Students, Co-Workers, Supervisors, or Others
Category 5:	Insufficient Evidence for Violence Potential, Insufficient Evidence for Infliction of Emotional Distress Upon Students, Co-Workers, Supervisors, or Others

letter, resulting in a search for Sheryl. Sheryl was eventually located at Robert's house after a frantic search by concerned school and police personnel. She was actively suicidal, partially precipitated by her fear of disclosing her pregnancy to her parents. She was then hospitalized by police and mental health personnel. At the same time, Tina indicated that Billy had been stalking and threatening Sheryl and her new boyfriend, upset about the prospect that she might get an abortion and that she had dumped him for a new boyfriend. When school police responded to investigate these concerns, they found Billy in possession of a fully loaded nine-millimeter handgun. He fought the arresting officers and issued more threats. He was charged with making terrorist threats, stalking, and carrying a concealed weapon. Billy was expelled from school and school officials secured a restraining order against him. Several weeks later Sheryl returned to a different school, after significant mental health intervention. For his own safety, her new boyfriend was also relocated. This case exemplifies the hospitalization issue and the arrest outcomes in two different types of Category 1 risk situations.

Category 2

Category 2 cases involve individuals who evidence high violence potential but do not qualify for arrest or hospitalization. In the Category 2 situation, the threat of violence has a qualification or condition associated with the threat. This means that the individual is going to hurt someone if some designated or inferred event in the future does happen or does not happen. In this circumstance, the reported behavior of the student, employee, or other person, while of serious concern to school personnel, is not reasonably likely to qualify for immediate arrest or involuntary psychiatric hospitalization. For example, a long term disabled school employee anticipating his upcoming disability pension hearing states, "If they decide against me, I know where they live and I will teach them a lesson." He then embarks upon extensive discussions with others about his violent fantasies, his detailed knowledge of their personal addresses and driving habits, and his past military training in surveillance and firearms.

Category 2 cases present a significant challenge to school personnel, campus law enforcement, and mental health professionals. In this category, the threat may or may not be explicit. An individual may make a threat and/or pose a threat for future harm (Fein & Vossekuil, 1998; Gelles, Fein, & Sasaki, 1998; Macdonald, 1968). Risk assessment specialists, particularly mental health consultants, play a critical role in distinguishing Category 1 from Category 2 cases, evaluating the level of risk to self and others as indicated by the student or employee's actions, and assessing options for continued school safety.

Category 3

Category 3 is defined as insufficient evidence for violence potential, but sufficient evidence for the repetitive and/or intentional infliction of emotional distress upon others. In the Category 3 situation, it is the threat of violence rather than the act of violence that is important. The threat of violence or other behaviors are intended to cause other students, co-workers, administrators, and/or others sufficient distress so that no interpersonal and/or school action will occur that would be adverse to the individual making the threat. These cases often involve intimidators who are extremely effective at making others take notice of their concerns. They believe that they are entitled to do so, and will often acknowledge to others that this was their intended goal, a goal that they will often perceive as justified. An example is the student who regularly bullies his classmates when he feels like they have not given him an appropriate degree of respect, angrily and abusively berating their personality ("You are a punk and a loser!"), using ambiguous and not so-ambiguous threatening language ("I could kick your ass" or "I'm gonna mess you up!"). While the bully denies that he would ever get violent, he is very effective at getting others to "walk on eggshells" to appease him. The Category 3 description also applies when the person denies any intention to cause distress, but the behavior is repetitive across time, and sufficient to cause distress in coworkers, classmates, and others. Many times the person fails to respond to limit-setting by district personnel.

Category 4

Category 4 cases have insufficient evidence of violence potential, but sufficient evidence for the *unintentional* infliction of emotional distress upon others. In the Category 4 situation, the threat of violence occurs and could reasonably cause emotional distress in other students/employees. The individual makes a single threat or threatening behavior, but does not have the intent or motive to cause distress in other students, co-workers, supervisors, or others. Subsequently, the individual is able to acknowledge the reasonable impact of his/her behavior upon the emotional health and welfare of the targeted people. The student further acknowledges and endorses the school and his or her parents' code of conduct that such behavior is unacceptable. S/he promises it will not occur again. For example, a high school junior joked to another student about how a "Columbine-type shooting might liven up their school's first fall dance" as he was complaining about the "brainless jocks." This other student, concerned about this statement due to another recent shooting, did the right thing and told a teacher who intervened and referred the boy to the vice principal. The vice principal convened a threat assessment team. Upon the TAT recommendation, she made arrangements for an interview of the student with security present. The teenager acknowledged making the statement, felt bad that he had caused others to become upset, admitted that it was in bad taste, and said he would apologize to put people at ease. When his mother, a single parent, was notified about the incident, she attended a school conference. With a campus-based police officer, they searched the boy's room, found no weapons or anything else to lend credibility to the statement, and his mother agreed to support the school's disciplinary suspension.

Category 5

In the Category 5 situation, insufficient evident is present for either violence potential or the infliction of emotional distress. This category indicates an unfounded allegation of violent threat by another student or co-worker(s) for unknown reasons. In one case, a teacher was referred to the police and an *ad hoc* school based threat assessment team after she accused students of attacking her and dousing her with fecal matter. After an investigation, it was determined that she had concocted the story, and she was charged and convicted of filing a false police report (Leonard, 1998).

These five categorical descriptions provide a consistent behavioral language for communicating the results of risk assessments. It is important to recognize that the categorical description of an individual applies to a particular point in time, under a given set of circumstances. An individual may escalate or de-escalate and qualify for inclusion in another category as these factors and interventions change.

The particular category system focused upon in this book is not the only one currently in use within school districts. For example, Fayette County Public School District in Kentucky has modified and adapted it into a similar five category system. Their system involves different descriptors: Category 1, Imminent Risk for Harm; Category 2, High Risk for Harm; Category 3, Moderate Risk for Harm; Category 4, Minor Risk for Harm; and, Category 5, Low/No Risk for Harm. Each of their categories has descriptors anchored by warning signs, known risk factors, precipitating events, and stabilizing factors present in the individual case (See Table 11).

Any risk assessment system utilized by a school district should be user-friendly, behaviorally based, and offer clear definitions of the categories to increase team member agreement (reliability) about the level of risk in any given situation. This will allow understandable communication between threat assessment team members when reviewing specific cases. Knowing and agreeing about the degree of apparent risk allows team members to move to the next important issue: intervention decisions.

Chapter Summary

Threat assessment teams (TAT) are multidisciplinary teams composed of an educator, mental health professional, school police

TABLE 11

Fayette County Risk For Harm Categories

Category 1: Imminent Risk for Harm

An individual is, or is very close to, behaving in a way that is, potentially dangerous to self or others. Examples include detailed threats of lethal violence, suicide threats, possession/use of firearms or other weapons, serious physical fighting, etc. Most of these individuals will qualify for immediate hospitalization or arrest.

Category 2: High Risk For Harm

An individual has displayed significant Early Warning Signs, has significant existing Risk Factors and/or Precipitating Events, and has few Stabilizing Factors. May not qualify for hospitalization or arrest at present, but requires referrals for needed services and active case management.

Category 3: Moderate Risk for Harm

An individual has displayed some Early Warning Signs and may be existing Risk Factors or recent Precipitating Events, but also may have some Stabilizing Factors. There may be evidence of internal emotional distress (depression, social withdrawal, etc.) or of intentional infliction of distress on others (bullying, intimidation, seeking to cause fear, etc.).

Category 4: Minor Risk for Harm

An individual has displayed minor Early Warning Signs, but assessment reveals little history of serious Risk Factors or dangerous behavior. Stabilizing Factors appear to be reasonably well-established. There may be evidence of the unintentional infliction of distress on others (insensitive remarks, "teasing" taken too far, etc.).

Category 5: Low/No Risk For Harm

Upon assessment it appears there is insufficient evidence for any risk for harm. Situations under this category can include misunderstandings, poor decision-making, false accusations from peers (seeking to get other peers in trouble), etc.

officer or security, and legal counsel. These TAT members take responsibility for reviewing situations of apparent risk, and generating intervention recommendations. The TAT may also provide important education to school staff, students, and parents about the warning signs of a potential problem, and where to report this information. TAT members must access collateral sources to identify warning signs, potential risk and stability factors, and precipitating factors associated with a particular case under review. The threat assessment process requires an understanding that there are multiple pathways to violence. At-risk individuals tend to become *organized, fixated,* and *focused* upon a specific target. S/he will demonstrate a *violent action imperative* that legitimizes violent problem solving and indicate an *urgency or a specific time frame* for his/her actions. These dynamic characteristics, in combination with other factors, suggest a higher risk for violent acting out. At-risk individuals can be assessed along a five category continuum: Category 1, High Violence Potential, Qualifies for Immediate Arrest or Hospitalization; Category 2, High Violence Potential, Not Imminent; Category 3, Insufficient Evidence for Violence Potential, Sufficient Evidence for the Repetitive/Intentional Infliction of Emotional Distress Upon Others; Category 4, Insufficient Evidence for Violence Potential, Sufficient Evidence for the Unintentional Infliction of Emotional Distress Upon Others; and, Category 5, Insufficient Evidence for Violence Potential or Emotional Distress Upon Others.

CHAPTER FIVE

General Intervention Considerations

Myth Six: There is nothing we can do to intervene with the potentially violent individual.

Intervention with students provides an ideal opportunity to make a difference. In contrast to adults, who may be more entrenched in dysfunctional patterns, experience confirms the malleability of youth who are beginning to demonstrate the early warning signs of increased aggression. Adult perpetrators of workplace violence have often demonstrated lifelong dysfunctional patterns of relating. If these problems had been addressed at an earlier developmental stage, the tragedy may have been averted. Whether an adult or a student at-risk, thoughtful intervention positively impacts the lives of many people.

Legal issues, criminal justice system resources, physical security, administrative protocols, information gathering, mental health liaison, victim management, campus stabilization, monitoring, and re-entry are important issues to consider in any intervention process with individuals at risk for school violence. An overview of these general concerns will be presented in this chapter. These response options must be adapted to the level of risk in a given situation.

Legal Issues

The liability, rights, and responsibilities of school, law enforcement, and mental health personnel in maintaining a safe school environment are affected by a variety of local, state, and federal statutes, regulations, constitutional requirements, and judicial decisions (See Table 12). School policies also play a key role in establishing liability and the responsibilities of district and other

111

personnel. Professionals involved in managing these situations seek to avoid liability for acts related to school violence, including the steps taken to prevent it, and should become familiar with the legal requirements in their jurisdictions.

TABLE 12

Legal Considerations in School Violence Threat Management
• Gun Free Schools Act of 1994
• Fourth Amendment (search and seizure)
• Fifth Amendment
• Family Educational Rights and Privacy Act
• Privacy Laws
• Laws Regulating Disclosure of Information Related to Juveniles
• Individuals with Disabilities Education Act
• Mandatory Child Abuse Reporting Laws
• Americans With Disabilities Act
• FedOSHA Requirements
• State Campus Safety Legislation
• State OSHA Requirements
• State Laws Related to Civil Commitments of Individuals and Juveniles
• Local and Educational Code Issues
• New Jersey v. TLO
• Other Case Law

The Federal Gun Free Schools Act (GFSA) of 1994 mandates that every state receiving funds under the Elementary and Secondary Education Act (ESEA) must have a law that mandates a minimum one year expulsion for any student caught carrying a firearm to school. It also mandates reporting to local law enforcement for appropriate action. The expulsion requirement may be modified on a case-by-case basis by the local chief administering officer. School districts do not violate the GFSA if they provide educational services in an alternative setting to a student who has been expelled from the student's regular school. All local educational agencies receiving ESEA funds must refer any student who brings a firearm to school to the criminal or juvenile justice system. The GFSA explicitly requires that it must be implemented in a manner consistent with the Individuals with Disabilities Education Act (IDEA).

Under the IDEA, school personnel may remove a student with a disability who carries a weapon, including a firearm, to school or a school function to an interim alternative placement for up to 45 days. This interim placement can be extended for additional 45-day periods if a hearing officer determines that it would be dangerous to return the student to his/her normal placement. Appropriate educational services must be provided to the student in that alternative site. IDEA does not permit discipline that changes a student's placement, such as an expulsion, if the student's behavior was a manifestation of their disability. IDEA does make clear that school personnel can report crimes committed by students with disabilities to appropriate authorities. If a student with a disability brings a firearm to school, a school district can comply with both the GFSA and the IDEA by using the provision of the GFSA that permits modification of the expulsion requirement on a case-by-case basis. The district must also ensure that the discipline of students with disabilities is handled consistent with IDEA (U.S. Department of Education, 1999).

The Fourth Amendment of the United States Constitution safeguards citizens against unlawful search and seizure. Law enforcement officers are subject to the "probable cause" standard, and must obtain search warrants without consent prior to searching a person, except in certain "emergency" circumstances. The Fifth Amendment protects a person from self-incrimination. A person also has a right, as reflected by the famous "Miranda" case law, "to remain silent, to have an attorney appointed, if you don't have one..." In many jurisdictions, the juvenile has the same right and can request his/her parent or guardian to be present during questioning.

Privacy is another issue. There are federal laws that bar the disclosure of medical information except under defined circumstances, and laws such as the Family Educational Rights and Privacy Act (FERPA) mandate the privacy of student records and prohibits disclosure of academic and disciplinary issues. This becomes particularly compelling in the aftermath of incidents, and how information may be accessed by team members as they grapple with warning signs in a given situation. Juveniles have many specific rights that serve to protect their privacy from being violated as it relates to school and the criminal justice system. Legal knowledge or consultation is helpful to prevent unknowingly violating the rights of the juvenile. Likewise, there are similar laws barring access and disclosure of confidential medical and personnel information pertaining to current or former employees. Those managing cases must be mindful of these important protections.

Many states have enacted laws that mandate programs to address school safety and documentation of the violence that occurs during the school year. California's Comprehensive School Safety Plan was presented as an example in Chapter Three, Table 6.

Federal Occupational Health and Safety Laws (FedOSHA) mandate under the general duty clause that organizations shall "provide a safe work environment." Some states (for example, California through CalOSHA) have similar entities that address violence prevention. When episodes of lethal violence occur, they may result in investigations by these bodies, who may in turn impose sanctions and fines for failure to address safety hazards.

State child abuse reporting laws mandate reporting incidents of suspected child abuse, including physical and emotional abuse, sexual abuse, and child neglect, to appropriate authorities. School personnel, mental health professionals, and police are mandated reporters in every state. Child abuse intervention may be an important component of case management in some school violence risk cases. There are similar laws designed to prevent elder and dependent abuse. These may be applicable in cases involving out-of-control students abusing an elderly caregiver.

Schools boards will establish their own rules, often referred to as educational codes, that define how schools within a given district may operate and address the rights of students and employees. Decision-making needs to take into account these important parameters.

Civil Liability Exposure

From a civil liability standpoint, there are a number of areas of vulnerability for a school district, police or security, or parent or guardian of a problem student. Violation of any of the above statutes will create civil exposure. For example, violation of search and seizure laws by a school police officer may form the basis for a civil rights claim. There are other important issues to be aware of, many of which are seemingly in conflict, placing TAT members in the often uncomfortable position of choosing the lesser of two evils. One participant in a recent workshop described the decision-making process as the "headline test," meaning that an organization might make decisions based upon avoiding the more egregious newspaper headline. Legal consultation is critical in most situations.

The more serious basis for civil liability is incurred when students and/or employees have been harmed during an episode of violence on district property. The basis for these claims is failure to adhere to laws or policy resulting in the episode of violence; negligent selection, hiring, supervision, and retention of personnel resulting in violence by an employee or former employee; and negligent response to threats and acts of violence. These pressures and concerns push professionals in the direction of intervention.

On the other hand, exposure to liability may develop from wrongful accusations and discharges. In these situations, claims against school districts occur because of wrongful termination of employees or expulsions of students. Other times the cause for action may be defamation and violation of privacy rights, often as a consequence of poorly conducted investigations which may have trounced upon the individual's due process rights and protections.

Civil liability may similarly originate from claims that the district or police violated student rights. There are a variety of ways that a district may expose itself: dress or uniform codes which fail to accommodate a person's religious beliefs; or ignoring rights in privacy and matters of record-keeping and the release of confidential records. District and police personnel must attend to these important details in their intervention procedures.

Liability is not only incurred by the school district. Parents and guardians may be held liable and accountable for acts of violence by their child. Parents/guardians may also be held criminally or civilly liable for foreseeable youth violence they should have acted to prevent. In some instances, negligent storage of a firearm or negligently providing their child with a firearm forms the basis for liability. They may be held liable for failure to adequately supervise their child, failure to take corrective actions when their child displays problematic behavior, or failure to notify others of the potential dangerousness of their child.

There may also be legal repercussions for those reporting threats. In a recent California case, a female student from Quartz Hill High School reported another student for making a verbal threat against her. He was questioned by school officials, then threatened her again. The student's parents removed her from school due to their fear and safety concerns. Subsequently, the family of the student alleged to have made the threats filed a lawsuit against the complainant's family for making the report. The case is pending, and the outcome could have an impact on the willingness of students to report threatening behavior to school officials (Landa, 2000).

While our discussion is by no means comprehensive or an adequate replacement for competent legal counsel, it does highlight the range of issues that threat assessment team members need to consider as they contemplate prevention, investigation, and intervention. It suggests tumultuous seas, and often difficult situations. Fortunately, if professionals involved in these matters are able to document a reasonable process–one which shows thoughtfulness, and consideration of both sides of important issues–the integrity of the procedures will be protected. Safety is the primary consideration, with individual rights and other issues running a close second.

Columbine-Related Lawsuits

The parents of one of the victims in the aftermath of Columbine filed a 250 million-dollar wrongful death lawsuit against the parents of Harris and Klebold. They also communicated intent to sue two manufacturers of the guns used by Harris and Klebold. Twenty families filed notices of "intent to sue" local government agencies, including the Jefferson County Sheriff's Office and the school district. The basis of these claims likely will be that the school district was negligent in failing to keep the school safe and to respond to warnings about Harris. The Sheriff's office may be subject to claims that that they were negligent in responding to complaints received about his activities.

In an interesting twist, Dylan Klebold's family also filed a notice of their intent to sue. They claimed that the Sheriff's office may have been negligent by failing to inform them of the 1998 complaint filed with their office in which Harris was alleged to have threatened to kill another student; and that the Sheriff's office had knowledge of Harris' web site in which he reportedly posted diagrams for building bombs, made threatening statements, and talked about mass homicide. Their contention is that had they known, they could have taken steps to prevent it. Their letter of intent to sue also claimed that the Sheriff's negligence caused them to be subject to substantial damage claims, vilification, grief, and loss of enjoyment of life. Their attorney stated

116

that they will only seek damages equivalent to the damages sought from them in suits by victims.

Paducah, Kentucky-Related Litigation

The parents of the three girls killed by Michael Carneal filed suit in state and federal court, initially naming more than 50 defendants: Carneal, his parents, students who had seen the guns and told no one, and school officials who ignored behavior that should have been cause for disciplinary action against Carneal. The plaintiffs are seeking a total of 120 million dollars in damages for pain, suffering, mental anguish, loss of earning capacity, and punitive damages. The judge dismissed all teachers, school officials, and five of the students as defendants, leaving Carneal, his parents, a neighbor from whom he took the weapon, and 11 students who allegedly had knowledge that he was going to carry out the violent act.

The plaintiffs also filed a separate suit in federal court seeking 130 million dollars in damages, naming 25 media companies as defendants. The suit claims that Time Warner and the makers of the film *The Basketball Diaries*, and 11 other companies making violent computer games including *Doom*, conditioned Carneal by exposure to violent media.

Thurston High School Shooting-Related Lawsuits

The parents of one of the severely injured survivors of Kip Kinkel's shooting spree filed a 14.5 million-dollar lawsuit against Kip Kinkel and the estate of his parents, Bill and Faith. The suit alleges that Kip was negligent in entering the school and discharging a firearm, and that the parents were negligent in providing him with firearms and failing to supervise and control his access to them.

Jonesboro, Arkansas-Related Litigation

Families of the five killed by 11-year-old Andrew Golden and 13-year-old Mitchell Johnson are suing the shooters and their parents for negligent training and supervision. They are also suing the manufacturer of the guns they used for not equipping them with trigger lock devices, and Golden's grandfather, from whom the boys took the weapons.

Unions and Attorneys

Dealing with employees and former employees as potential threats to school safety requires consideration of some additional intervention issues. When it comes to disciplinary actions, it is likely that TAT members will have to contend with union involvement and employee disciplinary hearings. These processes are rights to which employees are entitled. Each juncture of review and interaction between district representatives and the employee must be anticipated, and the district must review issues of safety. Former employees may be gone, but they have not necessarily forgotten their concerns. It may be difficult for them to truly be away from the district, as they wind their way through appeals, worker's compensation procedures, equal employment opportunity complaints, wrongful termination, or other litigation based upon perceived adverse employment actions. Tracking of their involvement in these processes is imperative.

Union representatives are often a necessary part of the landscape, and if handled properly, may serve as allies in dealing with volatile current or former employees. Concerns about a problem employee may be respectfully communicated (with legal counsel blessing) to the union representative, who can then serve a stabilizing function in the at-risk person's life. Union representatives have as their constituents other employees, so they have a vested interest in maintaining control of their client. The union representative has the unique opportunity to become aware of deterioration in his/her client that might impact the safety of others. It is useful to consider special training in warning signs for union representatives. The representative has often played a critical role in bringing important information forward or getting their client needed intervention. Similarly, attorneys representing employees and former employees may perform the same type of function, and open lines of communication about these issues are essential in high-risk cases.

A recent National Labor Review Board (NLRB) decision has determined that non-union employees may request the presence of a co-worker during investigatory interviews. Previously, unrepresented employees did not have this right. The district, however, is not obligated to inform the employee of this right prior to any interview and may decline to allow an attorney to be present (Kraemer, 2000).

Criminal Justice System Issues

Law Enforcement Liaison
An ongoing relationship with local law enforcement is an asset in managing school violence risk. In high-risk cases, school district liaison with law enforcement will enable the location of the school and circumstances to be relayed to local police so that it may be

flagged as a "special location." In the event the school summons police, responding officers will be more informed and concerned than had they responded without such a briefing.

Some municipalities have specially trained detectives or investigators assigned to handle threat or stalking cases. For example, the LAPD has the Threat Management Unit. Schools with these resources may avail themselves of highly trained, proactive, and interested professionals. These special resources increase the likelihood that school-based crimes will be taken seriously, and prosecuted in a manner helpful to restoring order and control of high-risk behavior.

There are also innovative programs which pair mental health workers with police officers to investigate and respond to situations where a disturbed citizen may need to be involuntarily hospitalized. This allows for field based response, including to school campuses. The LAPD has the Systemwide Mental Assessment and Response Team (SMART) and Mental Evaluation Unit (MEU) to provide intervention when mentally ill citizens may be a danger to themselves or others. It is important for schools to become aware of available resources. If no such resources are available, it may be useful to cultivate them, so that there may be in the future.

Fortunately, many schools have their own school-based police, school resource officers, or private campus security. Schools need to insure that these professionals are adequately trained so that they will have the tools necessary to address school safety.

Some counties have district and city attorneys who are knowledgeable and interested in threat, stalking, and domestic violence cases or those situations that require prosecution of a high-risk person. Identifying and using these resources when the occasion arises will increase the likelihood of an effective response. There often are victim/witness funds for counseling and support services, important adjuncts that the district may be able to use.

Restraining Orders

Restraining orders are a potential intervention tool that should be considered in high-risk cases. Most restraining orders require preparation of documentation and forms articulating the need for the order, legal filing of the paperwork, serving and implementation of the temporary order, followed by a court proceeding during which the recipient can protest. Typically there is some lag, often a few weeks, between the serving of the temporary order and the court proceeding that may grant a permanent injunction. Law enforcement may sometimes initiate emergency protective orders that serve a similar purpose, but they only last for several days. This gives the victim an opportunity to apply for longer duration restraining orders. Many police officers, district attorneys, and city attorneys know about these orders. At other times school district legal counsel can provide assistance in the application process.

Most persons who are subject to a restraining order will not fight the order, nor show up for the court proceeding. In those cases in which they do, it is important to monitor their response in the court situation; it can be very telling about their next steps and how likely they are to honor the order. The initial serving of the temporary order may also serve as a barometer of response. One stalker responded to the server by failing to answer the door despite being home. A surveillance to facilitate the serving of the order was initiated, and when the stalker walked towards his car, he was surprised to be handed the order, declaring without reading it, "This is not going to stop me, it won't!"

Permanent restraining (protective) orders are good for a specified time period once granted, often for several years or longer. In drawing up the request for an order, the school district should be thoughtful about the specifics: where the person is prevented from approaching others, and openings the at-risk person may use as a window of opportunity to continue his/her harassment or engage in violent behavior. In some jurisdictions only an individual may secure a restraining order, while in others, orders on behalf of the organization, referred to as corporate restraining orders, may be obtained. The advantage of a corporate order is that the district is not entirely dependent on the cooperation of the victim/complainant, but may step in and deflect the level of perceived direct confrontation between the victim/complainant and the at-risk individual. Declarations from witnesses and complainants will still need to be attached to the order.

It is important to remember that a restraining order is only a piece of paper. While they are very successful at stopping problem behavior in at-risk individuals, there are cases where the recipient will escalate in response to being served with the order. Applicants for restraining orders should be advised about security precautions they might take, which will be discussed later in this chapter. Security procedures to insure safe passage to and from the courtroom for any hearings should be considered, and the victim/target should be reassured of the district's concern for his/her safety and well-being during this process. Some jurisdictions have provisions within the law that preclude the person that is subject to a restraining order from owning or possessing firearms or other weapons. Knowledge and follow-up about weapons limitations is critical.

Physical Security

Adequate physical security may be a deterrent to at-risk individuals, as the Jewish Community Center shooting described in Chapter One makes abundantly clear. The shooter, 37-year-old white supremacist Buford Furrow, had considered attacking several other targets before deciding upon the Jewish Community Center because of their lax security. Other targets had included the Simon Wiesenthal Museum of Tolerance and the University of Judaism. Furrow abandoned the idea of carrying out his violent action plan against these latter institutions because he thought their security was too tight. In fact, he had toured the Wiesenthal Museum to survey its vulnerabilities beforehand.

Physical security refers to those intervention and prevention techniques that make the potential target less enticing to would-be criminals. In some security circles, this is referred to as "target hardening." Security procedures and techniques may be rated as minimal, moderate, or stringent, and there are an array of methods to address the physical security needs of our campuses and off-campus activities. Not all are appropriate for every situation and school, and it is important to appropriately match the strategies to the particular situation.

Access Restriction

Devices or methods can prevent uncontrolled access to the campus or off-campus activities. Perimeter fencing and other physical barriers can dissuade potential intruders. Barriers should be formidable enough to discourage an easy jump or climb, and prevent crashing through by explosive laden vehicles. At the same time, too much unsightly fence and/or barbed wire will conjure up a feeling of vulnerability among students and staff, an outcome that may be averted by some degree of prudence and aesthetic balance. It is also important to consider locking mechanisms for classrooms, offices, and other areas on campus. In some situations, it may increase safety to

121

be able to quickly impose a lockdown situation in response to some signal, preventing an intruder from being able to gain entry and access to potential victims. Master keys *must be available* for law enforcement and emergency personnel in the event of a school based crisis.

Visitor sign-ins, central reception areas, campus security patrols and parent patrols also create boundaries. Requiring visitors to sign-in at a central reception area prior to entry onto the campus will deter "pilgrims" from freely walking onto school grounds, and control the chaotic anonymity of unmonitored comings and goings. Having a singular point of entry and egress, will also be particularly useful when there is a student or staff member who is not allowed onto campus. Discrete posting of a photograph at likely points of attempted "boundary probing," enables key staff members on a "need to know basis" to serve as boundary maintainers and lookouts.

Campus Police/Security

Campus police and security personnel serve as effective deterrents simply by their presence and visibility. They are attentive eyes and ears, questioning those who do not appear to belong on campus. School resource officers (SROs) are police that are assigned to schools or a cluster of schools within a district. Their availability can be a real benefit to prevention and intervention efforts, particularly if they are selected for interpersonal skills with students and staff alike, as well as their competence in school crime and crime prevention issues. Concerned parties feel more comfortable bringing information forward to someone they know, rather than any police officer or stranger. Campus police and security can also play a credible role in pre-incident consciousness raising about warning signs and reporting procedures. If it is a local law enforcement operating procedure to be armed, police personnel assigned to the campus should honor that employment responsibility. There have been incidents in which the SRO has had to be the first responder to a shooting on campus, taking responsibility for apprehending an armed perpetrator. In some of these incidents SROs have done so without possession of their weapon, a harrowing position that they have vowed to never be in again! SROs, and other campus-based security professionals, have the ability to get to know students, staff, and parents, and can help establish campus boundaries.

Some schools use parent volunteers to enhance and extend their available eyes and ears and create a greater sense of shared responsibility for school safety. Both parent patrols and campus security personnel should be carefully recruited, screened, and trained.

Identification

Schools must be able to identify who does and *does not* belong on campus. Adults in many workplaces are required to wear work identification. There should be a system in place so that it is relatively easy to identify those who are students, staff, visitors, and intruders. Such control is essential. If there are identification badges, there should be rules for how they are displayed, and procedures for their surrender when job or student status changes. Failure to remove an identification card might allow a forbidden, at-risk person to enter a school campus. There have been several situations in which former employees have failed to turn in their identification and then used that identification in ways that were deadly. The most tragic example was the 1987 crash of a PSA airlines flight in California in which 44 people died. The culprit, a recently terminated employee, used his identification to bypass the airport magnetometer, allowing him to bring a weapon on board the aircraft to seek revenge on his former boss and company. He confronted and killed his former boss once airborne, then shot and killed the flight crew, causing the plane to crash.

Uniforms are another way to enhance the physical security of a school campus. They enable staff members to easily recognize who does or does not belong on campus. Uniforms may also be designed in such a way that they reduce the likelihood of weapon concealment. They may also deter gang-related shenanigans on campus, although kids are still fairly resourceful in "customizing" their uniforms so that their "individuality" might be observed. Research has shown that uniforms, however unwanted by students, actually reduce incidents of violence and other related problems.

Electronic Security Devices

Some physical security devices alert personnel to the presence of persons or items that may threaten the safety and well-being of students and staff. Metal detectors, surveillance cameras, and police dogs can work. There are walk-through types of detectors, and hand-held wands that may be used on a case-by-case basis. Whatever the methodology, it is essential that exceptions be avoided; even the best methods are compromised by poor compliance. Walk-through metal detectors rely upon the requirement that everyone, including staff,

123

pass through them prior to entering the campus. Hand-held varieties are used on a case-by-case basis with a sweeping motion around the person, enabling the identification of metal objects such as knives or guns. In the aftermath of the tragic shooting by the six-year-old boy in Flint, Michigan, some parents and school staff members demanded metal detectors, believing that they could have identified the boy's weapon and potentially averted tragedy.

Surveillance cameras serve as a deterrent to violence, increasing potential perpetrators' sense that they may get caught. Cameras can provide important evidence in the event of actual violence or crime. Police dogs are not ordinarily used except when a specific problem is identified, most often drugs or explosives issues. The dogs are used to "sniff" for the presence of these items on campus. If these methods are considered, care should be employed to avoid potential civil rights issues that pertain to lawful and unlawful searches.

Staff members should have the ability to make an emergency telephone call from their classrooms, and many districts are installing telephones to accommodate this need. Some districts are issuing cellular phones, while others may have radio communication or an intercom system to communicate in a variety of threat scenarios. If cellular phones are going to be issued for emergency notifications, staff should be well aware of how the emergency call will be fielded by the particular cellular phone carrier. Some carriers do not transmit the call to the local municipal police department without specifically programming it that way. Many will go to the state's highway patrol, who will then patch the call to the local agency. This delay is a concern. Many of these incidents are over within 15 minutes to a half an hour, with most of the lethal violence occurring in the first two to three minutes (Meloy et al., 2001; Hempel et al., 1999).

Alarm systems allow the campus or other specific areas to be electronically monitored for unauthorized breeches during and after regular school hours. This can serve as a deterrent to routine crimes such as burglaries, or more serious crimes, such as a perpetrator sneaking in after school hours to booby trap an area with explosives. Procedures and codes for disabling these alarms should be known to responsible parties, most importantly school administrators and the school resource officer. During a violent event, alarm noise and related issues have the potential to compromise the safety of responding officers. They can impede police access or telegraph their whereabouts as they are responding to the threat. Water from fire sprinklers and deafening alarm noise complicated officer response and rescue efforts at Columbine. Responsible parties must be able to override the system.

For intervention with the at-risk person, specific systems and procedures need to be established to prepare for rapid control of the situation if the person escalates. One-way pagers or panic buttons should be discreetly accessible, and on-site security personnel should be scripted to respond if they have to enter a room during an intervention. In the absence of panic buttons in the intervention room (often the administrative office of the campus), a relatively inexpensive way to address the issue is to acquire a battery operated remote doorbell. These may be purchased at many hardware stores. The chime device is monitored by the security officer in a nearby room, while the button may be discreetly kept in the pocket of the intervener during the high-risk interview.

Intercom systems provide a means of communication during emergency situations. In the Buell Elementary situation, the principal used the intercom system to rapidly initiate a classroom lockdown situation so that the six-year-old boy could be identified, contained, and turned over to proper authorities. Intercoms can also be used to disseminate other important emergency information. There should be several points of access to the intercom to prevent a circumstance in which the primary access is taken over by the perpetrator or unilaterally damaged, offering no back-up plan for communication. They should be two-way systems that can receive and send messages from within classrooms to other locations on campus.

Signals and Drills

Emergency signals and drills teach students and staff how to secure the campus in the event of an armed intruder. It is not a good idea to have drills in which children are potentially traumatized by enactments of armed gunmen entering the campus and harming people. On the other hand, intruder drills, in which kids and staff are taught to secure the environment in response to an intruder, may be helpful. In these scenarios, staff and students are taught a signal, such as a sound or warning, which instructs them to respond to the directions of those in charge and/or follow common sense reactions, not some hard and fast procedure like in a fire drill. There are cases in which the perpetrators have manipulated rigid drill procedures to set up their victims. For example, on March 24, 1998, 13-year-old Mitchell Johnson and 11-year-old Andrew Golden pulled a fire alarm and shot other children from their middle school who were appropriately responding to the emergency staging area. They killed a teacher and four girls, wounding nine other girls and another teacher. Johnson and Golden planned an attack by capitalizing on their fire drill procedures.

There is also a need to develop an "all clear" signal. Those designated to give the "all clear" signal should be identified prior to any incident to prevent potentially deadly misunderstandings.

In some situations it may be good to flee, in others to secure the room, in others to hide. General guidelines and common sense are the rule in drills surrounding these scenarios, and flexibility must be built into all rehearsals.

Coat Checks

In cold climate geographic regions, it is not uncommon for a school to have a routine coat check area. Coat checks are a relatively non-invasive way to insure that a student or staff member does not have a hidden large weapon, such as a rifle, machete, or larger handgun. People get used to turning in their coats. This serves as a subtle deterrent to weapon possession and concealment.

Blueprints

Blueprints of the school should be updated and available to law enforcement, not just "in the office." In the worst case scenario of a shooting and/or hostage incident on campus, the office may not be accessible, and the police Special Weapons and Tactics (SWAT) team will want to have a current schematic of the school to help in their deployment of officers. All common systems–electrical, mechanical, and water shutoffs–should be listed. Videotapes of the school layout may also be useful.

Administrative Protocols

General

District rules, disciplinary procedures, student or employee status changes, special classes, and administrative directives may all be important to the intervention process. Each district has different administrative options at its disposal. Student discipline for rule violations may range from warnings and detention to suspension and expulsion proceedings.

Removal Protocols

There are a number of ways to facilitate the removal of at-risk students or employees from district property. Many districts have procedures that allow for the person to be suspended and sent home pending investigation or review. Schools have various rules concerning assignment prior to a due process hearing, especially if the case involves a student with a disability. Each district should be clear about their parameters. School administrators can give "administrative stay-away" or "cease and desist" orders to at-risk students and employees in lieu of more formal restraining orders. This will serve to set a boundary on a student or staff member pending an investigation or disciplinary proceeding.

Students may also be transferred to different schools within the district, including alternative school settings for problem students. Home schooling may also be an option. At-risk employees may be disciplined or transferred in certain instances.

Notifications

Depending upon the circumstances, parents, guardians, emergency contacts, and potential victims may need to be notified by district personnel. Any situation in which a student is having problems at school will require notifying the parents or guardians. Emergency contacts may need to be notified by district personnel in the event of a serious problem involving an employee. If threats are made or posed to a given student, employee, or other identifiable persons, arrangements will need to be made to notify the potential victims and the police. Care needs to be taken in all of these situations to avoid violation of privacy rights and defamation of character issues. Legal consultation is always a good idea prior to such notifications.

Boundary Setting

Based upon district rules, boundaries may be clarified verbally and in writing to students, parents, and employees. Such limit setting helps emphasize the school's commitment to safety. When individuals lack the ability to regulate their own behavior, they often will respond to external controls. This can also help to establish that progressive discipline was attempted, so that if the person continues to escalate, more serious consequences may be implemented.

Boundary setting can also be in the form of a return-to-school or work agreement, a behavioral contract between the school and the student and family or employee. Parameters for behavior and potential consequences are outlined in such an agreement. These agreements are often implemented after a person has been suspended and it has been determined that it is safe for them to come back.

Criteria for Return to School/Work

TAT members should establish criteria for an individual to return to school or work if they are removed from the school due to risk concerns. In certain cases, this will be inappropriate if the individual has done something too egregious, potentially harmful, or illegal. In most cases, however, the person will eventually qualify to return to school or work. Criteria might include proof that the individual no longer poses a safety threat, and proof of satisfactory completion of remedial activities, including mental health treatment.

Information Gathering

Information-seeking is driven by the need to further assess behaviors and issues related to an individual's school violence risk. When a person is reported to have engaged in problem behaviors, it is important to gather first-hand information, as well as review other relevant information pertaining to the situation. In some instances this information will be gathered by district personnel, while in others the investigation will be addressed by security or law enforcement personnel.

Witnesses/Reporting Parties

Reporting parties and witnesses to problem behaviors of at-risk individuals need to be interviewed to verify and substantiate their concerns and observations. It is not uncommon for information to get distorted during the communication process. These interviews will help clarify what actually occurred, and avoid inaccurate, second-hand reports. Additional information will sometimes come forward that may enhance or decrease perceptions of risk. Scheduling should attend to the likelihood that certain collateral data sources, as discussed in Chapter Four, may tip the at-risk individual to the investigation. This becomes very important if there are concerns that the person's awareness of an investigation might serve as a precipitating event for acting out.

Background Review

Information pertaining to the at-risk individual's past history of problems may be available in school files, criminal justice records, or other sources. To the extent that it is legal to do so, such information should be accessed to enhance assessment and decision-making. Past incidents, discipline, and intervention attempts may be documented. Knowing what has previously worked reduces uncertainty, saves time, and avoids repetition of previously unsuccessful interventions.

Subject Interview Guidelines

Interviews of the at-risk individual are an important part of the threat assessment, but they are also an intervention tool. In many cases, simply addressing the person's concerns can help stabilize the situation. The decision to interview the at-risk individual is an important one, and TAT members must address beforehand the process and content of the interview, as well as the team's contingencies given the results of the interview. These contingencies may include any of the response considerations discussed in this third section. Team members need to consider what the goals or objectives might be in any decision to move forward to conduct an interview. This is usually driven by a need to better understand the circumstances and hear the subject's side of things, and often offers the opportunity to observe and learn of his/her concerns which may have been distorted by other reporting parties.

Once the goals and objectives are identified and the purpose of the interview is deemed appropriate, other issues come into play. Team members must address safety and security concerns, determine the location and timing of the interview, establish who is going to conduct the interview, and script which specific content issues will be covered. In addition, some thought needs to be given to interview termination. For example, if the person should escalate and become disruptive, assaultive, self-destructive, or make threats during the interview, discontinuance would be indicated. In employee situations, if the person should become tearful or upset, statements such as, "You seem upset, if you like we can take a break, would you like to take a break or continue?" may be necessary. If this procedure has to be initiated more than once, then discontinuation needs to be seriously considered, and arrangements made to meet again at a later date. This is to avoid potential liability for "stressing" the person or the perception of a "coercive interviewing" situation. It may be necessary to involve union representatives in an interview with an employee, while in student situations, it may be necessary to involve the parents or guardians. Interviews with outsiders who may pose a potential threat will usually be deferred to the appropriate law enforcement agency.

Questions during the interview will focus on understanding the circumstances precipitating concern about the individual. The interviewer(s), often a school administrator and member of security, will set the stage with a statement about the district's commitment to safety, the need to thoroughly and fairly investigate all safety concerns, and then inquire about the person's understanding of the purpose of the meeting. This is one way of setting the tone, and gives the person an opportunity to tell their story. If the subject responds with an, "I don't have any idea why" type response, one approach is to outline the district's concerns and then give an opportunity for the individual to tell his/her side of the events in question, as well as to express his/her concerns. At some point the subject may be asked what s/he thinks the district's options are for handling the situation. This begins the process of probing their thought processes, perhaps laying the groundwork for them to accept any negative repercussions. It may also become apparent that they have not anticipated consequences, a point that might elevate concern because it increases the chance that the subject has been "blind-sided" and will destabilize in response to district actions. The person may be presented with a series of "what ifs": their perceptions of how they will respond to a range of district options, again allowing the opportunity to observe and listen for potential problems. This may actually help soften the blow of any potential negative consequence by giving the issue some "settling in" time. It is problematic if there are intimated threats, or if the person has "no idea" how s/he will handle the situation, appearing to suffer from impaired coping. While these content areas are not all inclusive, they can reduce the guesswork involved in figuring out what the person's "violent action imperative" might be, if any, under a range of hypothetical scenarios, and the district can then adjust their management strategies accordingly. See Table 13 for a sample interview protocol.

Interviewers should note discrepancies between the individual's statements and non-verbal behavior or valid information from collateral sources. Such discrepancies should be reconciled through follow-up interviews and investigation. If there are reasonable explanations for the inconsistency, it may assuage concerns. On the other hand, such discrepancies may suggest an elevated risk level, or that the individual is not a credible information source. For example, if a student who has communicated intentions to harm others and tried to access weapons denies these behaviors, or lightly dismisses them without any believable explanation, risk may be enhanced. More careful monitoring may be suggested.

This type of meeting also allows for the setting of any boundaries such as discipline, stay away orders, and the like. The

TABLE 13
Sample Subject Interview Protocol
(Adapted from Fayette County Public Schools)

Whater interviewing an individual about safety concerns, one approach is ask questions which move from general introduction, to fact finding, to recognition of concerns, to assessing support networks, to developing an outline of next steps. The following questions are intended to provide a sample structure for the kinds of questions that may need to be asked. Individuals using this outline are encouraged to use their professional judgment and experience, and consult with legal counsel when tailoring questions to each unique circumstance.

1. "Seems like you've been having a hard time lately, what's going on?" *(to establish rapport and trust and open dialogue in a non-threatening way)*
2. "What is your understanding of why you have been asked to come to the office?" *(to review factual events)*
3. "We are concerned about (behavior of concern). What's your side of it?" *(to give the person opportunity to be heard, and understand the situation better)*
4. "What is your understanding of why school staff are concerned?" *(to determine if student is aware of effect behavior has upon others)*
5. "What has been going on recently with you at school?" *(to look into possible precipitating events such as peer conflict, student/teacher interactions, failing grades, etc.; follow appropriate leads)*
6. "How are things going with your family?" *(to look into events such as conflict, divorce, deaths and losses)*
7. "What else is going on with you?" *(to look into events outside of school such as police involvement, medical issues, threats)*
8. "Who do you have to talk to or assist you with this situation?" *(to determine what supports or stabilizing factors may be available or in place such as mental health professionals, peer groups, family support, church groups, etc.)*
9. "Given (whatever is going on), what are you planning to do" or, "What are you thinking about doing?" *(follow up on appropriate leads, including level of detail to stated plans, ability to carry out plans, violence intent, weapons access, etc. NOTE: if there is imminent risk take immediate action to maintain safety by contacting law enforcement)*
10. Close with a statement that describes short term next steps *(i.e., "I'll need to contact your parents to talk about..." or, "You will be suspended for two days, then we'll...")*

interview may be closed with, "That's all for now, I'll contact you when___ or you may contact ____ if you have any questions." Once the interview is concluded, TAT members should be briefed and agreed-upon contingencies (follow-up) initiated.

This interview might occur at the final stage of an investigation into the subject's conduct at school, or upon consideration of a return to the school after a threatening situation, as part of a re-integration planning procedure. Other times, an abbreviated interview may occur at the front end; for example, a student or employee is demonstrating problem behavior and they are initially addressed by district personnel.

Most at-risk individuals will need to be interviewed at some point by a member of the district staff. Preplanning, scripting, and contingency planning are critical to insure a successful outcome. Success, in turn, occurs when the team acquires reliable and valid information about the subject.

Dealing with Difficult Parents

When parents or guardians refuse to cooperate with the district in managing a potential risk situation involving their child, the team must be astute. Sometimes, there may be issues of abuse and neglect in which the lack of cooperation may be but one symptom. In those cases, involvement of the appropriate child protective services agency may be indicated. A different team member might be more appropriate and skilled at other times in securing parental assistance and support. In still other cases, the team will help the district recognize that the school will have to serve as the surrogate parent due to the impossibility of motivating the actual parents to appropriate action. Working creatively with a variety of social systems, including school counselors, teachers, after-school programs, and law enforcement, may be necessary.

Other At-Risk Individuals

With other at-risk individuals who have no connection to the school, such as chronic complainers and eccentric neighbors, creative intervention is required. There are people in every school district community who have emotional and mental disorders that get acted out with their surrounding neighbors, and occasionally the school and its members become the focus. Relatively minor campus issues may provoke: student trash on the person's property, student noise, loitering, trespassing, and the like. These issues can begin an ongoing complaint campaign which, in some cases, may erupt in violence. In other cases it can create a serious level of fear and distress on the part of those who are the target of the person's complaints, accusations, and attempts to control. Many of these cases have dynamics similar to stalking (Meloy, 1998; Mullen, Pathe, & Purcell, 2000).

A monitoring procedure can follow chronic complainers: someone with knowledge about threat assessment issues who can read and review the correspondence, and file and document communications. If there are indicators of an abnormal focus or warning signs, a TAT investigation and review process might need to be initiated. Working with law enforcement is important, since police will need to follow-up about any serious threat. Law enforcement representatives may conduct a neighborhood canvas–without increasing the person's paranoia–by asking members of the community about any general concerns related to safety or existing neighborhood tensions. This provides a forum for other information to come forward which might rise to the level of a criminal matter, such as terrorist threats or brandishing of weapons. Frequently such information is available, but people are afraid to say or volunteer anything without being prompted, out of concern that the individual may "go off." Sometimes surveillance by law enforcement or neighborhood watch groups may be indicated to enhance documentation necessary for prosecution. In this monitoring process, school representatives and law enforcement should be alert to symbolic gestures, such as protest activity with a violent undercurrent (burning an effigy or violence charged rhetoric), which apart from a legitimate form of expression, may actually represent fantasy rehearsal, lessening inhibitions towards acting out.

An empathic response set may also work. In this model, the person's concerns are taken seriously, and they are addressed where possible. For example, if the person complains about a problem with trespassing, a district representative is designated to liaison with the complainer. This representative may help the person come up with strategies to address his/her legitimate concerns, such as suggesting a fence, or the district making announcements and enforcing certain off-limits areas. If there are students or staff that are inflaming the situation by "messing with" the complainer for effect, the district liaison should discourage the inflammatory behavior. The goal of this intervention category is to insure that the person feels heard, and to the extent possible, his/her concerns are addressed so they do not have to escalate. By designating a primary point of contact for the individual, the district is establishing a useful feedback mechanism to monitor for escalation (G. Lipson, personal communication, April 15, 2000).

Interfacing with Mental Health Professionals

TAT members will likely have to interface with mental health professionals involved in the treatment and evaluation of at-risk students and employees. With appropriate releases, information from these sources is critical to evaluations of risk and decisions about returning the student or employee to the school environment. The following, non-exhaustive list of questions/issues may be used by the *treating or independent evaluating professional* to guide their assessment and feedback to the TAT decision-making process:

1. What exactly happened (from subject and collateral source points of view)?
2. How are discrepancies between the subject and other's perceptions of the events in question resolved?
3. What are the essential aspects of the student/employee's relationship with the school?
4. What does it take for the student/employee to safely function in the school setting?
5. Are there any circumstances that warrant a "duty to warn" intended victims and the police?
6. Does the student/employee accept responsibility for the circumstances that led to the concerns of others and for addressing these concerns?
7. Have you assessed whether there is a developing violent action plan, violence intent, planning, and preparations including efforts by the individual to acquire, prepare, or use a weapon?
8. Have the issues that precipitated the student/employee's deterioration and potential lethality been resolved, and how?
9. What is the student/employee's game plan for preventing a repeat of their potential lethality or other problematic behavior and is s/he participating in this game plan?
10. What degree of confidence do you have that there will not be a repeat of potential lethality or other problematic behavior?
11. Are you aware of any circumstances or situations that might precipitate a repeat of potential lethality?

12. What behaviors might be indicators of a repeat of potential lethality and suggest the need for evaluation and/or intervention?
13. What information have you used to base your opinion?
14. Is there any information that you believe to be helpful that you have not been able to acquire, and if so, why not?
15. Have you considered a course of family therapy by another therapist as an adjunct to individual treatment?

TAT members can reduce the uncertainty that often accompanies mental health system involvement by addressing some or most of these questions/issues with the treating or evaluating mental health professional. It also takes the team beyond simple "Johnny is okay to go back to school or work" letters.

Clinical Issues and the At-Risk Individual

Clinicians who treat high-risk individuals need to operate at the highest level of ethical and professional practice. It is essential to seek collateral information from reliable sources, such as the school and parents, in order to become aware of high-risk behaviors and verify improvement. Appropriate releases should be secured and informed consent procedures should be followed to support collateral data collection.

Common issues which might become the focus of treatment include: personality disorders or abnormal traits; intense anger; obsessional and ruminative thought processes; the tendency to externalize blame; limited coping skills; dysfunctional patterns of relating to others; control and power issues; violent fantasy coping mechanisms; abandonment issues; and dysfunctional family issues. In some cases skill in dealing with thought disordered individuals will be required. The use of adjuncts to the treatment, such as referral to a psychiatrist for medication to treat depression or symptoms of thought disorder, or referral for substance abuse treatment, may be indicated. Family therapy may also be appropriate.

Special attention must be paid in these cases to client *transference* and the therapist's own *countertransference* reactions. It is not uncommon for an at-risk individual's dysfunctional expectations to get projected onto the therapist (transference). If identified and addressed therapeutically, this offers a great opportunity to make some inroads into the problem. On the other hand, missed opportunities or countertherapeutic maneuvers (countertransference) may compromise the relationship, removing an important stability factor in the person's life.

Treatment Versus Evaluation

Clinicians involved in these matters should also be clear about their role: whether they are involved as an evaluator or as a therapist. Evaluators offer a relatively impartial view of risk and other issues. There is always a dual relationship or inherent conflict in a treating therapist perceiving that s/he can somehow perform both functions. TATs may have to insist on independent evaluations from a non-treating mental health professional in some cases.

Mental Health and the Duty to Warn

Mental health professionals who deal with potentially dangerous individuals, also need to be aware of "duty to warn" laws and ethical issues that mandate or allow breeches to confidentiality and privilege in defined situations. "Tarasoff" or "duty to warn" laws apply to most situations in which a person communicates a serious threat of harm towards a third party and it is observed by their therapist, who then must disclose the threat to police and the intended victim. The ethical codes of most professions allow an exception to confidentiality to avert danger to self or others. Mental health professionals are often uncomfortable about these mandated and allowable exceptions to confidentiality and privilege, fearing that they will jeopardize the relationship with their client. Properly implemented Tarasoff warnings, particularly if the parameters are outlined to the client before therapy begins, create the opportunity for appropriate boundary setting when the client is incapable of self-containment. These laws, and the related issues surrounding them, vary by state and specific mental health profession, and the practitioner should learn the specifics of how it applies in his/her jurisdiction.

Case Example: Sullivan v. River Valley School District

In January 1995, Richard Sullivan, a 17-year teacher for the River Valley School District in Michigan, began to engage in behaviors that caused his coworkers and superintendent concerns about his ability to work in a safe and appropriate manner. While up to that point he had been a discipline-free employee, he began to engage in disruptive and abusive outbursts at school board meetings, including verbally inappropriate behavior, shoving paper in the faces of school board members, and refusing to stop when requested. He also disclosed confidential grade information to a newspaper and used inappropriate language about another teacher.

When the superintendent attempted to discuss and resolve these issues by arranging a meeting, Mr. Sullivan refused to attend. The superintendent sought informal consultation with a psychologist, who recommended a mandatory formal fitness for duty evaluation, which was later supported by the school board. Mr. Sullivan refused to comply with the school board's mandate, prompting tenure charges for misconduct and insubordination. Ultimately, the charges against him were reduced to a three-year suspension without pay by the Michigan State Tenure Commission.

Mr. Sullivan responded to these events by suing under the Americans with Disabilities Act, alleging that the school board regarded him as disabled and illegally suspended him for refusing to take the tests. The district and appeals' courts supported the school district's actions, the Federal Sixth Circuit Court of Appeals ultimately rejecting Mr. Sullivan's claim that the school board regarded him as disabled. The Court also opined that an employer's perception that health problems are adversely affecting an employee's job performance is not tantamount to regarding that person as disabled. Finally, the Court ruled that an employer is free to insist upon a fitness for duty evaluation where it is "job related and consistent with business necessity" and where "there is genuine reason to doubt whether an employee can perform job-related functions" (Cohen, 2000; Sullivan v. River Valley School District, 1999).

Work Fitness Evaluations

The above case example demonstrates an important consideration in the intervention process as it relates to employees–mandated work fitness evaluations. It is comforting to know that there is recent case law supporting the rights of employers to address the fitness of employees to do their job. Many public service agencies have procedures within their organizations to mandate a "work fitness" examination of an employee when there is some question of their ability to perform essential job tasks in a safe manner. This often times entails either a medical fitness or a psychological or psychiatric fitness evaluation. Work fitness procedures need to be well understood by TAT members, the circumstances under which they may be ordered, and who to retain for the evaluation. It is critical that the identified professional know about workplace violence, the assessment of dangerousness, job tasks of the at-risk individual, and the culture and mission of the organization. The evaluator should be licensed, conversant with the laws governing these assessments and the legal limits of the feedback process, possess the technology and skills to perform competent work fitness evaluations, and clearly communicate the parameters of the evaluation to the employee being evaluated. These professionals should also have procedures to safely evaluate high-risk individuals, such as, offices equipped with panic buttons and other security measures. Many school districts have lists of such evaluators, or have a so-called "district doctor" for that purpose.

Professionals involved in these kinds of evaluations should request appropriate collateral information pertaining to the individual being evaluated, including documentation of the identified concerns, and read it *before* the evaluation. Familiarity with, and the use of psychological testing, is also helpful. Informed consent, and any releases required by the law should be addressed prior to the evaluation.

Victim Management

Relocation

Victim safety issues are an important intervention consideration. In cases where the at-risk individual has focused upon a specific student or member of a work group, and there is the luxury of having alternative school or work sites for the targeted individual(s), this should be arranged. In the worst case, high-risk scenario, relocation may be essential for the long or short-term. Other security measures should still be employed at the target site, and the victim should not return to the school or work-site (such as for social events or paydays). While relocation may create negative repercussions for the victim, safety is the ultimate goal.

Personal Security Enhancement

Potential victims in high-risk cases should be aware of their established routines and the extent to which they may be learned or already known by the subject. Security personnel and law enforcement, when appropriate, may provide counsel in these situations about how to become more vigilant of one's surroundings, and initiate variation in these routines to avoid becoming an easy target.

Some of these measures might include issuing the victim a cellular phone and/or panic button for an on-campus alarm system. Inquiries might also be made into their home security measures, including precautions taken by family members. Some determination should be made as to what risk, if any, may be posed outside of the school setting. When there is risk to the potential victim at home, it is prudent to address home safety as well.

It is not a good idea, as a matter of practice, to have readily available personnel address rosters that could fall into the wrong hands. There have been situations in which staff rosters were freely distributed so that holiday greetings could be exchanged, only to find inappropriate and distressing contacts by unstable coworkers or clients. These practices should be thoughtfully scrutinized for their appropriateness in the specific environment and their potential for misuse.

Victims and other persons (particularly staff members) may be counseled to secure a post office box, unlisted phone number, and the like, in order to increase anonymity and make it more difficult to be located by a high-risk person. In some aggravated cases, organizations may decide to offer security personnel during time-limited "windows" of vulnerability. It would be costly and impractical to keep these interventions in place for the long-term, unless situation and circumstances warrant this level of concern.

Managing Telephonic Harassment

There are a number of ways a victim can deal with inappropriate and harassing telephone calls in stalking and threat cases. Many telephone companies will cooperate with police in setting up a phone trap, which enables the tracing of the origin of annoying or repetitive telephone calls. These interventions are typically brief. If the annoying caller is episodic in his/her harassment, the trap may be removed before the caller renews his/her pattern of calling. Caller identification services are appropriate for less sophisticated or less manipulative perpetrators who do not take precautions to avoid being caught. This type of service, which may be obtained from the local telephone company, enables the identification of the caller through a box that attaches to the telephone, or a display on the telephone itself. "Call blocking" is a way of blocking calls made from a particular number. If the person is using multiple locations from which to call, it may be impossible to identify and block them all. It may also prevent the gathering of investigative information needed for prosecution. Changing the phone number to an unlisted number may end the calls, but prevent noticing signs of escalation, as well as eliminate the documentation necessary for prosecution. Timing of these interventions is usually the critical issue. Team members, in conjunction with law enforcement, may base their choices and decisions upon the relative priority assigned to making the problem "go away" versus accomplishing a successful arrest and prosecution. Sometimes a decision is made to keep the problem number, logging calls, having an answering machine and caller identification to support the investigation, and obtaining another unlisted number that will then become the victim's permanent number. With caller identification boxes, investigators recommend having a camera to take pictures of the telephone number and time and date display on the box for evidentiary reasons. Documenting contact with the at-risk individual is essential, since this information is necessary to understand the dynamics of the case, its potential risk, and to further prosecution.

Campus Stabilization

In situations where the at-risk person was disruptive, there is a high likelihood that students and staff are going to become aware that something has taken place. Parents are often going to become aware, and in worst-case scenarios, the media might even catch wind of what has occurred, necessitating press releases and the development and dissemination of scripted statements. It becomes important to determine what, if anything, can be told to assuage any fears or anxieties that others might have, and at the same time remain sensitive to privacy issues. Consistent statements which facilitate a return to normalcy should be prepared. For example, a response similar to the following could be prepared for concerned parents inquiring about a particular school violence threat. "Today there was a threat that came to the school's attention, and a prompt response resulted in a gun being found. The individual was removed from campus without further incident. We are confident that the school is safe, and our safety procedures are in place. Unfortunately, we cannot release any other information due to privacy issues." These communications may be shared with staff members during a staff meeting or through an intradepartmental memo. Teachers and other staff then will not be placed in the uncomfortable position of not knowing what to say to their students, parents, or other staff members, and they will avoid contributing to rumor. Consideration should also be given to crisis counseling for students or staff.

Monitoring

Monitoring refers to the process of determining whether the person is escalating or de-escalating in response to interventions across time. Monitoring activities are diverse and include a range of strategies. Feedback mechanisms, also known as "trip wires," may be established to determine if the individual is going to violate physical or psychological boundaries. For example, if the person is banned from coming onto campus, their photo might be distributed on a "need to know" basis among security and reception staff so that if they show up, they will be deterred from entering. Such "boundary probing" is often a sign of escalation. Security and reception staff would then be able to communicate important information to TAT members about the person's failure to adhere to a boundary, perhaps setting in motion other interventions.

As the at-risk person participates in consensual plans for remediation of his/her problem behavior, there is a need to assess his/her participation. TAT members should arrange follow-up inquiries to confirm compliance with designated procedures, such as mental health treatment.

If the person has been arrested or involuntarily hospitalized, TAT members need to anticipate release dates. Such releases may mean an enhancement of security procedures. Cases are not usually managed in one day. They often evolve over weeks, months, and even years. Identifying ways to take their pulse as they change is essential.

Readjustment

Information from monitoring and other sources may indicate that the person is escalating in response to a new precipitating event, or that s/he is de-escalating due to participation in mental health treatment or as a consequence of other interventions. Risk assessments need to be modified accordingly as criteria for return-to-school or work are fulfilled by the student or employee. These readjustments should result in changes to intervention procedures. For example, if a high-risk person has been banned from school for a period of time, then participates successfully in treatment reducing his/her risk, the ban may need to be lifted so they can again attend school. Any pictures and standing orders to detain them need to be turned in or rescinded.

141

Re-entry

If an at-risk person has been removed from campus for a period of time, and it is determined that they may once again attend school, re-entry to the school environment needs to be addressed. TAT members need to consider if the person will be allowed to go back to the same campus, and identify ways to increase the likelihood that re-entry will be successful. This can be troublesome, particularly if there are people at the campus who are anxious or fearful about the individual's return. Legal consultation may help identify thoughtful ways of addressing concerned classmates' and others' questions, without increasing liability for violating the individual's privacy. In most cases, readjustment and re-entry are likely, so preplanning for this eventuality is a good idea.

Intervention: An Assessment Opportunity

Intervention may also be viewed as an assessment opportunity. Intervention is not a magical panacea that automatically stops or eliminates individual risk; rather, these events and processes are tests of what might work in each unique circumstance. Interventions have the potential to de-escalate or escalate the situation, and the school and potential victims should be aware of these potentials and take appropriate precautions. There is a window of vulnerability around these events which may range from minutes to hours to several weeks. It depends on the person, circumstance, and type of intervention. Most commonly, these windows last a matter of several days.

For example, in the Springfield, Oregon case, several hours after being suspended from school and sent home to his father, Kinkel murdered his father and mother. He returned to school the next day and opened fire in the cafeteria. Kinkel's disciplinary suspension was a precipitating event, creating a short-time high-risk window of vulnerability. Intervention increased risk with tragic results, and interveners failed to assess that possibility.

Chapter Summary

There are many general intervention issues to consider in school violence risk situations. Legal concerns form an important backdrop, since there are a variety of liability exposures which impact decision-making. Interventions fall into several broad categories. Criminal justice system resources include law enforcement response, restraining

142

orders, and effective prosecution of offenders. Physical security interventions include access restrictions, campus police or security, identification procedures, electronic security devices, signals and drills, coat checks, and the availability of school blueprints to police resources. School district administrative protocols such as disciplinary and removal procedures, notifications, and boundary setting techniques play an important role in containing risk. Information from witnesses, background reviews, subject interviews, and others feeds the intervention process. Mental health intervention strategies such as treatment, evaluation, and work fitness evaluations are often employed. There are special clinical and "duty to warn" considerations that impact the involvement of mental health practitioners. Victims and potential victims need to be managed, and the campus may need stabilization after an event is addressed by TAT members. All situations require some degree of monitoring. Threat assessments and interventions should be readjusted in response to new information. This often allows the removed, at-risk individual to reenter the school environment, once their level of risk has diminished and they have complied with any "return-to-school" criteria.

CHAPTER SIX

High-Risk Case Intervention Considerations

Intervention Considerations by Risk Level

Intervention needs to match the level of apparent risk in a given situation. Overreaction or under-response are a problem in their own right. First and foremost, any immediate and obvious safety threats need to be quelled. This entails an initial determination of what level of apparent risk is present, based upon the available information. Information-seeking is a critical part of this determination. Depending upon the initial level of risk, short-term decisions will need to be made until definitive information about level of risk is assessed. The next decision is whether a TAT consultation should even occur. If the situation appears to be high-risk, then prompt TAT consultation should be arranged. If it is a lower level of initial apparent risk, then there is greater discretion about convening all or part of the team. Recommendations will be made by the TAT about the need for a security response, additional information gathering, notifications, student/employee status changes, monitoring, and readjustment of risk level and interventions. (High-risk intervention considerations for Category 1 and 2 cases will be addressed throughout the remainder of this chapter. Moderate and lower risk considerations will be discussed in the next chapter.) To avoid redundancy, *readjustment* and *re-entry/reconciliation* will be discussed in detail at the end of the next chapter, since these are important to consider across all risk levels.

Category 1: High Violence Potential, Imminent Risk

The Category 1 level of risk refers to those cases which have high violence potential, and the at-risk individual should be arrested or hospitalized. There is an assessed risk of imminent danger to self or others which qualifies the individual for involuntary hospitalization or commitment procedures, and/or the person has violated criminal statutes which qualify him/her for arrest. If the person qualifies for both, and depending upon the state, jurisdiction, and his/her behavior, arrest will occur first, while in other situations, involuntary hospitalization will take primacy.

Case Example Number One

In October 1999, one 14-year-old boy and three 15-year-old boys from South High in Cleveland, Ohio, were arrested for planning to open fire on October 29, 1999, the day of the school's homecoming dance and football game. Tipped off by a student, officials confiscated eight guns from two of the suspects' houses, two maps that showed positions for each shooter in the school, and a list of possible students to recruit for the planned massacre. According to the assistant prosecuting attorney, they "planned to kill an indiscriminate number of people; anyone who was present in the building" ("Four teenagers admit," 1999). Two of the 15-year-olds pled guilty to conspiracy to commit aggravated murder, while the 14-year-old and 15-year-old pled guilty to inducing a panic. The maximum penalty for all four is incarceration until the age of 21.

Case Example Number Two

Leonard is a forty-one year old maintenance employee at an elementary school in a Southern California school district. One day it was brought to the principal's attention that Leonard was talking and acting strangely. Usually a quiet person who did his own thing, some of the kids told their teacher that Leonard had arranged a series of bibles and religious books on the floor in the hallway near the stairs and was talking about religion. They described him as "wild-eyed" and scary. The principal and campus security responded to follow up on these concerns and found Leonard as he was described. He attempted to engage them in conversation about Jesus Christ, urging them to repent and to "save the children." He proceeded to tell them about the important insight he had gained through his spiritual awakening. "We are all connected and all the religions of the world are the same: Mohammed equals Buddha equals Confucius equals Jesus." Leonard gave the responding personnel assorted letters and written materials related to these ideas. There were several references to suicide and violence.

Leonard, during the course of his discussion with these responding personnel, was very peaceful. He stated, however, that the end time was near for him, possibly several weeks away. He added, "More will be revealed. My divine mission, martyrdom for the children will be fulfilled. It is honorable." During this discussion, Leonard confided his recent purchase of a small caliber handgun. He stated he would never bring the weapon to work unless the conspiracy was an immediate threat. "I prepare myself for a battle of spiritual proportions." Leonard could not articulate who was behind it, but felt the insight would come soon and said, "I will know it when I see them." An emergency psychiatric evaluation was arranged and Leonard was involuntarily hospitalized as a danger to self and others. Leonard's emergency contact person was notified of the situation and he was suspended from work. He was given a directive specifying that he could not come back to the campus until he was medically cleared and his return was approved by district personnel. Leonard was asked to surrender his keys and identification. He was given a single point of contact in this written notification, and campus police and reception staff at the front desk were notified about the fact that he was not to be on district property until further notice.

Leonard's personnel file revealed a similar psychiatric episode fourteen years prior that resulted in a psychiatric hospitalization and an eventual return to work. He had 18 years as an employee of the district. After two months off work, Leonard called the district office point of contact requesting to return to work. "I'm feeling much better thank you, may I come back to work?" He got a note from his doctor releasing him to go back to work, and signed a release so that district personnel could contact the doctor. His treating psychiatrist addressed issues pertaining to his safety. However, the district insisted upon an independent review with their psychiatric evaluator who conducted a formal work fitness evaluation. The district doctor cleared Leonard to return to work, and the district moved him to a facility with limited access to children, issued him new keys, and returned his work identification, upon the TAT recommendation.

Category 1 Response Considerations

The example cases demonstrate the imminent danger aspect of Category 1 cases. They also highlight the variable outcomes. The students at South High had the intent and means to carry off their violent plans. They were organized, fixed, focused, and demonstrated a violent action and time imperative. They certainly qualified for arrest, conviction, and incarceration. Leonard had deteriorated into a serious episode of mental disorder, exhibiting delusions with violent content. His disordered and paranoid thought made him unpredictable. He was potentially dangerous to himself and others and had a rapidly developing violent action imperative. Supporting

147

this, he had purchased a gun, and was getting closer to an implied time or urgency imperative. He had done this prior to becoming clearly focused upon anyone in particular. Anybody could potentially be behind the conspiracy, and he had already sought to arm himself. He was ready to take a pre-emptive strike against someone–or anyone. Leonard required emergency mental health intervention for active treatment of his psychosis.

Security Response

A security response is usually also required in the high-risk Category 1 case. In case example one, police were involved in restoring safety, while in case two, campus security responded. If one suspects that there is this level of imminent risk, campus security and/or police should take primary responsibility for safely approaching the at-risk student/individual. The immediate concern is to isolate the individual so that s/he may not cause any harm to anyone else, and to contain any destructive behavior. It is of concern that some security officers are unarmed and lack sufficient authority to detain and/or arrest. Security or police personnel should be prepared to handle any potential escalation, including a situation in which the individual might provoke a confrontation in order to force law enforcement to harm them, a situation referred to as "suicide by cop" (Mohandie & Meloy, 2000). Prudent officer safety practices should be implemented.

Isolation and containment should be to an area that is out of sight of any audience. This protects the privacy and prevents loss of face to the at-risk individual, and avoids unduly traumatizing any observers. On some occasions this might involve evacuating a particular area within the school setting, while at other times the high-risk person may be brought to another area. Strive to minimize the potential for escalation while at the same time preserve the person's dignity. Occasionally, a ruse may be used to lure the person to a safe setting for intervention. Deception should be employed only under circumstances that afford no other, more desirable alternative. Common sense and reason should prevail.

The next order of business is to facilitate a removal procedure appropriate to the situation in order to restore the campus setting to safety. Considerations may include an arrest procedure, as in case example one, or a civil commitment/involuntary hospitalization process, as was employed with Leonard.

Involuntary Hospitalization

In some jurisdictions, there are local mental health personnel who will respond to the school to perform emergency psychological evaluations and initiate commitment procedures. In other situations, the person has to be transported to the nearest hospital for evaluation. Law enforcement personnel or specific mental health professionals are empowered to perform this critical task. Familiarity with regional emergency evaluation resources is essential.

Information regarding the events leading up to the involuntary hospitalization evaluation should be shared with the mental health professional. This evaluator needs full knowledge of these circumstances so that s/he will attend to the situation with the proper degree of concern, thus insuring that the student or employee receives the best care. Generally, it is not going to be sufficient that the professional base their evaluative opinion solely upon the word of the person to be hospitalized. It is not uncommon for individuals facing involuntary hospitalization to distort information, not perceive any kind of problem, or be downright antagonistic to the idea of hospitalization. Initially, persons may appear compliant with the procedure, then arrive at the admitting room with a different version of events, as they have thought about the implications of their situation. They are no longer willing or able to honestly reveal their thoughts and intentions. A TAT member, often the mental health consultant, should be delegated the important responsibility of liaison with the hospital admitting room staff.

In addition, the team should consider the appropriateness of securing a release of information so that the district might receive information about important issues related to the safety of school personnel, and the return of the individual to the school environment. A more immediate concern, particularly when there have been "danger to others" issues and/or threats, is to remind hospital personnel that the school is aware of existing "duty to warn" obligations. A point of contact may be offered to these staff members to help the hospital make appropriate notifications in the face of additional threats made by the individual towards school personnel, students, or others at the campus. This is one way of reinforcing an *escalation feedback mechanism*: methods for monitoring precipitating events and boundary probing behaviors. If at all possible, advance notice by the hospital of the individual's pending release would be desirable so that necessary security precautions at the campus might be initiated. There will be a hearing in some cases to determine if the individual will be kept beyond the initial short stay. Monitoring continued involvement of the at-risk person in "the system" is important. It prevents the school from being blind-sided by an early release.

Arrest Considerations

Arrests are sometimes appropriate and necessary to contain individuals at high-risk for school violence. The first example case illustrates how criminal justice involvement was used to re-instill control and order. Rather than waiting for more serious crimes to be committed, today's law enforcement and criminal justice organizations recognize that lesser crimes are often precursors to violent acting out. Districts should be ready to address this option should hospitalization attempts fail or result in premature release.

Some criminal behaviors are relatively minor and are referred to as *misdemeanors* within the U.S. criminal justice system, while some are considered more serious, and are referred to as *felonies*. It is important to determine the applicable criminal statutes in a given district's jurisdiction. It would also behoove the school to develop a liaison with local law enforcement before there is a problem so that proactive resources within the agency may be identified. This helps to avoid a "cold call" to the police agency that could result in a response such as, "Call us after you've got a crime." In many departments today there are officers, detectives, and investigators who believe in the former proactive approach. Team members should identify these critical resources.

There are many criminal statutes that can apply to school violence risk cases (See Table 14). Threatening statements are at the top of the list. In many states and jurisdictions, there are laws against making what are sometimes called "terrorist threats" or "terrorist threatening." The name sounds fancier than how it usually is defined. A terrorist threat is often defined as a statement or behavior that leads a victim to be in reasonable sustained fear of their personal safety or that of their loved ones. Jurisdictions differ as to the specific elements of these charges: for instance, they may delineate that the person intended to put the victim in fear, and that the statement was unequivocal, specific, and communicated directly to the victim. In other places, these conditions are not necessarily required to achieve an arrest or conviction. Local law enforcement should be aware of their applicable statute published in the state's "penal code." Some states have specific threat statutes that apply to threatening school officials.

TABLE 14

Arrest Considerations in High Risk Cases
• Terrorist Threats
• Threatening a School Official
• Brandishing a Weapon
• Carrying a Concealed Weapon
• Possession of an Unregistered or Illegal Firearm
• Possession or Manufacture of an Explosive Device
• Criminal Harassment
• Stalking
• Annoying Telephone Calls
• Hate Crime
• Assault and Battery
• Trespassing
• Burglary
• Malicious Mischief
• Vandalism
• Violation of Parole or Probation Conditions
• Violation of a Restraining Order
• Conspiracy to Commit Murder

Brandishing is a charge reserved for situations where a person has inappropriately displayed a weapon, usually some sort of firearm. Carrying a concealed weapon is related to this crime, which is unlawful in most states without a special permit.

Criminal harassment and stalking are similar arrest charges. In some jurisdictions, they mean the same thing–the repeated and unwanted contact of a victim that places that person in reasonable fear for his/her safety or the safety of his/her family.

In some school violence risk cases the person might also qualify for arrest for assault and battery, reserved for situations in which the at-risk individual has physically attacked another person. The charges may be more serious if there are visible physical injuries or a weapon was used. There also may be arrests for attempted assault. If the individual has harmed another person, and the basis for their attack is suspected to be racism or sexism, they may also qualify for a hate crime charge. These charges rely upon the acquisition of proof that the person was motivated by a specific hatred. Therefore, capturing statements, drawings, and writings that demonstrate any existing biases is critical.

Persons may be arrested for other crimes such as trespassing, burglary, and vandalism. Trespassing is most often a low-grade offense reserved for those who have illegally entered onto school property. Burglary usually involves theft without victim confrontation, such as when a perpetrator enters onto school property and steals items from school lockers. Vandalism is the intentional destruction of school property through graffiti or more aggressive means.

If the person is already subject to a restraining order or bail conditions that prohibit the reported behaviors, then intervention will typically involve an arrest for violation of such conditions. Documentation and confirmation of the violation is important, so the team should be prepared to offer evidence of any infractions.

Access Restrictions

Hand-in-hand with the at-risk person's removal from the campus are other security enhancements. Personnel should be told on a "need to know" basis that a particular individual is not cleared to be back on campus and if seen, certain procedures should be initiated. Security personnel and key individuals such as receptionists should be made aware of these contingencies. A picture might be distributed to help in the identification process. At the same time, legal counsel should be sought in the individual case so that privacy might be adequately protected.

Restraining orders are often used to set boundaries. In the first example, arrest, conviction, and incarceration of the threatening students clearly prevented them from coming back onto the campus and posing a threat. A restraining order could have been used in this case if they were expelled but somehow released. In the second case, an administrative "stay away" order was employed. In all likelihood, a restraining order would have been sought only if Leonard violated the boundary or made specific threats. The less invasive and easier to rescind access restriction was employed.

It might also be helpful to script out some response if the person should inappropriately show up on school property. Statements such as, "Leonard, please have a seat, I'll call so-and-so, they said if you showed up that they would want to talk to you," might serve as a surprise delay tactic if the at-risk person is expecting shock and is confronted instead with a, "We've been expecting you, please wait right here," type communication. At that point the staff person might have a signal or code to use when s/he calls campus security or the police.

Identification and keys were temporarily surrendered in Leonard's case to help restrict access to the school. Similar issues should be considered in high-risk cases where the person is barred from being on district property.

Weapon Issues

In many states, weapons possession, usually defined as firearms, is illegal if one has been involuntary hospitalized or committed for psychiatric or mental disorders, or subject to certain types of arrest. The specifics of these laws are vary across jurisdictions. For example, in California, a law enforcement officer may remove any weapons from the home of someone who has been involuntarily hospitalized. However, the person may qualify for getting their weapons back unless they are held beyond 72 hours. Then they are prevented from owning or possessing a firearm for five years unless they petition the courts (California Welfare and Institutions Code, Sections 8100-8104).

Whatever the specific legal parameters, retrieving any remaining weapons is very important in these cases. Team members should inquire and follow-up. While weapons removal cannot prevent a person from illegally acquiring a new weapon, it certainly reduces the chances that they will get one. Fortunately, waiting periods and background checks that accompany firearm registration and purchases are designed to help identify those who should not have weapons.

No intervention process in a high-risk case is complete without assessing for weapons possession and access. Law enforcement team members may be able to access information about registered firearms. Information derived from other sources, including interviews with the subject, may help to reduce uncertainties in this area. Accessibility should be looked at broadly, as there are many sources from which an at-risk individual might secure a weapon. For example, a student's parents might be asked about weapons in the home, whether campus police could help them search the student's room, and which friends or relatives have weapons in their homes. An agreement might be reached: any existing weapons in the home are removed temporarily, or permanently, so that risk may be reduced.

The availability of weapons other than firearms should also be assessed. Potentially hazardous materials for making explosives and sharp objects like knives and machetes, or blunt objects, such as clubs or baseball bats, may be relevant in some cases.

Post-Arrest/Release Considerations

In the event of the arrest of a high-risk individual for any charge, there are still issues to address. Due process afforded to arrested persons demands that team members monitor the person while in the criminal justice system. Will the person make bail? If so, it is possible to request that certain conditions be attached, sometimes referred to as *enhancements*, often identical to conditions which might be included in a restraining order. Such modified bail conditions may have significant consequences for the person should s/he choose to violate and renew his/her problem behaviors. S/he will then be subject to immediate arrest and significantly increased bail or no bail, improving the likelihood that s/he will remain in jail.

Juvenile offenders may be subject to different arrest and release procedures. In some states laws have been modified to take a strong stance against youthful offenders. If they are over a certain age and presumed to have the capacity to form criminal intent–depending upon the nature and severity of the crime–they may be treated as adults in the criminal justice system. Prior to release they may have to post bail. In other jurisdictions, juvenile offenders are treated differently, including the fact that they may be released with or without bail to their parents after arrest. Other states have a mixed approach to juvenile offenders, so it is important to find out how juveniles are handled in any given state.

The timing and outcome of the various court proceedings should be monitored, particularly conviction and sentencing. If convicted, it is important to determine if the person will be sentenced to jail or prison, or some other situation such as probation, community service, and counseling. Monitor this process so that the school and potential victims are aware of the pending release. Further, there may be the opportunity for school officials to advocate with the court for stronger conditions or controls that the court may impose as part of any sentence.

Probation and parole officers serve as resources to influence the behavior of the high-risk individual. Contact between the district and these professionals, usually through campus police or security as appropriate, can be helpful to keep the person contained and in control.

Surveillance

Surveillance–the monitoring of the high-risk individual–has been incorporated into the short-term management strategies recommended by some TATs in unusual and extremely high-risk scenarios. There are obvious potential abuses and liabilities stemming from invasion of privacy, depending upon how the surveillance is conducted. Some situations demand consideration of this alternative because of the potential for short-term violence. One high-risk student, arrested and expelled for weapons possession and terrorist threats, emphatically stated his intentions of "getting even" after being released from jail. He was surveilled for several days after his release, and was observed in his parents' garage, manufacturing a pipe bomb and handling a semi-automatic handgun. In this case, police investigators were used to conduct the surveillance, given the high likelihood that this offender would engage in antisocial and illegal behavior after release. He was re-arrested and returned to jail.

School/Employment Status Issues

When the person is involuntarily hospitalized or arrested, the team should decide his/her leave status. The team should arrange whatever documents are necessary to notice the individual or their family (in student cases) about their leave status, and what procedures are involved to facilitate a return to work or school. These criteria become an important part of the monitoring and re-entry process. These criteria may also include an independent evaluation by a mental health professional prior to any return to school or work. Some districts will even pay for these evaluations rather than quibble and suffer from a lack of crucial information.

On those occasions which involve an employee, it may be helpful and necessary to use a union representative or appropriate emergency contact. Any correspondence that specifies the individual should not be on campus should also include a campus point of contact and telephone number, indicating that, "If there are any questions you may contact ____ by telephone." Without a point of contact, there is no way for the at-risk person to address any legitimate concerns they s/he may have, and also less chance that we get the courtesy phone call that the person is getting upset and escalating. This is another way of establishing an escalation feedback mechanism.

Notifications

In all student cases, parents or guardians should be notified of the situation. An understanding approach is helpful, one which attempts to involve the parent in a collaborative way towards stabilizing the situation. Some parents may be quite surprised by their child's difficulties, while others may be angry and defensive, feeling guilty and resorting to blame as their way of coping. The team member engaging with the parents should be interpersonally adept, and less likely to invoke negative feelings. In some cases, the campus police or security officer may be the appropriate person, since some families will defer to these roles as a matter of custom or practice. In other cases, there may be a team member who has dealt with members of the family on previous occasions and built up some degree of rapport.

Another issue to consider is whether parents are prepared for violence towards themselves at the hands of their child. There are a number of cases in which a student turns his rage upon his parents prior to attacking school personnel or other students; for example, Luke Woodham and Kip Kinkel. Sometimes there are concerns about the parents' potential to become abusive with their child in response to notification about their child's problem behavior. In these situations, appropriate consultation with child protective agencies might be warranted, prior to any notification. It may also come to the attention of school personnel that an employee might pose a potential risk to their intimates or others outside of the school milieu. In these situations, notification of any potential victims needs to be seriously considered.

Monitoring

It is imperative that the status of at-risk students or employees be monitored to determine whether the person's level of risk—a dynamic rather than static phenomenon—is decreasing or increasing, so that intervention may be appropriately adjusted. The person's involvement in expulsion hearings, disciplinary hearings, appeals processes, worker's compensation procedures, other litigation, and the criminal justice system may result in escalation. A case is always monitored for additional warning signs. While the individual is precluded from being on campus, feedback mechanisms need to be established to determine if the individual is attempting to violate boundaries. Such "boundary probing" is often a sign of escalation. In Leonard's case, this would have been exemplified by any attempts to enter the campus prior to his official return. On the other hand, if the person fulfills their return-to-school or work criteria, TAT members need to readjust their assessments of risk, and initiate re-entry for the now formerly at-risk individual.

Category 2: High Violence Potential, Not Imminent

Cases described as Category 2 level are high-risk for violence potential, but the at-risk person does not qualify for arrest or involuntary hospitalization or commitment procedures. There is substantial risk, but no evidence to support that the threat is imminent. Often there is a qualification or a *quid pro quo* to the stated or implied threat. This determination involves a judgment call. The behavior in question, such as a threat, falls just short of the criminal statute definition, as often happens in conditional threat situations: "If you don't give me that promotion, I will hurt you," or "If you go with Johnny to the prom, I am going to kill you." The person making these statements should be taken very seriously and further assessed to determine whether there are risk factors present, such as weapons possession or past violent behavior. Approach behaviors and potentially destabilizing precipitating events should be assessed. At other times, the individual may demonstrate behaviors indicative of a conditional risk without articulating a clear, "If you do this, then." There is enough behavioral evidence that they may engage in violent behavior under certain evolving conditions.

Case Example: Threatening Communications Part II

In the fall, 1999, a mid-western high school was confronted with the following situation. High school sophomore Jennifer Sampson reported to her parents that she had received a series of distressing communications from another sophomore Suzie Jones. The communications involved e-mails, letters directly handed to Jennifer, and letters passed to Jennifer through third parties. (Excerpts of these communications were presented in Chapter Four on pages 98-100).

157

Jennifer's parents were horrified when they realized that their daughter was being sent these e-mails and letters. Jennifer was terrified that Suzie was going to harm her and had no idea why Suzie was so focused upon her. In fact, they had never had any relationship other than the occasional "hello" exchanged in the hallway, and there had never been any overt rejections–or betrayals–at least not in the real world. It was clear that something was very wrong.

Jennifer's parents called the principal and informed her of their concerns. The principal convened the threat assessment team. The principal, campus police officer, school counselor, and district legal counsel were all present for this meeting.

Team members acquired some initial information from Jennifer's parents, Suzie's mother, school counselor, and favorite teacher. Suzie told the school police officer and principal during the initial interview that she was tired of being disrespected by Jennifer. She denied any intentions to harm her, and downplayed the seriousness of her communications. When asked about her explanation for why she had been preoccupied with Jennifer for so long, she shrugged her shoulders and teared up. She was placed on suspension from school pending disciplinary review. Jennifer's parents considered obtaining a restraining order against Suzie. Jennifer's parents wanted to know what the school was going to do to protect their daughter, and kept her home from school pending a satisfactory resolution.

Suzie was a good student, but a quiet loner. She lived with her mother and father, and her father was reportedly an alcoholic. Suzie didn't mix well with the other kids, and had been in treatment with a psychologist until about one month prior to her series of communications when her parents decided that she no longer needed to continue. She had suffered from depression and suicidal ideation in the past. For her school picture, Suzie wore a message shirt stating, "Kill 'em all and let God sort 'em out." Her favorite band was *Korn*, and her mother reported that she had been repetitively listening to the song *Falling Away From Me*, from their album titled *Issues*. TAT members downloaded some of the lyrics from one of the band's websites and learned that the song had several references to suicide and intense pain (Korn, 1999).

The important warning signs present in this case demanded that the threat assessment team immediately confer. Suzie made multiple contacts with Jennifer in a short period of time, without any apparent precipitant. She made a number of statements that indicated a highly detailed violent fantasy life focused upon another student. Suzie was clearly obsessed with this girl, and the obsession had lasted for some time. She expressed strong themes of rage and anger. Her behavior caused significant distress to Jennifer.

The important risk factors were her level of obsession and willingness to "step outside of the box" and make these inappropriate communications, suggesting a lack of impulse control and restraint. She identified with violent ideas and had an active violent fantasy life, with apparently limited positive coping skills. Suzie also had been treated for depression in the past, and suffered from suicidal ideation. There were guns, knives, and swords in the home. There was evidence that she had engaged in some degree of *aggression immersion* (Meloy & Mohandie, 2001): she repetitively played the more intensely violent *Korn* songs, and other violently themed music. Her communications were *organized, fixed,* and *focused,* and demonstrated a *violent action imperative,* but no apparent *time imperative.*

Stabilizing factors and potential precipitating events were also considered. Her father was not an effective parent due to his alcoholism, but there was no evidence of abuse and Suzie's mother was highly invested in taking care of her daughter. Suzie's family had financial and health care resources. They could afford and were willing to get Suzie into mental health treatment. Her father was willing to keep his knife and sword collection, as well as his guns, at his brother's house–locked in the gun safe for the foreseeable future.

Intervention itself was viewed as a potential precipitating event. There was a disciplinary process to consider, and when Suzie was sent home, the school police officer and a school psychologist spent some time talking with her mother about the need to arrange an emergency session with mental health for short-term residential treatment. The school principal contacted the mental health professional at the facility. She communicated her concerns and provided copies of the e-mails and letters so that the treatment staff might understand the situation better and tailor their treatment accordingly. "Duty to warn" expectations were communicated to both the facility and Suzie's therapist.

Additional information requested included a signed release of information for school representatives to talk with Suzie's therapist. There was a clear and articulated expectation that treatment progress and issues related to safety would be communicated to the school principal.

After all of these issues were considered, it was determined that Suzie represented a high, but not imminent risk for violence potential. Several interventions were arranged: 1) disciplinary suspension; 2) short-term residential treatment, which her mother agreed to arrange for Suzie so that she might get stabilized on medication; 3) follow-up treatment with her former psychologist and a new psychiatrist to monitor problematic symptoms; 4) an independent evaluation by another psychologist to address her return to school; 5) alternative school arrangement at another campus which afforded more individualized attention and prevented contact between Suzie and Jennifer, the target of her obsession; and, 6) monitoring for any signs of destabilization in the form of other communications.

Two weeks after Suzie's removal from school, the decision to bring her back to school had to be made, counterbalanced with the obvious risk of her obsession reactivating by any contact with Jennifer. Because Suzie's parents were actively involved in getting her to treatment, the district favored suspension as opposed to expulsion. Prior to her return, the district had the positive recommendation of Suzie's treating therapist and an independent psychologist. This resulted in a readjustment of her risk level downward, as criteria for re-entry were fulfilled. Suzie and her mother met with the principal after she was cleared to return to alternative schooling, and the rules for her return were explained. She was cooperative and agreed to abide by the parameters. Suzie did well in her alternative schooling, had some friends, and made no further contact or approach behaviors towards Jennifer. Her parents, while preferring that Suzie attend regular schooling, understood and accepted the arrangement to allow a period of observation and stabilization. The school district continued to monitor the case, and at the time of this writing were introducing Suzie to another school campus because of her compliance with her return-to-school agreement.

Case Example Number Two

During the 1999-2000 academic year, a high school in the Green Bay, Wisconsin region was confronted with a very difficult situation. School officials became concerned about one particular student, Bruno Johnson, an 18-year-old senior with a history of serious mental problems and learning difficulties.

Bruno came to the attention of school officials in the eighth

160

grade, because he had sent threatening letters and was found to possess detailed writings that graphically described the manner in which he wanted to kill various students and staff members. The letters were sent to a teacher and student at the school, prompting a search of his locker where the other materials were found. Accompanying these explicit descriptions were drawings of equally compelling shock value. During an interview, Bruno acknowledged making the statements and writing the letters, describing them as fantasies he had no intention of acting upon.

His parents at that time were not responsive to the fact that their son had engaged in highly distressing behavior, and that he likely suffered from serious mental problems. In fact, Bruno would not talk in the principal's office if his computer was on, because he was afraid the device might be filming and recording their interaction. The parents discounted and minimized these important warning signs during a parent-school conference, and stated that Bruno was normal compared to his four brothers and sisters. Begrudgingly, and at the insistence of the school, they took Bruno to one session with a psychiatrist who indicated that, "with medication he should pose no danger to others." The parents, who were from another culture, found the notion of psychiatry shameful and did not comply with medication and follow-up visits. For this reason, Bruno was disciplined and transferred to a highly monitored alternative school setting, and for a period of time after the initial intervention, his behavior stabilized. He was reintegrated into a regular high school.

In his ninth grade year, Bruno sent out 30,000 junk e-mails to all of the school computers and caused significant disruption. Once again, a parent conference was arranged, and his parents minimized his intentional sabotage. Bruno claimed he was testing his skills, and that he was simply playing a prank. He was suspended for several days.

Bruno had difficulties in his classroom studies as well. He didn't listen, was often disruptive, and failed to complete assignments. He exhibited significant concern, however, that he should pass his classes so that he might graduate. Efforts to work with his parents to get Bruno into remedial tutoring and treatment failed, and his school performance remained consistently poor.

So poor, in fact, that by the beginning of his senior year, Bruno was a "senior" on paper only. In reality, he barely had enough credits to qualify as a freshman. He became obsessed with the idea that he needed to graduate with his small group of friends, and started to pursue his school academic counselor about what she could do to "fix" his grades so that he would graduate with his class. He was completely out of touch with the reality of his dilemma, believing that she could, in fact, reverse his multiple course failures and incompletes. Bruno began to intimidate the school counselor and made veiled threats to her: "Something bad will happen if I don't graduate."

The school academic counselor was terrified of Bruno. He had a way of staring at her with an unblinking gaze. It was like he could see right through her. He would stand too close, clench his jaw, and on a couple of occasions when she attempted to broach the subject of getting a GED instead, she thought he might assault her. On one occasion she heard him mutter under his breath, "I'll show them, I'll kill." She reported her concerns to the principal.

An *ad hoc* threat assessment team was convened. The team was highly concerned about Bruno's unrealistic focus upon graduating, the conditional threats he had made, and his developing belief that the academic counselor was the person impeding him. His history of explicit violent fantasies, poor family support, and lack of treatment for what the first psychiatrist had diagnosed as paranoid schizophrenia, were very ominous. Bruno was *organized, fixed* and *focused*, and demonstrated a *violent action imperative*, with no *time imperative* articulated. When Bruno was interviewed by the assistant principal and school police officer, he expressed anger at the academic counselor, reiterating his belief that she could change his grades. He was vague when asked the question, "What do you mean bad things will happen if you don't graduate?" Bruno had no concept that graduating with his peers was not going to happen.

With the input of their legal counsel, psychologist consultant, and campus-based law enforcement, district administrators decided to compel Bruno to withdraw from school, barring him from being on campus or attending classes until they had some assurances that he was stabilized and receiving adequate psychiatric treatment. In addition, the guidance counselor was transferred to another school–she welcomed the move–and counseled by school police about how to enhance her personal security at school and home. School officials were concerned about Bruno showing up at a school event, and arrangements were made to enhance security at these venues, on and off campus, until the end of the school year. The school initiated a formal administrative order barring Bruno from district property. This was explained to Bruno and his parents during a parent school conference. This order indicated that if he or his family had any questions, they were to address them in writing through the mail or by telephoning the principal. Plainclothes school police observed Bruno as he entered school property for the serving of this order, and stood watch nearby in case he might escalate. While Bruno and his parents were unhappy with this outcome, other procedures by which he could obtain alternative schooling, including the pursuit of a GED diploma, were communicated to them. Bruno indicated he would abide by the order.

Security and key reception personnel were told that he was banned from district property, and his picture was distributed. Several months after the order was initiated, Bruno showed up on campus and was quickly intercepted as he headed towards the cafeteria during lunch break. He was politely escorted by responding security personnel to the principal's office, and gave permission to be searched. He was unarmed, and the principal reiterated, with security present, that he was not to be on the district property. Bruno's parents were called to pick him up. Once they arrived, the boundary was reinforced with them as well. They were told that a formal restraining order would be sought if he showed up again prior to an approval to return. He has not yet returned. The case continues (Note: because of the true location of this case, IDEA did not apply).

Category 2 Response Considerations

The above case examples demonstrate the distinction between Category 1 and Category 2 levels of risk, and the factors that were considered as part of that determination. Suzie presented with important warning signs, risk factors, stabilizers, and potential precipitants that firmly planted her in the Category 2 level of risk. There were no indicators of imminent risk. This case exemplified the tailoring of intervention options to stabilize the situation and which ultimately led to Suzie's successful return to school. Similarly, Bruno's case demonstrates these types of concerns, as well as longer-term case management.

Security Response

If an at-risk individual is assessed as a potential Category 2 level of risk, some degree of security response should be strongly considered. That response may involve the presence of security during any initial interactions with the individual, and notifying

163

security and reception personnel of the name and description of the person if s/he is prohibited from entering the campus for a period of time. These responses were implemented in both example cases.

Subject Interview

Interviews of the subject were initiated at various points in the assessment and intervention process. Interviews often uncover critical information about the subject's actual behavior, motivation, and intentions. It is important to understand the subject's point of view of the events in question and to get their side of the story. There may be reasonable explanations for their behavior. It is also helpful to give the individual a chance to feel heard, lessening the chance that s/he might feel pressured to do something more dramatic to get attention. A return-to-school interview is usually appropriate, allowing school personnel the opportunity to assess compliance with return-to-school criteria, reaffirm rules for re-entry, and probe for any potential problem resurgence. Conferencing with the parents should accompany the student interview.

Removal from Campus

Removal of the person from school district property is a strong consideration in cases that appear high-risk, pending a thorough assessment of the level of risk actually present. This may involve an administrative decision, or be a natural consequence of the school's disciplinary system. Medical removal may apply if the person is obviously too impaired to attend school as a student or work as a school employee.

Boundary setting techniques such as stay-away and restraining orders should be considered in these cases. In the case examples, the less invasive administrative stay-away order was employed. However, if Suzie had failed to abide by the stay-away order, the next step would have been a restraining order. Similarly, the school officials in Bruno's case decided that one more boundary probing activity would necessitate securing a formal restraining order.

Notifications

Parents or guardians should be notified after the problem is identified and an initial decision is made to remove the student from the school premises. Care should be taken to watch for parent or guardian responses that are potentially violent or dysfunctional. The last thing these situations need is to be further escalated by an untoward parental response. In Suzie's case, her mother helped to stabilize the situation, while in Bruno's case, cultural issues precluded the family's willingness to participate in an adequate plan to contain his behavior. Therefore, the school intervention team bore an added burden of containment and needed to take more responsibility for boundary setting.

Parents or guardians may need to be cautioned about their child, and whether the student might be capable of harming them. The Kinkel case discussed in the previous chapter is a tragic example of the need to assess for that type of risk. The parents should be asked whether there are guns or other weapons in the home, and if so, reminded to adequately secure or remove them.

Psychological Consultation

Psychological consultation is usually necessary in Category 2 cases. Consideration should be given to an immediate evaluation of dangerousness to self or others warranting an involuntary commitment procedure and placement in a residential treatment facility. A timely emergency evaluation and ongoing treatment by a mental health professional on an outpatient basis might be indicated instead. In some cases, these evaluations will be performed by the psychological consultant to the team, while in others they might be conducted by an outside evaluator. Whichever option is utilized, any exceptions to confidentiality and privilege should be explained at the outset to parents and the individual, and treating mental health professionals should avoid the complications of a dual relationship.

In addition, there are laws in most states regulating the provision of mental health services to minors and the need for parental consent. Formal consent will often be necessary for all but the most obviously emergent circumstances.

Similar issues appear in adult cases of employees or staff members. If the person does not qualify for hospitalization on an involuntary basis, there is a need to refer the person for a work fitness evaluation and/or mental health professional through an employee assistance program (EAP) so that limited feedback may be provided. Typically, feedback will be arranged with this mental health professional around four issues: 1) did the person make it to their mandatory appointment; 2) are there any safety issues to self or others; 3) is the person able to work or are there modifications to their work status that are necessary; 4) what kind of follow-up, if any, is being recommended. Other issues that impact work and safety may also be the focus of the evaluation. Again, it is critical that the employee be aware of the proposed disclosures and exceptions to confidentiality.

Monitoring

The Category 2 case examples underscore the need to continue tracking the student or employee's status and his/her response to intervention. Methods to assess the individual's compliance with return-to-school criteria and procedures must be implemented. Such feedback is an integral part of insuring the safety of others, and success upon re-entry for the at-risk individual. "Trip wires" to detect boundary violations indicative of potential escalation need to be established. For example, in Suzie's case, Jennifer and her mother were instructed to notify the principal if Suzie attempted to approach her in any way.

Chapter Summary

Cases that are a high-risk for violence potential may or may not be imminent. In either situation, removal of the individual from the school is usually indicated until there is some assurance of reduced risk. It is critical to have security or police involved in removal procedures to ensure safety and control. In Category 1 cases, initial intervention usually involves involuntary hospitalization or arrest. In Category 2 cases, the person will not usually qualify for arrest or hospitalization, but is often precluded from being on campus until s/he has complied with established return-to-school or work criteria. These criteria may include attendance with, and feedback from, a mental health professional. The individual's access to weapons should be assessed and restricted. High-risk individuals should be monitored to assess their compliance with boundaries and return-to-school procedures. Family members or emergency contacts should be notified and involved in the intervention process as allowed by law and as needed to facilitate safety, stabilization, and the individual's ultimate return to the school environment.

CHAPTER SEVEN

Moderate/Lower Risk Case Intervention Considerations

Category 3: Repeated/Intentional Infliction of Emotional Distress

The Category 3 level of risk case occurs when there is insufficient evidence for violence potential, but sufficient evidence for the repetitive and/or intentional infliction of emotional distress upon others. There is no evidence to support that the person intends violence. The individual repetitively engages in behaviors, however, that would cause reasonable people emotional distress, or acknowledges intentionally engaging in behaviors or making statements that would cause emotional distress in others. In the most typical pattern, the person is making veiled threats and intimidating statements, expressing attention-seeking anger, getting in people's faces, and creating the circumstance where people are "always walking on eggshells" while in his/her presence. When questioned about his/her conduct, s/he may acknowledge engaging in the behaviors to "make my point." S/he tends to self-justify and blame others for the need to resort to these extreme measures, making statements like, "Good, it's about time somebody noticed people are upset around here, if it takes me walking around pissed off to get their attention so be it, it's not okay to mess with me!" In other cases, the person denies the intent, but over time repeats the behavior, even after receiving corrective feedback. This strongly suggests that s/he is intentionally doing it for effect. S/he should know by now the behavior is not acceptable.

Case Example One

On March 2, 2000, a middle school teacher from South Carolina found a note on the ground outside of her third period class. The note contained threats to "nuke" the school and harm various teachers and students. The writer of the note indicated that s/he felt mistreated by people at the district, and that they should be punished for making his/her life miserable. Swastikas and racial slurs were doodled on this piece of notebook paper, along with drawings of skulls, dripping blood, and tombstones. The teacher took the note immediately to her principal.

A partial meeting of the threat assessment team was arranged and tasks were delegated. The principal, a school psychologist, the teacher reporting the threatening communication, and a school police officer were present at this meeting. Team members participated in person and by conference call. After reviewing the communication, the team members were highly concerned about who would leave such a note, and the teacher voiced her suspicions about one student in particular who had had some recent behavior problems in class, and may have made drawings and doodles similar to those on the note. The team determined that the first order of business was to identify the writer, if possible, so that information about other warning signs, risk factors, and potential stabilizers and precipitants could be gleaned, and a reliable estimate of risk could be made.

The school police officer took responsibility for investigating the student, discreetly accessing other writing samples from previous assignments handed in, and examining the student's desk in various classrooms for similar doodles and drawings. After reviewing these items, it became quite obvious that the student had been the author of the threatening communication. The team then met to discuss their options for handling the situation.

The student's name was Mark Johnson, a 13-year-old eighth grader with average academic performance, few hobbies and interests, and a limited circle of friends. The teacher noted that he had seemed depressed and distracted of late, and was easily frustrated. A decision was made for him to be interviewed initially by the school police officer and the school psychologist to determine, what, if anything, he might say about the letter. The basis for the interview was a disciplinary investigation of threats at school, a possible violation of school policy. While the threats had not been communicated directly, some determination of his intent in writing this material was needed.

Mark was called into an office and gently presented with concerns about the note that had been found. He initially denied writing the note, but when the police officer showed him the note as compared to his writing assignment, Mark finally admitted that he had written the note and stated that it must have, "dropped out of my backpack." He was questioned about his motivation for writing the note and he stated, "I don't know, I'm just mad and bummed out all the time." He became tearful, and the school psychologist noticed that he had cut marks on his arm. Mark was asked about the cut marks and admitted that he had self-mutilated. "It makes me feel better, the pain goes away," he told the team members. He denied that he wanted to kill himself or anyone else, but admitted to feelings of hopelessness and anger. A decision was made to immediately contact the boy's parents immediately and arrange for a parent conference.

The note was shown to his parents, and they were surprised to learn about their son's difficulties. They had no idea that anything was the matter, and took the situation very seriously. Mark's parents agreed to take him to a psychologist, and signed a release of information so that the school could get some assurances that he had been seen for evaluation, therapy, and potential risk or danger. The parents agreed to provide a copy of the letter to the psychologist. In addition, the school police officer talked with them about weapons access in the home, which they denied. His parents agreed to inspect their son's room and check out his computer for more information. They also reviewed his Internet bookmarks, as well as his Internet history that lists frequent and recently accessed sites. Fortunately, this search revealed nothing more than some soft-core pornography websites. They did find more swastikas, morbid drawings, and racist posters in his room.

The psychologist determined that Mark was depressed, referred him to a psychiatrist for medication, and scheduled additional sessions for Mark and his family. Mark was reportedly able to identify his anger and understand how others had been concerned and distressed by his violent fantasies. He was quickly returned to school and scheduled for meetings with the school counselor on a weekly basis. Prior to his return, the psychologist and psychiatrist both indicated that Mark had been stabilized and that they were continuing to treat him. They welcomed any input about his school behavior. He and his parents sat down with the school principal and his school counselor to discuss appropriate school behavior parameters. At the time of this writing, he was doing well and there had been no further episodes of distressing behavior.

Case Example Two

Mr. Jones is a 15-year teacher with a district in the Pacific

Northwest. He was recently given an evaluation that criticized his job performance, particularly his lack of respect for students, parents, and coworkers. At times he engaged in yelling and abusive language towards these individuals. One morning, Ms. Smith was talking to Mr. Jones and she reported a series of interactions to the assistant principal.

Mr. Jones was crying in the break room between classes. She saw him and went to talk with him about it. He told her it was "pointless" and that he didn't know what he was going to do about his problems at the school.

Mr. Jones reportedly told her, "That goddamn principal Gomez, he's never liked me and I've got a good notion to kick the living shit out of him, next time I see him!"

Ms. Smith became alarmed and told Mr. Jones, "Don't do anything stupid, just take your evaluation as a 'lesson learned,'" to which Mr. Jones stopped talking and said, "thanks for listening, you've always been there for me."

When the assistant principal heard this information, she became concerned about these behaviors, the well-being of Mr. Jones, and others on the campus, especially Mr. Gomez, the principal. She reported the threatening statement to Mr. Gomez, and Mr. Gomez tasked the assistant principal with reviewing the situation with members of their *ad hoc* TAT. A decision was made to locate Mr. Jones, and the assistant principal and a campus security person responded to the break room and his classroom with no results. Mr. Jones failed to return to school after lunch.

TAT members became more concerned, and also had to provide coverage for Mr. Jones' class. They had no idea whether Mr. Jones was serious about his statement to "kick the living shit out of Gomez" or simply was "blowing off steam" with a colleague. Erring on the side of caution, they discreetly informed security that if Mr. Jones was seen on campus, that he should be tactfully directed to the assistant principal's office, and arrangements were made to determine his whereabouts. A decision was made to re-interview Ms. Smith to ascertain how and what actually was communicated. Mr. Jones' personnel package was located and quickly reviewed.

It was learned that Mr. Jones' wife had left him six months before, and he had been going through a bitter divorce and hotly contested custody battle. Ms. Smith told investigators that he had recently been arrested and convicted for driving under the influence of alcohol, and that Mr. Jones was someone who often confided in her. Therefore, it was not his intent to have the threat communicated to the principal. He was "blowing off steam," in her opinion.

Some initial concerns were raised about the need to warn Mr. Jones' ex-wife of his problem at the district, given his relationship problems and family difficulties. Team members considered whether they should contact his ex-wife or not, but decided against it as he had not articulated any statements or demonstrated any behavior indicating a focus upon her. Team members were concerned that it might further inflame the situation and cause him unnecessary difficulties. Ultimately, they decided to call Mr. Jones at home. As arrangements were being made for that telephone call, the school receptionist notified the assistant principal that Mr. Jones had just called in sick saying he "wasn't feeling well."

Team members breathed a sigh of relief, but still had concerns to address. Would Mr. Jones be allowed to come back to work, could he safely work around the principal given his level of expressed anger, and how were they going to deal with his history of inappropriate behavior? They decided to send Mr. Jones to their employee assistance program on a mandatory basis, requesting limited feedback. If there were serious questions raised about his safety and potential to create additional emotional distress in others, then he would be referred for a formal work fitness evaluation according to district procedures. There were also disciplinary issues raised when he left his classroom unattended, and past unprofessionalism to reconcile and address. Reconciliation between Mr. Jones and the principal Mr. Gomez was necessary for re-entry to be viable. The potential for a mediated meeting between the two, with low-key (portable panic button, security stationed nearby) safety contingencies was discussed.

Mr. Jones came to work two days later with a note from his psychologist to account for his time off sick. During an interview with the assistant principal, Mr. Jones acknowledged making the statements, but says he did so out of frustration and anger, and that he had no intentions of having that statement shared with others, nor of harming anybody. He was not particularly concerned that others had become upset and worried. He denied weapons ownership or possession. He agreed to sign a limited release of information so that the school could have some assurances that he was okay, given the circumstances. His psychologist verified that he was not a danger and had voiced no reportable threats towards Mr. Gomez or anybody else.

The psychologist confirmed that Mr. Gomez had difficulty seeing the impact of his verbally abusive behavior upon others. The psychologist stated that he was continuing to schedule sessions with Mr. Jones, and that Mr. Jones had begun Alcoholics Anonymous to address his alcohol issues.

The principal, with input from the TAT, decided to accept the psychologist's opinion as enough assurance, and recommended that they offer the EAP as an alternate place for Mr. Jones to get help if he voluntarily chose to do so. A meeting was arranged between the principal and Mr. Jones, and the principal heard Mr. Jones' concerns and clarified his expectations about appropriate conduct in the workplace. Future misbehavior would result in further progressive discipline. Mr. Jones agreed to honor this clarification, and stated that he understood the consequences for stepping out of line again.

Category 3 Response Considerations

These two case examples demonstrated issues consistent with a Category 3 level of risk. Mark Johnson wrote a threatening note, implied identification with violent symbols, and made racial slurs, creating distress and concern on the part of others. He admitted a level of anger and depression that was part of his motivation. It may be that his behavior was a "cry for help," to draw attention to his depression. He had no stated intent or ability, however, to make good on his threats. Mr. Jones was more prolific in his history of angry and abusive behavior, and coupled with his inappropriate statements and lack of concern for the impact upon others, repetitively created distress. Further assessment determined that he had no intentions of harming others. Both of these cases illustrate the way the TAT process can prevent overreaction by seeking appropriate information about the context and meaning of behavior. The examples also point to how interventions may be tailored to address moderate to lower risk cases.

Security Response

If one assesses a Category 3 level of risk, there may be a need for some degree of security response. Such a response is not likely to be dramatic, but might simply entail having procedures in place should the person choose to escalate. The one-way panic button or pager in the pocket of the person intervening is a good idea, with security personnel nearby. Simply having two people present during the intervention phase may suffice. TAT members working with security should generate a planned and scripted approach to take control if the individual engages in any intimidating behaviors during the intervention. This might include the manner in which they will enter the room, introduce themselves, and respectfully and firmly set boundaries. For example, they might come in and say, "Hello Mr. Jones, I am security Officer Smith and this is Officer Brown, you seem upset. Could you please step back from Mr. Gomez, lower your voice, and sit down, so we can figure out what's going on."

Removal vs. Limits

Another decision needs to be made: whether it is acceptable for the individual to remain on campus temporarily, pending further assessment and investigation, or removed until that process is completed. This decision is usually impacted by the egregious nature of the behavior. In the two example cases, it was decided that assurance from a mental health professional was in everyone's best interest prior to allowing either Mark Johnson or Mr. Jones back onto school property. In other cases, a simple clarification of the boundaries of acceptable conduct might be appropriate. If the decision is to remove the individual, the basis is usually a serious violation of disciplinary rules, an ongoing pattern after earlier warnings, or the results of a work fitness evaluation procedure. If the person is allowed to remain or granted permission to return, a return-to-school or work agreement should be initiated: a behavioral contract with specified consequences for misconduct. This agreement is formulated during a meeting between the principal or assistant principal and the student and his/her parents, or with the employee of concern.

Notifications

Parent/guardian notifications should be made in most student cases. The team needs to think about who will make the notification, motivating the parents to participate actively and supportively in any interventions. The contact person should be alert to signs of any counterproductive behaviors, and have well-thought, common sense responses to deal with these problems. An example: "Mr. Johnson, your son Mark was involved in an incident in school today that caused everyone a great deal of concern for his well-being and the safety of others. I'd like to meet with you so that we can come up with some ways to better understand this and help him get back on track. I need your help." Notifications inform, but they also serve to set a collaborative, problem-solving tone with the family.

173

Notification in Mr. Jones' case also let Mr. Gomez know that Mr. Jones had expressed some angry statements about him. This allowed Mr. Gomez to take some precautions until the situation could be further assessed, including notification that the assistant principal would be used for the initial intervention.

Information Gathering

As with all potential risk situations, it is imperative to seek more information. The TAT should obtain firsthand verification of the reported misbehaviors, talk to any potential witnesses, and review all known collateral information. In addition, a review of the student or personnel records will help to determine if the behavior is acutely aberrant or part of a chronic pattern, and what interventions have been attempted. Information reduces the uncertainty of blindly dealing with the problem situation.

In Category 3 cases, such information can reaffirm that there is a lower degree of risk. It is useful to assess weapons possession or access, as well as any history of impulse control problems. In the examples, an understanding of the context and meaning of the individuals' behavior helped design appropriate interventions.

Subject/Parent Interview and Conference

Part of this process is an interview of the individual who has been engaging in the distressing behavior. Such inquiries involve legal or practical considerations, like the need for union or parental representation during the meeting. Interviews help to clarify the person's perception of the events in question, as well as their motivation, intention, and willingness to correct the problem behavior. These types of meetings should be organized and behaviorally focused. Simple, matter-of-fact presentation of the problem behavior should be outlined for the individual (and his/her parent or guardian in student cases). The meeting should provide an opportunity for any input or explanations. This enables district personnel to listen for any responses that may suggest a longer-term problem or more serious concerns, such as the person responding, "I still don't give a damn about THAT, I am giving NO promises that I won't do it again. If he pisses me off again, I will MESS HIM UP!" Barring any such misbehavior, this can be followed by explanation of the consequences for the current behavior and any subsequent reoccurrence. This is a progressive discipline approach–a soft probe for more pervasive

174

problems–and lays the groundwork for further disciplinary intervention should the person continue the behavior. This type of meeting should not be held prematurely. Any necessary investigative or administrative proceedings required to address the issue should occur first. This information can play a key role in decisions to allow the person to remain at school with a return-to-school/work agreement, or other decisions involving discipline, suspension, expulsion, or transfers.

Return-to-School/Work Agreement

Team members need to develop a written contract that identifies acceptable and unacceptable school behavior, and the student or employee's commitment to abide by the school's rules in the future. Consequences for failure to do so are also indicated. The student and his/her parents (or employee) and the principal or other appropriate school representative then sign the document, and copies of the signed contract are distributed accordingly. This type of intervention may increase the personal responsibility and compliance of the individual. In any event, it certainly creates documentation of attempts to manage and control the behavior should more serious discipline or intervention be required.

Mental Health Consultation

Psychological referral may also be in order. While some persons may pursue counseling on their own, as in the second case example, many times there is a need to arrange for an appropriate mental health intervention in Category 3 level cases. Mental health intervention should be required when there is a pervasive pattern of problem behavior, or the person fails to care or understand that others are impacted. This will often entail referral to a mental health professional with an arrangement for limited feedback, so that the district can gain important information about the person's ability to refrain from distressing behavior towards others. In employee-involved situations, the team may recommend a work fitness evaluation as described in Chapter Five. Monitoring the results of evaluation and treatment is important. This follow-up and liaison activity is best suited for the psychologist on the TAT or a human resources person.

There should be a release signed by the student's parents, or in the case of an employee, signed by the employee. The TAT psychological consultant can then insure that important collateral information is in the hands of the evaluating professional. Even if the person has not signed a release, most professionals are willing to listen to the input of others while "neither confirming or denying" the fact that they are the one professionally seeing the person. This at least insures that the professional is aware of the issues.

The following series of issues may be addressed with this evaluator or treating mental health professional:

1. Inquire of student/employee psychotherapist whether student/employee understands the events that led to prior problem behavior or violent acts;
2. Inquire of student/employee psychotherapist whether the student/employee understands the distress of others;
3. Question student/employee psychotherapist about what degree of assurance or confidence they have that student/employee will not engage in additional problematic behavior;
4. Inquire whether student/employee has a specific plan to prevent additional problematic behavior;
5. Question student/employee psychotherapist as to whether student/employee understands the potential consequences of a recurrence.

Apart from providing valuable information about the individual's progress, these questions provide a structure for the liaison with an evaluator, communicate that the case is a priority to the district, and notice that the school is concerned and attending to the management of the case.

Restraining/Administrative Orders

In some Category 3 cases districts may want to secure a restraining order. The difficulty is documenting the "reasonable fear" of the victim/recipient of the distressing behavior. Victim behaviors that support the fear component, such as changes in the person's routine, heightened vigilance, or increased security measures, must be identified and documented in the restraining order to convince the court to issue it.

A lesser form of intervention than the restraining order is an administrative order. The student or employee is directed to "cease and desist" his problem behavior, stay away or have no contact with the victim/recipient, or abide by any other legitimate limits that the organization deems necessary to contain the situation and establish control to end the problem behavior. Similar to return-to-school or work agreements, such orders may be an important first step in reducing the person's misbehavior and provide documentation of progressive attempts to manage the situation.

Monitoring

It is important to monitor and track student/employee status and response to intervention attempts, so that future interventions may be modified accordingly. If the person is to return to the school environment, the reactions of those s/he distressed need to be managed. Scripted statements, sit-down sessions, or even apologies may be needed. Sometimes the person may need to be transferred to another district site, depending upon the extent of the distress that s/he created in others. Monitoring will determine the person's compliance with any agreed-upon game plan for preventing future problem behavior. Consequences, as appropriate, should be fairly and swiftly applied. Finally, team members should identify behaviors that would qualify the individual for more serious risk and the corresponding intervention contingencies.

Category 4: Unintentional Infliction of Emotional Distress

The Category 4 level of risk is defined as *insufficient* evidence for violence potential, but *sufficient* evidence for the *unintentional* infliction of emotional distress upon others. These situations often involve one-time, "I put my foot in my mouth" episodes in which someone says or does something in a moment of emotion or as a poorly conceived practical joke. When the person is confronted with the inappropriateness of their behavior, s/he recognizes and acknowledges the impact s/he has had upon others. S/he will usually accept full responsibility for the behavior, and is willing to participate in a game plan for putting people at ease again, as well as accept the just consequences. S/he truly did not intend to create the distress. Persons engaging in this behavior most often suffer from temporary or permanent lapses of judgment.

Case Example One

On April 12, 2000, five students at Monroe High School in Los Angeles, California, told another student that they were planning to attack classmates, a school police officer, and a teacher to mark the one-year anniversary of the shooting at Columbine High School. This student brought forward his concerns about the plans, resulting in the suspension of the five students, an ongoing investigation, and widespread concerns about violence at the campus. The mayor disclosed the investigation during a question and answer session after his annual State of the City address, resulting in worried parents and reporters descending upon the school.

Detectives soon determined that the boys had been joking about their threats, and detectives found no evidence that they were planning an attack. No charges were filed, but the students will face likely punishment, given the number of people who were affected and the unnecessary expenditure of public resources to address the safety concerns precipitated by the prank (Gettleman, 2000).

Case Example Two

On November 4, 2000, an *armed* school police officer from a high school in the Midwest told his lieutenant, as he was getting his equipment to begin his workday, *"give me my mother fucking gun before I kick your ass!"* This event came two days after the workplace violence shooting at the Xerox plant in Honolulu, Hawaii, that left seven employees dead at the hands of a coworker. The lieutenant told the officer that it was inappropriate to make those kinds of statements and that he had to ask the captain for his gun back. The school police officer assumed a martial arts stance, pulled his baton out of his belt, twirled it aggressively in the air before placing it on his arms in a battle-type stance, and stated loudly, "That's okay, I don't need a gun to be dangerous!"

At this point, the lieutenant informed his captain about the threatening statements and unusual behavior. A decision was made to intervene. They took the officer into the captain's office and explained their concerns about his statements and then referred him for a mandatory evaluation to a psychologist. They explained that the appointment was mandatory according to the organization's work fitness procedures, and then escorted the officer to the psychologist's office, "just in case."

After the lieutenant explained to the psychologist the behavioral concerns preceding the referral, the psychologist met with the officer. The psychologist explained the limits of confidentiality and that personal information would be shared with the lieutenant and captain if it pertained to his potential risk, as well as any other recommendations. The officer indicated he understood these issues and proceeded to tell his side of the story.

178

The officer confirmed that he had made all the statements and behaviors attributed to him, and even demonstrated for the psychologist his baton behavior. He stated that he hadn't intended to scare anybody, that he was just "messin' around," denying any intent to harm. After a careful consideration of the risk factors, stability factors, and potential precipitating events, the psychologist formed the opinion that this officer did not pose a threat to others or himself at the current time, nor had he intended to create the distress generated by his behavior. In fact, he acknowledged his judgmental lapse, and was able to see that, on the heels of another workplace violence incident, it was not funny. The officer indicated that he was willing to do anything to reassure his supervisors and coworkers about his safety, and stated that he felt bad for making others uncomfortable. He offered to apologize and identified the need for disciplinary consequences for his conduct. The officer did, in fact, apologize when he returned to the workplace, and to date there have been no more incidents.

Category 4 Response Considerations

These case examples exemplify the Category 4 level of risk, and how intervention responses were used to address the problem behaviors which initially caused distress and concern in others. The joke, in case example one, caused significant disruption. Follow-up information-seeking, as a component of the intervention process, determined that it was a misguided prank rather than a higher risk case as it initially appeared. Interventions were appropriately downgraded. Case example two involved a similar "prank" issue. Further assessment was part of the intervention to rule out more serious concerns. In response to intervention, the individual acknowledged his judgmental lapse, and was concerned about the impact his behavior had upon others. He accepted the consequences of his behavior and sought to make amends.

Security Response

In these cases, there is rarely a need for a security response. In the first case example, the security response occurred because the case initially appeared to be high-risk (Category 1 or 2). Once information establishes a lower level, security will not be required to safely manage the situation. If there is a fact that suggests otherwise, such as weapons possession or availability, like in case example number two with the armed employee, then protective measures

179

commensurate to the situation need to be arranged. The issue most often, however, is the need to reduce any security procedures that may have been initiated.

Background Reviews

It is helpful to conduct a cursory review of background records and information to rule out a more pervasive problem. Occasionally, one might assess a case to be a low-key Category 4 level of risk. Upon further review, TAT discovers several other instances of the same behavior that continued to occur despite intervention attempts. In these cases, upgrading to a Category 3 or higher level of risk, and progression in the disciplinary and intervention areas will be indicated.

Removal versus Limits

When a probable Category 4 level of risk case is identified–often by one or more members without the whole TAT being convened–decisions will need to be made about the egregious nature of the conduct, and whether temporary or permanent removal from school property is necessary. In case example one, the students were suspended because their conduct broke the rules and disrupted the school, but not because they were dangerous. Allowing these "pranksters" immediately back to school might send a bad message to other would-be practical jokers.

After conferring with the parents and the student, or the employee and the union representative, a decision will usually be made to allow the person to remain at school or work after experiencing appropriate consequences and agreeing to certain behavioral parameters. Return-to-school/work agreements are an important intervention tool in these situations.

Return to School/Work Agreement

Behavioral contracts and administrative orders establish boundaries for the person's conduct. S/he may make amends to those individuals s/he distressed as part of the contract or order, or as something s/he simply does to "make things right". This begins the process of effective re-integration and may help to reduce the attractiveness of further acting out behavior.

Mental Health Consultation

A referral to a psychologist is frequently considered, usually to address judgment issues that led to the poorly conceived practical joke or "foot in the mouth" issue. Many times these mild acting out behaviors indicate a cry for help, drawing attention to some problem in the person's life that needs to be addressed. The clinician should review with the person whether s/he clearly understands the consequences of any reoccurrence, helping them to acknowledge that, upon returning to school, they are on "thin ice."

Notifications

In student cases, parental/guardian notifications will be in order, although in all likelihood they will probably not need to attend any conference. An exception: when the behavior is so disruptive that there is some question about the student's ability to continue in school.

Monitoring

The monitoring process is the final stage of intervention. A determination needs to be made about what additional information might trigger a reclassification into Category 1, 2, or 3. A team member should be designated to track the student or employee's participation and compliance with any agreed-upon contracts or plans, including counseling and restraint from engaging in any more counterproductive behavior. Monitoring is facilitated by establishing appropriate feedback mechanisms.

Category 5: No Evidence for Violence Potential or Distress

Category 5 cases have *insufficient* evidence for violence potential and *insufficient* evidence for emotional distress. In these situations, it has been determined that there were no threats and no one poses a threat. There is no legitimate distress. This category often includes blatantly false reports. While most cases reported to TATs have a legitimate basis, there are a small percentage of situations that, upon follow-up investigation and review, are discovered to be false.

A cautionary note is in order. It is critical to treat all situations initially as if they are legitimate until evidence proves otherwise. The potential physical, psychological, or other harm of accusing or inferring that a true complainant has "made up" the allegations is unacceptable. It is far safer to risk being initially fooled, then return to confront a false accuser at a later point.

There are a variety of reasons why persons might report that a threat exists, or that they have been a victim of some crime, when, in fact, no such events occurred. At the less pathological end of the continuum, it may simply be that they misunderstood or overreacted to the event. There are many cases where this innocuous explanation has been the source of the false report. One recent case, for example, involved a language difficulty, and the complainant simply misunderstood and reported a threat based upon their innocent misperception.

Other situations involve persons who are obviously mentally disturbed and subject to hallucinations, paranoia, or delusions. They make complaints based upon these false sensations and distorted perceptions. Fortunately, these cases are easy to identify, and intervention usually follows a mental health track. However, even here caution is important, as occasionally what sounds "paranoid" may actually have occurred.

The cases that are most difficult to manage, potentially explosive, and professionally challenging, are when persons knowingly make the allegation and stage their false victimization. Usually the motive is to get attention, create an alibi, or seek revenge. These cases often involve unnamed or unidentifiable perpetrators. If the "perpetrator" remains unidentifiable, the game may continue longer without a forced confrontation or discovery. When there is a falsely named perpetrator, other motives certainly may apply; however, revenge and other payoffs or secondary gains may be more prominent (Mohandie, Hatcher, & Raymond, 1998). The following case examples illustrate the dynamics of these cases and the issues related to detection and intervention.

Case Example One

In spring 1999, Jane White, a part-time employee of a California school district, noticed a white piece of paper on the floor of the main office. She asked a student to hand her the paper and discovered it was a store receipt with a written message on the backside. The message stated, "Move all the fucking cars away from the parking lot by 10:00 or they will explode!" She reported this to her supervisor, and police were notified. The campus was searched and no explosives were located. The investigation quickly focused upon the employee due to idiosyncrasies that were present in the verbatim written message (and which are omitted here for privacy reasons).

The initial investigation revealed that Ms. White had secondary employment in a retail setting, and, not coincidentally, there had been four bomb threats to that work site. One of those threats took place subsequent to the current threat, and each of the threats coincided with Ms. White's work hours. The written notes were submitted for forensic handwriting analysis, and a polygraph examination was arranged by local law enforcement. Ms. White's husband called to cancel her scheduled polygraph examination, claiming that she was ill.

When investigators finally had the opportunity to confront Ms. White, they presented her with the results of the handwriting analysis, which indicated she had written some of the notes. She confessed to fabricated threats, and was charged with five counts of false bomb threats.

Case Example Two

In July 1997, Shannon Barron, former teacher with Dominguez High School in the Compton, California Unified School District, reported that she had been attacked after an English class by four students who doused her with two buckets full of fecal matter. Distraught, she reported the crime to school officials, campus police, and ultimately, local law enforcement. Various holes quickly appeared in her version of events leading to the allegation that she had concocted the story. Ms. Barron was charged with filing a false police report. According to police, her statements were inconsistent, she was never able to identify any of her alleged attackers, and no witnesses ever came forward to corroborate her story.

She became very upset when her story was challenged, secured an attorney, and filed a 3.5 million-dollar lawsuit against the district and local police department. Forensic evidence, however, was compelling, and she was prosecuted by the district attorney's office. The bulk of the human waste had been found inside Ms. Barron's slacks, and there were no signs of splashing that would be expected from something being thrown on her. This misdemeanor trial lasted more than a month, involved 24 witnesses, and at least 100 hours of police time. Prosecutors argued that she had soiled herself and then invented the story of an attack to hide her embarrassment. She was ultimately convicted of filing a false police report, fined, sentenced to six months in jail, and mandated to attend counseling. She sobbed as the verdict was read, and Compton police Lieutenant Danny Sneed commented, "This whole trial was about clearing the good name of students at Compton Unified School District." He added that prosecution was important to deter other people from wasting police resources (Leonard, 1998).

Case Example Three

During June 2000, a fourth grade teacher became concerned when she reviewed the following writing assignments allegedly submitted by several students:

The Burned Schoolhouse

Once upon a time there was a building that was called "Schoolhouse." It was a very boring place to go. All the kids hated the schoolhouse. The kids did not like the teachers. They told their parents to at least take them out. They also told their parents how rotten they were. They said, "All of the teachers make us starve, take long naps, and make us jealous. They don't really care about us, they are just there to get paid. They only let us play outside for five minutes. When they took toys, they took them and burned them." The kids got so mad that they got beer bottles and threw them all over the schoolhouse. After they did that, they burned down the whole entire schoolhouse. Nobody ever saw the schoolhouse again.

Signed Johnny, Bobby, & Gary

The Burned Teacher

Once upon a time there were three kids named Johnny, Bobby, and Gary. They didn't like any teachers because they bossed them around. They got so mad that they wanted to burn the teacher. Every day the teacher separated them. So one day they got in a gang and were thinking how they were going to burn the teachers. So then the boys saw the teachers in their cars, and the boys brought gallons of gas and put the gas on the cars then burned them. The boys came out on America's Most Wanted.

Signed Johnny, Bobby, & Gary

The teacher was concerned, based upon this writing assignment, that these three 10-year-old boys might pose a risk to the school and herself. She informed the principal of her concerns and a TAT was convened.

The children were interviewed and their parents were notified about the writing assignment. It was learned that this creative writing

184

assignment took place two days after the post-Lakers game riots in Los Angeles. The media broadcast many images of rioting fans looting businesses, throwing rocks and bottles at police, and burning property.

One boy took responsibility for writing the short stories. He did not intend to cause distress, nor was he planning to set fire to the building. He had no documented history of firesetting, but had some minor conduct problems. His parents agreed to take him to counseling as a precaution.

The other two boys cried when they were interviewed and clearly had nothing to do with the writing of these short stories. There were no other warning signs, risk factors, or potential precipitants to acting out. Their parents were concerned. The teacher in fact was not distressed, but was being cautious. It was determined that this was a Category 5 case where the complainant may have overreacted in the interest of safety.

Category 5 Response Considerations

The first two cases demonstrate purposeful fabrication of false reports of violence or threats. The third case illustrates circumstances occasionally encountered in post-Columbine America, where a complainant, in good faith, reports a concern about violence potential. Subsequent investigation fails to support any basis for concern for violence potential or emotional distress. The investigation may instead uncover inappropriate behavior, which can then be addressed. Cases of inappropriate behavior are easy to identify through existing review methods, while the first two examples may be more challenging to discern.

Recognizing the False Case

Recognizing the false case is an important first step that must precede response considerations. This recognition usually comes on the heels of a thorough investigation and inquiry which then fails to substantiate the reports of the complainant, and identifies factors consistent with false victimization. There may be many of the following indicators present:

1. Complainant is overheard bragging about or discussing the falsity of their claim.
2. Forensic or investigative evidence is inconclusive, or is

inconsistent with the complainant's account of events.

3. Complainant gives inconsistent stories and conflicting statements about what has occurred.

4. Complainant has reasons to create the false accusation; motives may include attention, revenge, alibi for regretted or embarrassing activity, or reconciliation of a failed relationship.

5. Complainant has a history of lying or misperceiving events.

6. Complainant behaves in a manner that is in stark contrast to how one would expect a true victim to behave.

7. Complainant reports outrageous or preposterous stories that are highly unlikely, and conflict with known and typical case patterns.

8. Complainant's "reporting rhythm" coincides with stressors in their life: new reports or complaints occur when there is a lull in attention, the need for some new piece of information to account for a discrepancy, or in the context of interpersonal or life problems.

9. Complainant has a history of attention-seeking, manipulation, and dramatic behavior.

10. There is a "gut" or intuitive sense on the part of those investigating that the claim is false or grossly exaggerated.

While none of the above items automatically imply that the person making the report has lied, these may be indicators of a false report. Once there is a determination that the report is false, then the team needs to identify action steps to address the person reporting the case. The first two case examples featured several of the above indicators which flagged the attention of investigators.

Interviewing/Confronting the Complainant

Given the importance of an investigation to determine the veracity of the threats, law enforcement or campus security will usually take the lead role in the investigative procedures, confrontation, and initial intervention procedures. Due to the nature of the allegations, the team should hand off the case to police or security for investigation. Investigators need to decide how to initially confront the victim/complainant with the results of the investigation, and the fact that the situation did not occur in the manner that s/he described or reported. The temptation is to hammer the complainant with the way resources have been wasted. Strategy is the operative word here, however, because there are a variety of reasons why the person may have made the report, and none of them will benefit from an angry, nonprofessional confrontation.

The easiest cases to handle are those where the complainant has made the false report due to a simple misunderstanding. If it is determined that these are the reasons for the false report, then the team may recommend that the situation simply be clarified for the person. A matter-of-fact discussion of the facts with someone designated by the team may be appropriate, with an ear for the reasonableness of the complainant's response.

If someone is purposefully engineering behaviors to report, intervention requires careful consideration to avoid unnecessary escalation into counter-accusations, high drama denials, complaints to the media, and lawsuits. Some of these complainant responses may be unavoidable due to the complainant's heavy investment in the secondary gains of the falsehood. However, if the team and investigators have "all their ducks lined up," regarding the facts of the case, many of these responses may be squelched. The person will be thoroughly convinced about the futility of the charade.

Readjustment

Once the determination has been made that the case is false, the complainant confronted, and the threat laid to rest, there is still the issue of assuaging any hurt feelings or removing any consequences that may have been initiated, as a precaution, against any named "perpetrators." If a specific person was unjustly and falsely accused of having made the threat, and that person was subject to consequences and investigative procedures during the investigation, they should immediately be told of the findings and offered an apology for their hardship and inconvenience. If possible, they should be told that there will now be an investigation of the false complainant and, as appropriate, that that person will be subject to legal or other consequences. Acknowledgment and validation of the impact of being falsely accused is an important part of healing. This communication should come from a ranking person within the district, often the principal and/or assistant principal, in cases involving employees; in cases involving students, other messengers may be better. The important issue is to get the information to the falsely accused, the true victim, as quickly as possible to alleviate ongoing hardships, before s/he learns about it from other sources. In student cases, parents and guardians should be told as well, and offered understanding for the unnecessary difficulties the false report may have created. Those involved in making these notifications should expect anger and outrage, rather than gratitude; and should be prepared to listen to a litany of complaints about the unfairness of these events, and angry demands for punishment of the offender. School or police representatives should let the true victim of the false report know what his/her options are.

One might consider a mediation session between the parties so they could sit down and "bury the hatchet." This is a most sensitive matter, and the utmost care should be utilized to insure that both parties are sufficiently mature and motivated to handle the interaction. Well-executed, it can potentially avert the bad feelings and resentments that might otherwise fester and turn into ongoing and lasting rivalries and conflicts between students, or between members of the staff. The damage to trust and feelings of anger and betrayal, however, are usually too severe on the part of the aggrieved party for this to have any degree of success. If the criminal justice system is involved, this process should be discouraged. This approach is most appropriate for the "simple misunderstanding" cases.

If the false accuser is suffering from delusions or other psychotic symptoms, then one needs to consider whether the complainant or "victim" may act out in response to some misperceived threat. Intervention should cautiously parallel a process which now assesses whether s/he might pose the risk, and if so, at what level.

In student cases, a parent/guardian conference will be part of the intervention, with the interveners attempting to get the parents in agreement with the game plan for remedying the problem. With employee or other cases where an adult is the focus of concern, referral for a work fitness or mental evaluation may be in order. Motivating the person to comply may involve the following type of communication: "There may be a number of explanations for why a person may report these concerns ranging from 'it happened' to 'psychological problems.' We have to rule out all possible explanations, therefore, we are referring you to a psychiatrist/psychologist."

Many jurisdictions within the U.S. and elsewhere have laws against filing false police reports or making anonymous threats, and most organizations will impose discipline commensurate with the level of disruption created.

Anonymous Threat Investigations

Anonymous threats of violence are a related issue. These cases can involve varying levels of risk that may extend from no risk whatsoever, to a high level risk. In certain countries, such anonymous threats should be taken far more seriously because of a history of terrorist acts. A recent issue in the U.S. has to do with threats involving weapons of mass destruction (WMD) or nuclear, biological, and chemical (NBC) weapons. These types of threats have grown more frequent. They often involve some agent, such as anthrax, or a bomb, placed in a building imperiling its occupants. Fortunately, WMD and NBC threats are nearly always bogus (false positives). However, due to the potential for irreversible devastation, immediate law enforcement involvement is indicated. In the U.S., most typically the FBI will conduct these investigations. They will provide a final assessment of the legitimacy of the threat.

Investigative Issues

District personnel should be prepared to conduct immediate and safe evacuation procedures as recommended by the FBI or responding law enforcement agency, and provide important information to investigators. This information might include:

1. What did the communicator specifically say, as close to *verbatim* as possible?
2. Do you have the recording or actual correspondence sent by the communicator?
3. What was the sex and approximate age of the communicator?
4. Were there any noteworthy or unusual background noises or other idiosyncrasies in the communication (accents, laughter, heavy machinery, music, etc.)?
5. Have these communications been received by anyone else or through any other medium?
6. Who else do you think we should talk to about the threat?
7. Are there any persons who have a motive to make this kind of a communication?
8. Who do you think the communicator is?
9. Have you noticed any recent unusual activity on or around the school campus?
10. Has anyone recently noticed any unusual packages or deliveries?

11. What steps has the organization taken in response to this?
12. Where can we reach you and other important key staff/witnesses during and after business hours?

The case example listed below stemmed from an anonymous phone threat and was later determined to be a Category 4 level of risk. It demonstrates the disruption these events can cause on school campuses.

Case Example

On March 1, 2000, Willowside Middle School in Sonoma County, California received a telephone call from an anonymous female caller who threatened to shoot other students, stating simply, "I'm gonna come down there and shoot everybody," before hanging up. School officials, concerned about the threat, closed the school and a charter school on the same campus the next day. An investigation was initiated into the possible identity of the anonymous caller.

When the school reopened, a Willowside staff member overheard a ten-year-old girl talking about the threat. Sheriff's deputies, present at the school as a deterrent, interviewed the girl and later arrested her.

They determined that the girl had made the threat "on a dare" and she admitted that she strives for attention, good or bad. The deputies noted that she did not intend to create distress or fear in anybody; rather, she had intended the threat as a practical joke. While she was remorseful, she was suspended for five days pending an expulsion for the rest of the school year. She was charged with making a terrorist threat, and could be sentenced to three years in Juvenile Hall if convicted. The case led to such disruption that the Chief Deputy District Attorney commented, "Authorities take all matters involving violence at schools very seriously...We want to discourage this type of thing from happening again."

Investigators noted that the girl did not have access to weapons, nor did she have any history of violence. They speculated that she may have been suffering from family problems, and confirmed that her parents were divorced and both had arrest histories. Investigators considered the possibility that her behavior was a cry for help to address more serious problems in the home, and investigated the possibility of child abuse.

The girl had allegedly told her friends that she had made the threat. Several of these friends vied for the $1000 reward that was offered for information leading to the arrest and conviction of the person responsible (Deputy Carpenter, personal communication, March 8, 2000). With the identification of the probable caller, parents, school staff, and students expressed a "sigh of relief" that the matter was over.

Campus Stabilization

Once it has been determined that the report of the threat is false, whether anonymous or otherwise, there is a need to modify any security responses that were implemented. Extra security, school closures, and other precautions should be stopped.

For any larger-scale disruptions that may have been created by the event, affected individuals need to be told that the threats were false and that there is no cause for alarm. Information to address the matter should be shared. This informs people that the situation is back in control, and that appropriate and thorough investigations were conducted. It may also discourage others from making false reports.

Mental Health Consultation

Mental health referrals are often indicated when persons make a false report. There is a need to address the underlying issue that led them to choose such drastic measures to accomplish their psychological goals. They need to learn alternate problem-solving skills to deal with their attention-seeking, abandonment, resentment, and other contributory issues. Those that have the best prognosis are false victims who admit their misdeeds and accept responsibility for the chaos and hurt they have caused. It is particularly important to let the treating professional know what the deception has been, since s/he may have been deceived as well. In student cases, parents or guardians play an important role in insuring adequate mental health intervention and keeping the lines of communication open with the treating professional.

Monitoring Critical Events

Monitoring is an important consideration across all risk levels. The case is not over after an initial intervention effort. There may potentially destabilizing events that are still unfolding in the student's life. For example, the parents may have disclosed that they are divorcing, a parent may get sent to prison, or the student may prematurely terminate psychotherapy. An employee placed off work pending a work fitness evaluation or disciplinary hearing may be

191

found unfit for duty or terminated. The at-risk individual may test the boundaries that have been set. Clear channels of communication are essential: checking in with the student periodically, inviting the parents to disclose this kind of information, and staying abreast of employment changes of at-risk workers. Assessment is an ongoing *dynamic* process.

Readjustment

We need to enhance or reduce our interventions according to common sense and good judgment. For example, a student is suspended subsequent to acting out and/or suicidal behavior. The parent agrees to send the child for a period of residential treatment, and during this interval the student is barred from entering the campus. "Trip wires" in the form of photographs are provided to key personnel on a need-to-know basis (receptionist staff and campus police). Subsequently, the parent notifies the school that their child has successfully completed the program and received a positive recommendation to return to school. The parent signs a release that enables the school to get key questions and concerns addressed, and a parent-child-school conference is arranged to discuss the parameters of acceptable conduct. At this point, the school decides to let the student back in–with clear boundaries.

School personnel obviously need to rescind the campus ban, and the student's picture should be reclaimed. *Failure to readjust has been the cause for action in civil suits,* and the notion makes good common sense. The degree of intervention should parallel the degree of risk at any given point in time.

Readjustment should also occur when the at-risk individual exhibits signs of escalation. Readjustment, in these circumstances, should parallel the considerations discussed earlier for a perceived level of risk. An at-risk individual may progress from "not imminent" to "imminent," based upon changing risk factors, stabilizing factors, and precipitating events. The person will hopefully respond to intervention attempts by risk reduction, moving from "imminent" to "no risk," and compelling the TAT to lower interventions and countermeasures as appropriate. TAT members should establish upgrade and downgrade criteria, defining what behaviors, statements, or other information should result in a reclassification of risk level. This is a fluid process that must adapt to change.

Re-entry/Reconciliation

In all of these cases, thought needs to be given to re-integrate persons who may have made or posed a threat, and might at some point be allowed back on campus. From a practical standpoint, when and where can they be safely allowed back? In the discussion of Category 1 cases, Leonard was allowed back to a campus where he would not have contact with children and could be individually supervised. This was subsequent to his completion of return-to-work criteria. The South High students were incarcerated and therefore precluded from returning to school. Had they been released, important decisions about their schooling would have been made. Perhaps they would be sent to an alternative school, encouraged to participate in home schooling, or urged to pursue their GED.

In the Category 2 case section, Suzie was allowed to come back to school because she and her family fulfilled the school's criteria for returning. In contrast, Bruno was not allowed back because of a failure to fulfill the school's established criteria (Note: because of the real location of Bruno's case IDEA laws did not apply). Similarly, Mark Johnson and Mr. Jones, our Category 3 examples, were allowed to remain on campus after some assurances about safety and notification of campus limits.

Once the decision has been made to bring the at-risk individual back, the feelings of others on staff or among the students will need to be addressed. In particular, feelings of anxiety and fear about additional episodes may be encountered. In situations involving those who falsely accused, how are these individuals going to make the necessary amends to be allowed back in, and how are they going to manage the wrath and distrust of others?

This is re-entry or reconciliation, because there is a need to facilitate the person's return to the environment and to repair relationships and trust damaged by the problem behaviors. Sometimes the person's return, as in the case of Leonard, involves a work site where the employee will not be involved in unsupervised access to children, and where district personnel can monitor him for a period of time to insure stabilization. Similarly, Suzie, who was obsessed with Jennifer, was not allowed back onto a campus where she would be near her obsession.

On the other hand, Mr. Jones was allowed to return to work after having lost control of his emotions. However, the district required specific assurances from his treating psychologist. A mediated meeting between him and his supervisor, principal Gomez, was arranged to facilitate reconciliation. If it became clear that they could not work out their differences, and Mr. Jones could not contain his anger, then he probably would have been transferred elsewhere, or become subject to other personnel actions.

Affected parties often need support or counseling for what they've been through, or coaching about how to handle interactions with the individual. Re-entry, re-integration, and reconciliation should be planned activities, which will increase the success of the overall process. In the best of all possible worlds, we will be able to come full circle, bringing the at-risk individual back and having them re-enter school without incident. A flow chart of the entire threat management process is presented in Table 15. It should be self-explanatory.

Chapter Summary

School violence cases that are moderate to low risk lack evidence for violence potential. Category 3 cases have evidence for the *repetitive* or *intentional* infliction of emotional distress, while Category 4 cases have evidence for the *unintentional* infliction of emotional distress. Intervention in these cases typically involves discipline and limit setting in the form of behavioral contracts between the school and the student and his/her family. Mental health referrals are often initiated. Category 5 situations have no evidence for violence potential and no evidence for the infliction of emotional distress. Category 5 cases often involve false reports that stem from the need for attention by the complainant, or from misunderstandings and overreactions. Intervention in Category 5 cases begins with recognition, and often transitions to gentle confrontation of the false complainant and the provision of appropriate mental health resources. Anonymous threat investigations, like false report cases, are usually conducted by law enforcement representatives. Information gathering is an important activity in cases across risk levels. Security response is usually minimal in each of these moderate to low risk categories. It is critical to monitor the at-risk individual's response to intervention to determine if his/her risk will diminish or increase. TAT members, based upon monitoring, need to readjust their assessments of risk and intervention approaches. Re-entry of the individual into the school environment needs to be anticipated in most cases. In higher risk

TABLE 15

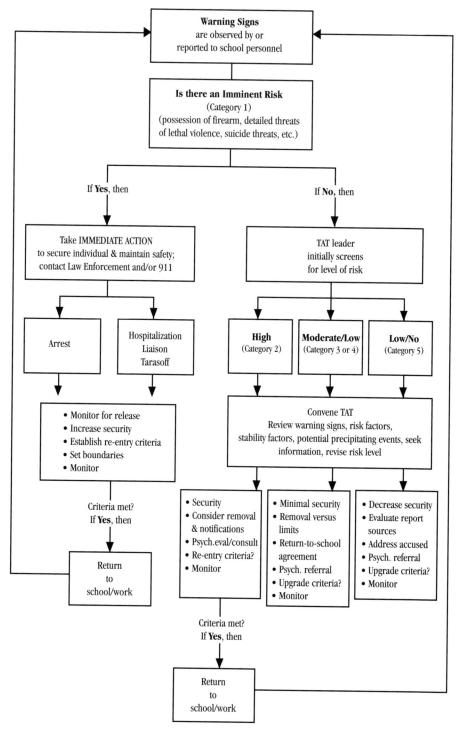

195

cases, TAT members must contemplate the best strategies to increase the success of the individual's re-integration into school. The reactions of classmates and others need to be anticipated, and as appropriate, reconciliation and mediation may be warranted. Once the at-risk individual is back in school, monitoring for warning signs begins anew.

CHAPTER EIGHT

Aftermath Crisis Management

Most tragedies can be averted with the strategies and issues identified in this book. Some lethal and serious events, however, will continue to occur. School districts need to have contingencies for worst case scenarios, and know what to expect and how to deal with the significant impact these events have upon students, families, staff, local authorities, and the overall community. Various concerns will have to be addressed as a consequence of school violence. Two case examples highlight the breadth of these issues.

McKinley Elementary School, Lisbon, Ohio

On March 23, 2000, a 12-year-old sixth grade student stood up in his classroom, pointed a gun at the floor, and told his fellow students and the teacher to "get down." A student walking down the hallway outside the classroom heard what was going on, and summoned another teacher for help. The teacher, Linda Robb, stood in the doorway of the classroom and asked the boy if she could talk to him. They walked out into the hallway and hugged, and the boy handed the weapon to her.

The boy was reportedly despondent because his mother was serving time in a state prison 150 miles away, and he wanted to be with his mother in jail. He acquired the weapon, a loaded nine millimeter semiautomatic, from his father, who had stored it on a dresser top with a fully engaged trigger lock. The boy was able to find the key and remove the trigger lock before taking the weapon to school.

After the boy surrendered, he was taken into custody.

Fortunately, no one was hurt. This event was a close call, and its aftermath was limited in magnitude and duration. The sixth graders were sent home and classes were canceled the next day. The school remained open for crisis counseling ("Ohio boy," 2000).

Columbine High School, Littleton, Colorado

On April 20, 1999, 18-year-old Eric Harris and 17-year-old Dylan Klebold, both seniors, assaulted the Columbine High School campus in Littleton, Colorado, killing 12 students, one teacher, and injuring 21 classmates before committing suicide. Both wore trenchcoats (initially), black cargo pants, and message t-shirts. Harris' shirt said, "Natural Selection," while Klebold's read "Wrath." They planned the assault for over a year, motivated by revenge, hatred, and a desire for notoriety. Fans of Hitler, and obsessed with weapons, explosives, violent music and movies, and the video game *Doom*, they sought death and destruction, hoping to be reborn as characters in their favorite game.

Multiple clues were left by these troubled teens as their resentment and rage grew. They laughed together in their homemade videotapes about the extensive "foreshadowing" and "irony" of the clues they had left behind. Harris had written a short story about what it would feel like to be a shotgun shell in a weapon, and told his friends, "Wouldn't it be cool to kill the jocks and blow the school up," several months before the fateful day. Klebold had written violent stories and asked a friend to purchase a weapon for him in January, 1999. Harris' room was reportedly littered with bomb making equipment–a tackle box with bomb-making supplies, six alarm clocks, and boxes of empty $CO2$ cartridges. They extensively chronicled their planning process in journals, notes, and videotapes, including one homemade "suicide" video to their parents in which they addressed their motivation.

A timeline of the Columbine mass murder illustrates the dynamics of an unfolding incident and the related aftermath:

1110 Harris and Klebold arrive separately at Columbine High student parking lot. Harris talks briefly to another student, tells him he likes him and to leave.

1114 They walk into the cafeteria, occupied by 600 students on "A" lunch, carrying two duffel bags loaded with two 20 pound propane bombs set to go off at 1117, the time most students would be present. If the bombs had been successful, they

198

would have killed dozens of students. They leave the building.

1119 Harris and Klebold begin firing at students from outside the building. The pair approach wounded students and shoot them again at close range. One of them shouts, "This is what we always wanted to do, this is awesome!" The first 911 call to police dispatch is initiated, reporting the explosion of a distraction device the pair had detonated several miles from the high school.

1122 Deputy Gardner, Campus Resource Officer was requested by a custodian over the school radio: "I need you in the back lot." Gardner is dressed in his identifiable uniform and responds by police car with lights and sirens.

1124 Gardner engages in a gun battle with Eric Harris, who is temporarily distracted from shooting other students. The first 911 call for the school incident occurs.

1125 Klebold is seen running behind students fleeing down a hallway.

1126 The pair detonate pipe bombs and fire weapons randomly inside the school.

1129 Harris and Klebold enter the library. One yells, "Get up!" Another "Yahoo!" In 10 minutes they kill 10 people, wound 12, and fire weapons out the window at responding police. Thirty-four other people hiding in the library escape injury. Most of the killing occurs during the first 15 minutes of the incident.

1132 Jefferson County Sheriff's Department receives first call from the media requesting information.

1133 Jefferson County SWAT commander orders SWAT deployment.

1135 Last victim is killed.

1136 Harris and Klebold leave the library and make their way around the school, looking in windows, and making eye contact with people trying to hide. They do not try to enter these locked rooms, nor do they fire through the windows. The pair are throwing pipe bombs inside the school. SWAT commander arrives on scene.

1144 Klebold and Harris return to their unsuccessful bombs in the cafeteria. Both try to activate the bombs. One is overheard saying, "Today the world's going to come to an end, today's the day we die."

1146 Fire originating from partial detonation of a bomb results in the activation of sprinklers inside the cafeteria.

1147 Denver's KMGH Channel 7 announces that the Jefferson County Sheriff has confirmed gunfire at Columbine High School.
1149 Denver Metro SWAT arrives on scene.
1150 Investigators arrive.
1151 Fire sprinkler alarm system is triggered resulting in strobe lights, deafening noise, and three inches of water is covering the cafeteria floor. The noise and mess complicate police rescue efforts.
1152 Authorization for immediate SWAT entry.
1153 First definitive description of suspect Eric Harris is given by police dispatchers.
1202 For the next several minutes, shots from library are fired toward police officers and emergency personnel outside.
1208 Harris and Klebold commit suicide.
1217 Victim services counselors arrive. They were assigned to the public library and a nearby elementary school; safe staging locations are identified for students and families to congregate while awaiting information about the status of loved ones/classmates (Jefferson County Sheriff's Department, 2000).

During the incident, police had to detain students and staff fleeing the building, and prevent students from re-entering the school. Victims hiding inside the school called 911 from school phones and personal cellular phones, providing important information about their whereabouts, often keeping an open line that provided police with current information. Some victims made signs or signals to identify their whereabouts, or the location of those who were wounded and unable to flee.

By day's end, 1000 law enforcement officers and emergency medical personnel were on the scene. They facilitated the evacuation of nearly 2000 students and over 100 faculty members and staff. It took several hours for police to clear the building, rescue the wounded and those who were hiding, and locate the dead. Police found several groups of up to 60 students and staff members hidden in locked rooms, closets, and the cafeteria freezer. Within two hours of the beginning of the incident, streets surrounding the school were totally congested with emergency, fire, police, media, victim advocates, mental health professionals, and the curious.

Nearly 150 counselors and victim advocates from law enforcement victim services agencies responded to the scene, assisting with students and families. Before Jefferson County law enforcement teams were relieved of duty, they met with their contracted mental health team (Jefferson County Sheriff's Department, 2000).

Columbine is the worst case scenario. The impact is devastating and universal within and outside the community. As the crime unfolded and ended, the school, community, United States, and world were left with the task of restoring safety and control, and the ongoing issue of healing for the survivors. No case is more poignant than Columbine to demonstrate the need for intervention in the wake of a planned and deliberate assault upon our collective psyche. Thirteen innocent people were murdered, the two boys who inflicted the carnage were dead, and 21 people were wounded. There are many issues that must be addressed to reduce the immediate, short-term, and long-term potential impact of a tragedy like Columbine.

Pre-incident Planning

Schools should prepare and have a plan for small scale and worst case scenarios. Incidents may be lethal multiple victim events, hostage incidents, bombings, snipings, intruders, and less lethal single and multiple victim events. The school district needs to have a clear, known plan for how to deal with each incident. Police need to identify their strategy and resources for responding to an unfolding episode of school violence. School district mental health resources need to be competent and well-versed in responding to needs during the aftermath. All of these important components must work in a cooperative and coordinated way with one another. Pre-incident planning will influence the extent of physical and psychological casualties resulting from an event, and will reduce the sense of helplessness in facing potential violence in our schools. Plans should address the following content areas which will arise during an event: incident survival, command and control, first aid, notifications, information accessibility, law enforcement response, staging areas, practical issues, stabilization, common psychological reactions, and mental health intervention.

During the Incident

Incident Survival

Staff and students may find themselves in a range of terrifying and dangerous situations during an incident. Potential victims learn

201

that the threat is occurring based upon gunshots, explosions, screaming, public announcements on school intercom systems, and the media. They may be confronted by the armed perpetrator, taken hostage, shot or otherwise assaulted. Nearly all of these methods of "finding out" occurred in Littleton, Colorado.

Survival is the operative word. While there are some guidelines gleaned from past experience, each situation is different and individuals will need to adapt. If there is an opportunity to escape, it is preferable. In other situations, survival may be enhanced by preventing the perpetrator(s) from having access to potential victims by locking or barricading a classroom. Sometimes potential victims may elude harm by hiding when total escape is not an option. If a phone is accessible to a hidden person unable to escape, contacting 911 and communicating the hiding location to police for rescue attempts is a good option. The police dispatcher may want the line to be kept "live" and open to allow for the exchange of critical emergency information. These different strategies were employed by survivors of the Columbine incident.

If these options are not available, and one is presented with the armed individual, generally a low-key, non-confrontational approach is going to increase survivability. This was the approach used by Linda Robb in case example one. Robb approached the teenager, engaged him in conversation, touched and talked him into surrendering, but it is preferable to avoid drawing attention to oneself. In some cases, a potential victim will have no choice but to engage in dialogue with the subject. It is imperative to attempt to defuse the situation, sincerely addressing the individual's concerns, and telling them in a credible fashion what will likely de-escalate the situation. Harris and Klebold would not have responded to these types of approaches, and students and staff clearly sensed this and responded appropriately by fleeing.

If the perpetrator is shooting and harming people, one should try to flee. If shot and unable to flee, some people have survived by playing dead, while others have managed to crawl and hide or escape to safety while the perpetrator is busy elsewhere. This strategy was employed by some of the wounded at Columbine.

Confrontation and attempts to overpower the perpetrator are strongly discouraged, unless those involved in such efforts are 100 percent sure they can accomplish the takedown. Consistently, such actions, if failed, will precipitate violent acting out on the part of the subject. In Columbine, the pair had no hesitation in responding violently to police intervention attempts, a response police are equipped and trained to handle.

If one is taken hostage, it is important to stay calm, and avoid doing or saying anything to inflame the situation. Again, it is critical to blend in as much as possible, not drawing any undue attention to oneself, and to go along with the perpetrator's directions. If the suspect tells you to leave, do so. If the person asks for ideas about how to get out of the situation or what to do, be prepared to tell them–respectfully and with concern–the importance of surrendering. Be empathic and sympathetic to their issues. Remember it is possible to understand and sympathize with their feelings without necessarily agreeing with their actions. The person is frequently upset at this point and operating on a high degree of emotion. An understanding and compassionate response which seeks to create and find common ground is helpful. Humanize yourself in the eyes of the perpetrator, somehow finding commonalities you share to prevent being objectified. As a hostage, know that professionals will be responding to intervene. Encourage and support constructive dialogue between the subject and police personnel as appropriate. These strategies were employed by hostages in the Eric Houston hostage situation described in Chapter One.

Command and Control

Police will have primary command and control until the incident is stabilized and preliminary investigations are complete. At the outset, the school or district needs to designate who will be responsible for declaring an emergency, making notifications, documenting actions taken, and liaisoning with law enforcement, parents, and the media. This is to counteract the chaos and confusion that is inevitable as a major incident is unfolding. Contingencies need to be established so that there can be informed and available backup staff persons to fill these key roles in the event the primary persons are not available. Specifics about notifications, important telephone numbers for internal and external resources, and emergency procedures and guidelines need to be accessible and known to these staff. Critical emergency information, the location of staging areas for emergency personnel and other responders, communications systems, and damage control/minimization procedures, must all be included. Each issue must be addressed as it relates to pre-incident, during the incident, short-term, and long-term post-event time frames.

First Aid

The ability to administer appropriate first aid must be addressed. Ideally, there are already procedures in place within the district, as well as accessible supplies. However, it goes a few steps further in school settings. Most schools have kids and staff with special needs, such as medication and allergies to particular medications. Somehow this information needs to be readily available for any potential emergency. It can make the difference between life and death. In addition, if there are students with sensory impairment or disabilities, such as a hearing impairment, provision must be made to convey emergency directions via sign language.

Notification Considerations

There will be an immediate need to notify the police, school administrators, mental health intervention team members, and staff and student emergency contacts. Logistically, staff must be designated to make these notifications, and in the worst case scenario, they need to be prepared to deal with very emotionally upset persons. It is imperative that some thought be given to any publicly released information. Scripting these communications will prevent misinformation. For example, a statement might be released: "Today a ninth grade student was shot by another student. The injured student is in critical condition and a suspect is in custody. Tomorrow there will be no classes but trauma counselors will be available. We expect classes to resume on Friday. As more information becomes available, we will keep you informed." Working with law enforcement to develop quickly acceptable scripts is helpful. Crisis counselors and religious resources may also be considered for stand-by activity and to assist in injury and death notifications. Victim advocates were essential resources for difficult notifications in Columbine.

Information Accessibility

In the moments after an incident, or while the incident is unfolding and awaiting resolution, important information must be accessible. Law enforcement may need blueprints of the school or building schematics in order to rescue victims and intervene. Master keys to campus facilities and alarm disabling procedures must be on-hand. Student and staff rosters with emergency contact information should be readily available. Current pictures of students and staff should also be available to police. This information will be needed to identify and account for likely perpetrators and victims, and for appropriate target and rescue identification, respectively. Given the substantial likelihood that an event may occur in the building, updated information of this nature needs to be accessible and easily retrievable in an outside location. Some districts are storing this information on compact disks, which allow large volumes of data to be consolidated and transported with relative ease.

Police will also need to know about the internal communications systems, including telephones and intercom, and the specific numbers attached to particular offices and classrooms, including fax lines, computer lines, and cellular telephones that may be issued to staff members. Any of these lines may be a potential forum for communication between the authorities and the victims or perpetrator. At Columbine, police had several open 911 calls from hidden victims within the school, so knowledge of the phone locations was critical to rescue efforts. Police may need to modify these systems in order to facilitate resolution, particularly if there is a hostage or barricade situation.

Law enforcement will also be interested in power sources, gas lines, and the location of items like television sets and radios, which could potentially transmit information to a perpetrator about the police tactical response. Police had the gas company turn off the gas at Columbine, out of concern that lines may have been ruptured and leaking as a consequence of the damage. Knowing the whereabouts of these items will enable authorities to anticipate potential problems.

Law Enforcement Immediate Response

If the unthinkable happens, there will be an immediate law enforcement response. Police will take responsibility for containing any violence that may still be ongoing, responding in an emergent fashion to end the aggressive behavior of the perpetrator. At the same time, they will be involved in facilitating the evacuation of innocent parties and the rescue of downed victims from the "hot" zone. Depending upon the nature of the situation, there will be varying levels of confusion as they attempt to sort out who the suspect (s) is/are. If there is ongoing gunfire or explosions, special response teams such as Special Weapons and Tactics (SWAT) teams and bomb squads may respond on the heels of first responding line officers. While the preference is to resolve the situation without further bloodshed, if necessary they can and will take escalating actions, including engaging the subject(s) with deadly force, to overcome and stop any violence. School personnel in positions of responsibility must heed the directions of these professionals and provide them with

205

information they require during these exigent circumstances. They will need information about the possible identity of the suspect and his/her picture, if available. In addition to the need to stop violent behavior, there is also the concern about mistaken identity or a suspect who may try to hide and escape in the ensuing confusion among fleeing students and staff. Law enforcement professionals will detain and search as necessary, prior to releasing innocent parties (staff and students) fleeing the target location. They do not want to take any chances of letting the dangerous person escape, should the perpetrator try to blend in among others.

Bomb squads from local and federal law enforcement were a critical component of the Columbine response because of the explosives issues. Numerous live bombs were found in and around the school and it took many hours to neutralize these threats. It is important that school officials recognize that police searches are thorough and often time consuming.

If a hostage situation ensues, law enforcement will contain the person(s) and effect the evacuation of surrounding areas. At this point, there will be attempts to initiate verbal contact with the subject so that they might convince the person to surrender without violence. Professionally trained negotiators will likely be deployed to relieve any first responding police or school personnel who may have established contact. This is not meant to slight the good work that any first responding officer or school staff member may have started, but there are established protocols in the field of hostage negotiations that will increase the chances of safe resolution. Research supports that time is generally on the side of the negotiators and law enforcement, favoring a peaceful resolution. School personnel should support requests of law enforcement involved in this process. Sometimes this will entail providing a quiet room for them to set up shop for the negotiation process, offering information that might be helpful to understand the motivation of the subject, and other information about any of the hostages and what relationship they may have to the hostage taker.

Once the situation is resolved, the school will become the scene of an ongoing investigation. Officers, detectives, or investigators will gather evidence to understand what happened, who was involved, and why. It is critical that these perimeters be established and maintained so that the investigation does not become contaminated. Full cooperation between the school and police is essential, a process

206

that may be facilitated by mutual respect for the roles and goals of both functions. Police and school personnel share the common goal of safety, and returning the school to order.

Police may demand information about the residences of known suspects to facilitate emergency searches of those locations. They will also be seeking to interview witnesses. It is critical to identify potential witnesses during the early stages post-threat containment. Running lists of who is who, and who saw what, may be kept in rough form, copies of which may be handed over to police personnel tasked with the investigation. At a later point, these lists may also prove helpful to school personnel as they perform their own post-mortem review of events. Such reviews may be for various purposes, including learning and litigation.

Police investigations may last for days and weeks after a lethal event. Accommodating their need for information, within the provision of applicable laws, is critical to expediting this process and a return to normalcy. Even if the event is non-fatal, there will likely be some law enforcement related disruption as investigations are conducted, but the scope will be on a smaller scale.

One way of preparing for these events is to plan drills with the various responding agencies when school is NOT in session. Working out the kinks beforehand in the deployment of emergency resources is essential, and these exercises will help identify weaknesses in the existing system.

Staging Areas for Responders

The school district needs to identify potential staging areas on each campus for responding emergency personnel. With 1000 emergency responders in the Columbine event, it is easy to see why these staging areas are necessary to facilitate incident command and control. Other people will show up at the campus: concerned parents, media representatives, and onlookers will have heard about the incident over the radio, by word of mouth, or through frantic calls from people at the school. Evacuated children and staff members will need to be accounted for, and appropriate checks should occur to insure that no suspects are among the group. Two thousand students were evacuated from Columbine. Staging areas for these different categories of people will need to be established. School personnel and police should identify useful locations around and on their school property for these various gathering places prior to an incident. Nearby safe public places, such as other school campuses and libraries, were used at Columbine. Law enforcement and emergency services personnel will necessarily occupy the closest "safe zone" to the innermost perimeter of the event, while other responders will expand outward in a larger concentric fashion.

Anticipating these different categories of responders, and setting up these areas, will prevent people who are wandering around in shock and full of anxiety from getting into places they simply should not be. Knowing who is where enables law enforcement and school personnel to arrange for helpful support services, information updates, and to reduce confusion.

Practical Issues

Both case example one and two make clear the importance of addressing certain practical issues. In the worst case scenario, as in the Columbine case, all classes will need to be canceled. In the first case example, classes for the involved students were canceled and parents were notified to pick up their children. A general explanation about the nature of the occurrence, and the restoration of safety, was explained to these parents. Prior to parents picking up their children, decisions needed to be made about how long the students need to remain for any police questioning, as well as the game plan for the next day, and over the following days and weeks. By the end of the first day, school representatives should communicate the school's plans for the next several days, and the availability of crisis intervention and counseling. A method for communicating the game plan to parents and students needs to be implemented. In large events such as Columbine, toll-free hotlines should be established to disseminate this critical information. Standard statements will be communicated by school staff members, flyers, and in some cases, radio, television, and the local newspaper.

When the immediate investigation is complete and the property is rendered safe, there may be a need for cleanup, to repair any damage or eliminate reminders of the violence. Decisions need to be made about how that is to be accomplished. It may not be appropriate, for example, to use traumatized custodians to clean up blood, or repair and repaint bullet and explosion damaged classrooms. In some jurisdictions there are companies that actually specialize in this sort of cleanup. Local law enforcement representatives may know about these resources. Restoration and reconstruction are critical to the healing process. Sending students and staff into bombed or bullet-ridden classrooms may re-traumatize them.

Stabilization Phase

Once the violence is contained and the situation is stabilized, the process of picking up the pieces begins. In nonfatal events, this is more contained and localized. Usually less people are impacted, and the level of trauma, while significant, is more manageable. A specific class or grade may be impacted as in case example one. In the larger event, there are many issues to address. More people are affected, and the level of trauma may be overwhelming to many, as in case example two. Re-instilling a sense of safety to those who are traumatized and in a state of shock becomes the next critical issue.

Post-Incident

Common Psychological Reactions

Psychological reactions to school violence can be profound and long-lasting depending upon the severity of the incident. In smaller scale incidents, such as case example one, the impact will typically be of less intensity and shorter duration. Depending upon the extent to which witnesses or victims were directly involved and perceived danger to themselves or someone they care about, reactions may vary significantly. Other factors play a role, too, including previous trauma, coping skills, prior mental disorder, available support, and spiritual belief systems. Larger scale incidents such as Columbine will have more intense and longer lasting effects on a greater number of individuals.

Feelings of vulnerability and helplessness are quite common. Most people live their lives with a certain illusion of safety and a sense of control over life events. That is normal. School violence shatters any such illusions and painfully reminds people of the reality that we are neither always safe nor always in control. Sometimes these feelings settle in after an initial feeling of denial, disbelief, shock, or numbness.

Fear, anger, grief, and confusion are common emotional reactions that accompany feelings of vulnerability. While most people are bombarded everyday with the fact that bad things happen to good people, personally becoming a victim or witnessing human violence (vicarious trauma) takes the realization to a whole new level. Anger is often expressed towards individuals and entities besides the perpetrator for causing or failing to prevent the situation. It is conceivable that some survivors might say, "Those jocks provoked

209

him, he just couldn't take it anymore, why didn't anybody do anything." To blame others for the incident serves to re-instill and maintain the illusion of control. Allocating blame enables denial to replace feelings of helplessness. "It was someone's fault, they have been punished, it won't happen again." Ultimately, however, healthy adaptation requires some acceptance of the fact that not everything can be controlled.

Divided loyalties and mixed feelings can lead to confusion and group conflicts. Survivors may feel sympathy for any victims while others express support and concern for the perpetrator(s) who may have been a friend or an acquaintance. Survivors may take sides in who they support. Taking sides can be very divisive, especially at a time when everyone is primed and "on edge" from their own human stress response. Resolution of such "splitting" (polarized feeling) and conflict relies upon the ability to validate that everyone, in fact, does suffer in these events, and that sympathy for the victims and the perpetrator is not as inconsistent as it seems. Mixed feelings are normal and acceptable, and reflect the highly complex issues that these events engender. It is important to set a tone of respect and tolerance for the feelings of others during the healing.

Loss and grief are primary issues when the incident results in fatalities. Family, classmate, and faculty responses will vary depending upon the degree of relationship and whether they witnessed a violent death. Stages of grief involve denial, anger, bargaining, depression, and acceptance. The person grieving may not pass through these stages sequentially, but s/he will tend to experience the total range of these identified phases.

Depression, anxiety, sleep disturbances, nightmares, and flashbacks are common victim/witness responses to the traumatic school violence event. It is not at all unusual for these symptoms to last for several weeks to several months. Most professionals however, recommend early intervention to mitigate the impact of the traumatic event. If symptoms are intense, persistent, or involve destructive thoughts or impulses, additional mental health care is warranted. An overview of these typical critical incident reactions is presented in Table 16.

TABLE 16

Sample Critical Incident Handout for Staff and Parents

Critical Incident:
Any event outside of the range of normal human experience

Events That Can Cause Stress Reactions:
- Death- child victim, rescue victim, emergency worker victim–especially school violence death–or traumatic loss of coworker, multiple deaths, suicide
- Threatening event–being physically or emotionally attacked, exposure to hazardous material, perceived safety threat, robbery, assault
- Extraordinary media coverage–death or threatening event with extreme publicity

Some Normal Signs and Symptoms of Acute Distress:
Physical
- nausea, upset stomach, tremors, feeling uncoordinated
- profuse sweating, chills, diarrhea, rapid heart rate
- muscle aches, sleep disturbance, dry mouth
- shakes, vision problems, fatigue

Cognitive
- confusion, lowered attention span
- memory problems, calculation difficulties
- poor concentration, flashbacks, distressing dreams
- disruption in logical thinking, blaming others
- difficulties with decision-making
- heightened or lowered alertness
- increased or decreased awareness of surroundings
- preoccupation with vulnerability or death

Emotional
- anticipatory anxiety, denial, fear, survivor guilt
- uncertainty of feelings, depression, grief
- feeling hopeless, overwhelmed, lost, vulnerable, helpless
- feeling abandoned, worried, angry, wanting to hide
- feeling numb, identifying with the victim
- feeling alienated, disenchanted
- panic, generalized anxiety
- intensified or reduced emotional reactions

Behavioral
- change in activity, withdrawal
- less or more communicative, increased smoking
- change in interactions with others, excessive humor
- increased or decreased food intake
- overly vigilant to environment, unusual behavior
- increased alcohol intake
- avoidance behavior
- acting out, antisocial acts, angry outbursts
- suspiciousness
- intensified fatigue, sleep increase or decrease
- more frequent visits to the physician for nonspecific complaints

Sample Critical Incident Handout for Staff and Parents

Grief and Bereavement Process:
- not everyone goes through all the stages in order
- denial–"this can't be happening!"
- anger–"how could something like this happen!"
- bargaining–"if only....!"
- depression–"this is sad"
- acceptance–"sometimes bad things happen to good people"

Coping After The Incident:
- eat well–AVOID CAFFEINE, ALCOHOL, SALT, SUGAR, AND FAT-drink more fluids (water and fruit juices), eat complex carbs, low-fat and nonfat foods, whole grain bread
- get rest but avoid boredom
- physical exertion or exercise as soon as possible after incident is over-moderate intensity to work out potentially damaging stress chemicals
- attend and participate in a debriefing
- view your reactions as normal reactions to an abnormal situation-anyone who experienced what you did may feel the same way
- allow yourself the freedom to talk about your reactions to what happened
- seek peer, clergy, or professional assistance as necessary
- allow yourself time to heal
- work on accepting that anyone in your situation would have responded similarly
- talk with your family, check in with your peers
- be gentle with yourself, move away from beating yourself up
- use crisis as opportunity for growth and positive change

Helping Students/Coworkers Cope With The Aftermath:
- offer listening and discussion opportunities regarding the incident
- for group discussions set parameters: tolerance/respect for feelings of others, confidentiality (except for safety issues) and trust, one person at a time
- discussions should be age-appropriate in method and content
- normalize and validate reactions
- share and model healthy emotional and coping responses to incident (tears, anger, and the like are okay, as long as it is modulated and in control)
- don't put child or student in position of having to care for the adult

When To Seek/Recommend Additional Assistance:
- intense feelings of discomfort
- significant symptoms that persist longer than six weeks
- suicidal thoughts or planning
- other self-destructive acting-out(sexual, aggressive, or substance)
- intense family conflict
- feel like your losing control of your impulses
- just want to check in to see if your "normal"

Where To Seek Additional Assistance:
- list options

Anniversary reactions and holiday blues are also associated with these events. Helpers should give thought to the calendar dates and seasons likely to precipitate a resurgence of trauma and grief. Anticipating these victim responses enables responsible parties to prepare victims to expect these reactions and provide education to cope more effectively. Professionals responding to these events need to address their own traumatic response: a side effect of helping victims. At the conclusion of their involvement, it is important for helpers to arrange for their own debriefing.

Mental Health Intervention

The school district needs to have a protocol for dealing with the emotional impact of these events. A critical incident stress debriefing (CISD) team needs to be identified or created to provide services to students and staff alike, as well as to persons who might show up at the campus distraught and out-of-control with their grief. The purpose of such a team is to be available for immediate deployment to the staging area of the campus immediately after an incident. Often these teams are geographically decentralized, with a district level team available as a backup and resource team. These teams usually consist of campus mental health personnel such as school psychologists or community mental health professionals and members of the clergy, who should be specially trained in critical incident debriefing techniques. This training is available from Jeffrey Mitchell and his colleagues at the International Critical Incident Stress Foundation, the National Organization for Victims Assistance (NOVA), or the Red Cross.

The CISD approach includes: immediate management consultation, on-site support services, defusing services, debriefing services, and follow-up and referral. These CISD resources should address the mental health needs of students, staff, parents, law enforcement, and other emergency services personnel. Law enforcement and other emergency personnel will usually have their own CISD professionals to address their special needs.

It is imperative that the mental health intervention effort be centralized. In many community tragedies, well-intentioned helpers, as well as the usual "ambulance chasers" and obviously unqualified, will show up offering "to help." Quality control is important, and screening out the inappropriate "pilgrims" is accomplished by having resources identified long before any tragedy. "Pilgrims" may be gently thanked for their concern and referred to other non-school places they might be of assistance, with the explanation that there are already teams available to address the needs of the school.

Immediate Management Consultation

Immediate management consultation related to CISD and crisis intervention issues should be facilitated by the lead mental health person to the district. Consultations with this resource person should be initiated by someone on the school administrative staff with enough horsepower to make decisions about bringing in the CISD team. The district staff person should inform the professional about the circumstances of the incident, issues unique to the situation, and the scope of the potential impact upon the student body and staff.

At this point, the consultant should provide initial guidance about possible ways of approaching the intervention process, and begin to discuss the logistics of service delivery.

Victim advocates and counseling resources to the Columbine situation were contacted within minutes of the initial 911 calls, and responded on-scene to help manage the trauma of over two thousand affected individuals within minutes after the shooting had stopped. They also generated ideas to help and manage distraught parents and others, who were calling and showing up at the scene, traumatized because they did not know the status of their loved ones.

On-Site Support Services

After an event is contained, or after a protracted hostage incident has stabilized, on-site support services will be needed. The school district needs to have an emergency contact procedure for notifying CISD resources. Any professional that a district is retaining should commit to provide 24-hour-a-day, seven-day-a-week coverage, and should be able to respond immediately to an emergency request (within 15 minutes by pager, an hour or so to get on-site). Those initial moments of a crisis are critical, and CISD professional input is essential. CISD resources should arrange for competent backup professionals in their absence.

On-site support typically involves CISD trained professionals, usually mental health professionals and chaplains, who are available to listen to the concerns and crisis reactions of students and staff. This intervention is referred to as "water cooler therapy" because it may simply be a short conversation with a professional in an informal setting. While seemingly insignificant, they are critical. The mere presence of professionals establishes an important reminder to all that something outside the range of normal human experience has just occurred. It assures affected individuals that they are expected to have reactions to the event, and that there are people who care and can be trusted to provide safety. On-site support also reduces barriers to future, more intensive help-seeking behavior, because individuals will have already met the helpers during the initial stages of an incident.

These resources may also help calm people who have little or no information about the status of a loved one. They can reduce and manage the uncertainty that contributes to distress by liaisoning with school, police, and emergency workers. These resources are then less impeded in their efforts to rescue and identify victims. If the information is news about the death or serious injury of a loved one, they can play a key role in sensitively notifying the family, and providing critical crisis intervention services to support adaptive grieving. They can disseminate important information about other available services to facilitate healing. All of these critical roles were fulfilled by Columbine crisis counselors and victim advocates.

Information about crime victim compensation should also be provided to all potentially affected individuals. Many district attorneys' offices have victim/witness funds to help pay for medical expenses, mental health services, lost employment, and burial expenses. In larger events like Columbine, methods may be implemented to streamline the bureaucracy that often accompanies the application process. It is desirable to reduce such barriers to help-seeking.

Outreach

Larger scale events benefit from mental health outreach. While many affected individuals will make contact with appropriate resources, some of those in the most need will not do so. It is imperative to identify every potentially affected person, and then attempts should be made to contact and determine individual needs.

Defusing Activity

In larger scale events such as Columbine, there will be occasional briefings about the status of loved ones for persons convened in the various staging areas. These briefings provide an ideal opportunity to offer information to affected individuals about the potential psychological impact of the event, and things that can be done to reinstill a sense of control and help the return to normalcy. These short (15 minute) presentations by crisis counselors are referred to as "defusings." Defusings help to "normalize" and educate potentially affected individuals about the emotional impact of these critical incidents.

215

In smaller scale events, such as the one described in case example one, more limited briefings can be arranged for the class as a whole prior to their leaving school for the day. If a group cannot be convened due to investigator meetings with students and staff members, then defusings may take place individually prior to each person's departure. Whether the event is large scale or small, parents and staff members should be given an educational handout about critical incident stress to supplement the information disseminated during any defusings. These handouts should identify follow-up resources and referrals. Table 16 is a sample CISD handout.

This particular intervention is important psychological "first aid" for potentially traumatized individuals. At the conclusion of these interventions, crisis counselors should remain available for those who may want to talk, both after these meetings and over the next several days to weeks. These interventions should be delivered in a manner consistent with local laws regulating the provision of counseling services to juveniles.

Debriefing Services

In the days following a traumatic event, the reality of what has happened will be sinking in for students, parents, and staff members alike. In fatal incidents, formal "critical incident stress debriefing" interventions will be necessary, typically delivered in group format by a mental health professional trained in the procedure. The purpose of the debriefing is to facilitate and accelerate normal healing processes. Individuals who attend such debriefings often experience improved recovery from the trauma. Generally these interventions are provided in group format with no more than 15 to 20 individuals. There are seven phases in the debriefing process. The mental health professional sets the stage through the *introduction phase* that orients participants to the purpose of the procedure. It is explained that debriefings facilitate and accelerate normal emotional healing. Certain ground rules are established to make the group a safe place to share feelings, including the issue of confidentiality, respect for feelings, and one person talking at a time. Then participants go through a *fact phase* in which they share what their role was in the incident and what they saw, heard, and did. Next comes the *thought phase*, in which participants share their first and worst thoughts in relation to the incident. After that is a *feelings phase*, during which participants disclose their first and worst emotional reactions; followed by a *symptoms phase* in which they share what they have noticed is

216

different since the event occurred, including any sleep disturbance, flashbacks, or mood changes. At this point the mental health professional will transition to a *teaching phase*, providing education about these normal reactions, identifying common themes, future expectable reactions, do's and don'ts to help recovery, and when and how to seek additional help if it should be needed. Finally, a *re-entry phase* is addressed, with each person sharing their personal plan for coping in the days, weeks, and months following the event. Some professionals may modify or adapt this basic format, but these elements are the gist of most procedures.

In fatal events, the debriefing process should be held after any funeral and memorial services. Funerals and memorials offer a great deal of healing in and of themselves, leaving unfinished business for the intervention process. Parental permission may need to be obtained to establish these interventions with juveniles.

Decisions need to be made about whether participation will be voluntary or mandatory, particularly as it may apply to staff members. The mandatory aspect usually applies only to attendance. Participants should be told they do not have to talk, a factor that may reduce resistance to participation.

Follow-Up Intervention

When the time comes for a return to normal routines, mental health and victim advocates will often be needed to help victim/survivors return to the school. The prospect of returning to school will often increase student and family trauma reactions that had decreased and stabilized. Walk-throughs, desensitization procedures, and return-to-school ceremonies may be important healing processes to consider. Mental health consultants can help with planning and implementing these interventions.

Referrals should be identified for those who need more extensive follow-up. Crisis counselors should anticipate anniversary reactions and victim responses to court and investigative proceedings, memorial services, and press conferences. They may need to accompany recovering victims to these events.

Crisis counselors should be aware that they might hear about other high-risk cases in the school, so it is important that they have some basic knowledge about suicide and violence warning signs. They may identify other students or staff requiring intervention by threat assessment team members.

While aftermath interventions may be formal, many informal

217

interventions will be occurring and should be encouraged, as long as there are cautions in place. Teachers may want to offer opportunities during class for students to discuss their reactions to what has happened. While this may seem to be taking kids away from the business at hand, the reality is that after major events, they will not be emotionally present for normal classroom activities. The teacher should set parameters for these discussions, including: one person talking at a time, respect for the feelings of others in the room, keeping what is said by others in the room, and the value that *violence has no place in school.* Similar discussions may be held for staff during meetings, and may spontaneously evolve in parent meetings with school staff. During such meetings it is common for another topic to be the focus of discussion and suddenly there is a need to talk about what has happened. It can then be suggested that a discussion might be helpful, laying out appropriate parameters: "It seems that this is on everybody's mind right now, how about we table the business at hand and spend some time on..."

If teachers are to facilitate these discussions, they should possess certain basic interpersonal skills so they do more good than harm. Staff members should receive in-service training about how to facilitate healthy classroom discussions. This provides some structure to those on the front lines who are helping to channel and express the grief, pain, and trauma.

Parents may request further information about how to handle the difficulties they are experiencing with their kids. Arranging for crisis counselors to provide information during an open forum setting may prove a helpful way of addressing this need.

The larger the event, the greater the likelihood the long-term impact will endure until there has been complete student turnover, and until the last staff member who was around during the event has retired. In a fatal event like Columbine, the event will live beyond even this time frame. It will become a permanent part of the organization's history and a wound to its collective psyche. For example, the 1927 Bath, Michigan incident is still remembered and memorialized in that community.

In smaller scale events, such as case example number one, there will a less far-reaching influence and impact, so the same interventions will be more limited. Addressing these various mental health needs after the fact will enhance the school's healing.

Media Issues

In the United States, school violence events generate a media frenzy. The first call from media representatives to police came within 22 minutes of Harris and Klebold's arrival at Columbine. The media began arriving and interviewing witnesses and victims on scene prior to the conclusion of the incident, broadcasting images of distraught individuals. It is safe to assume, particularly in large metropolitan areas when major networks show up at scene, that they do not have the community's best interests at heart. Media representatives are in the ratings business, and ratings are generated by high drama, intrigue, and controversy.

School and police representatives do need to share relevant information with the media to help manage the scene and prevent distortion and misinformation. In the Columbine case, the media became an important communication method for emergency information. The media broadcasted toll-free numbers, locations of staging areas for affected families, and victim service information. They also provided updates about locations that were off limits or inaccessible. At times, cellular phone service was not available due to high utilization, so the media performed an invaluable dissemination service.

Involved agencies should coordinate beforehand the release of scripted statements and any press conferences. Nothing makes a school district, police department, or district attorney's office look more foolish than conflicting information between the agencies or from different personnel within the same agency. Unnecessary misinformation can also cause additional trauma to survivors of the event. All press releases should weigh the impact upon survivors and ongoing investigations. The timing of the release of certain information in past cases can be in bad taste. For example, officials involved in the Columbine situation released graphic information and allowed the cafeteria surveillance tape to leak to the news media during the holiday season. Affected individuals were not notified prior to the release of this material, and were blind-sided by it. Such actions reinforce the powerlessness of victims and serve to re-traumatize them.

Students, staff, parents, and others should be told how to handle intrusions by aggressive media representatives. They have choices about speaking to these representatives, and they may decline to be interviewed. It may be helpful to offer friendly reminders about the

219

healing of others that may be impaired by careless or insensitive remarks. Freedom of speech is a right in the United States, so anticipate that some problematic information will be released. School and law enforcement personnel should be prepared to address the emotional ripple effects caused by such releases.

Longer-Term Issues

Some students and staff members may never be able to return to the school. Provision should be made for alternative schooling and work arrangements, including transfers. Some employees may become involved in workers' compensation cases, alleging psychological stress. Legitimate claims should be addressed as expeditiously as possible to enable treatment and recovery.

Investigations, criminal trials, recurrent publicity, and civil litigation should be anticipated. Civil litigation may go on for years, like the appeals for those convicted of these crimes and the release issues when juveniles have served their maximum sentence after only a few years. Agencies involved in these cases should anticipate the significant impact of these events across time.

School district and law enforcement officials will engage in critical self-examination efforts to determine how the situation could have been prevented and/or responded to better. Internal reviews to determine what went wrong can be helpful–provided the results do not cause greater liability exposure. If properly conducted with appropriate safeguards to prevent discovery during civil litigation, these reviews may lead to the prevention of future events.

Chapter Summary

School violence events may be large or limited. School district, law enforcement, and mental health professionals need to have coordinated aftermath management plans. Such plans will address incident response, logistical issues, mental health, and practical needs of the affected school. All efforts must be oriented towards re-establishing safety, and helping potential victims cope with their trauma. Critical incident stress debriefing (CISD) interventions are an important part of that effort. CISD interventions provide immediate consultation to the district, on-scene support services for distraught individuals assembling in staging areas, defusing, debriefing, and necessary follow-up. Media interest must be addressed responsibly. The impact of school violence is significant, and there are many issues to consider and implement to facilitate healing.

Closing Thoughts

This book has provided an overview of the breadth of issues to consider to keep our schools safe from violence–especially lethal violence. We try to understand the dynamics of the worst-case scenarios so that we might learn lessons from the past. Such knowledge helps to prevent similar events from unfolding in our own communities and affecting people we love and cherish, both victims and would-be perpetrators. While the reader may find some of the information in this book helpful, undoubtedly there are interventions that were overlooked–strategies the reader may have developed which have worked in individual cases with great success. The goal of this book has been to open a dialogue, raise awareness, outline some possible tools, and stimulate further research and development of methods to prevent the horror of human violence on our school campuses. May our efforts continue to successfully blossom.

References

American Psychiatric Association. (1994). *Diagnostic and statistical manual of mental Disorders* (4th ed.): DSM-IV. Washington, DC: Author.

Bachman, R. (1977). *Rage*. New York: Signet.

Begley, S. & Kalb, C. (2000, March 13). Learning right from wrong. *Newsweek*, 30-33.

Belkin, L. (1999, October 31). Parents blaming parents. *New York Times Magazine*, 61-67, 94, 100.

Borum, R. (2000). *Assessing violence risk among youth*. Journal of Clinical Psychology, 56, 1263-1288.

Braun, S. & Cart, J. (2000, March 1). 6-year-old Mich. Girl is killed by classmate. *Los Angeles Times*, pp. A1, A25.

Brown, R. (2000). *Assessing violence risk among youth*. Journal of Clinical Psychology, 56, 1263-1288.

Brown, T.R. (2000, February 8). Alleged Mississippi killer pleads guilty. *Associated Press*. [On-line]. Available: www.associatedpress.com.

Cart, J. (2000, March 2). Boy tied to girl's shooting lived amid guns, drugs. *Los Angeles Times*, pp. A1, A17.

Centers for Disease Control and Prevention. (1997). Rates of homicide, suicide, and Firearm-related death among children- 26 industrialized countries. *Morbidity and Mortality Weekly Report*, 46. Atlanta, GA: Author.

Center for Disease Control & Prevention. (1999, April 21). Facts about violence among youth and violence in schools [On-line]. Available: www.cdc.gov/od/oc/media/pressrel/r990421.htm.

Cohen, D.G. (2000). ADA permits mandatory medical testing of disruptive worker. *Workplace Violence Prevention Reporter*, 6, 8.

Douglas, J. & Olshaker, M. (1999). *The anatomy of motive*. New York: Scribner.

Dylan & Eric's refuge on the net. (2000). [On-line]. Available: http://millennium.fortunecity.com/jamestown/739/.

18-year-old jailed in Columbine High Internet threat (1999, December 18). *Los Angeles Times*, p. A19.

Ellsworth, M.J. (1927). *The Bath school disaster.* Bath School Museum Committee.

Fainaru, S. (1998, October 18). Killing in the classroom. Alaska school murders: A window on teen rage. *Boston Globe* [On-line]. Available: www.bostonglobe.com.

Federal Bureau of Investigation (1999, October). *Symposium on school violence.* Riverside, CA.

Fein, R.A. & Vossekuil, B. (1998). *Protective intelligence and threat assessment investigations: A guide for state and local law enforcement officials.* Washington, DC: U.S. Department of Justice.

Feldmann, T.B. & Johnson, P.W. (1996). Workplace violence: A new form of lethal aggression. In H.V. Hall (Ed.), *Lethal Violence 2000: A sourcebook on fatal domestic, acquaintance and stranger aggression* (pp. 311-338). Kamuela, HI: Pacific Institute for the Study of Conflict and Aggression.

Four teenagers admit planning massacre at school in Cleveland. (1999, December 23). *Los Angeles Times,* p. A22.

Gelles, M., Fein, R.A., & Sasaki, K. (1998, October). *Current approaches in threat assessment and threat assessment management in Federal Law Enforcement.* Paper presented at the International Association of Chiefs of Police Annual Conference, Salt Lake City, Utah.

Gettleman, J. (2000, April 15). 5 boys suspended at Monroe High in Columbine hoax. *Los Angeles Times,* p. B 6.

Gibbs, N. & Roche, T. (1999, December 20). The Columbine tapes. *Time,* 154, 40-51.

Gibson, J.W. (1994). *Warrior dreams: Violence and manhood in post Vietnam America.* New York: Hill and Wang.

Hatcher, C. (1994, 1995, 1996) Workplace Violence: A Risk Assessment Model. In G. Mathiason, S. Avila, et al. (Eds.), *Terror and Violence in the Workplace.* Littler, Mendelson: San Francisco. (1st, 2nd, & 3rd Editions).

Hempel, A.G., Meloy, J.R., & Richards, T.C. (1999). Offender and offense characteristics of a nonrandom sample of mass murderers. *Journal of the American Academy of Psychiatry and the Law,* 27, 213-225.

IACP (1999). *Guide for preventing and responding to school violence.* U.S.: Bureau of Justice Assistance.

Jefferson County Sheriff's Department (2000). *The Columbine report* [On-line]. Available: www.rockymountainnews.com.

Kachur, S.P., Stennies, G.M., Powell, K.E., Modzeleski, W., Stephens, R. Murphy, R., Kresnow, M., Sleet, D., & Lowry, R. (1996). School-associated violent deaths in the United States, 1992-1994. *Journal of the American Medical Association*, 275, 1729-1733.

Kaufman, P., Chen, X., Choy, S.P., Ruddy, S.A., Miller, A.K., Chandler, K.A., Chapman, C.D., Rand, M.R., and Klaus, P. (1999). *Indicators of school crime and safety, 1999*. Washington, D.C.: U.S. Departments of Education and Justice. NCES 1999-057/NCJ 178906.

Kellerman, A.L., Rivara, F.P., Rushforth, N.B., Banton, J.G., Reay, D.T., Francisco, J., Locci, A.B., Prodzinski, J., Hackman, B.B., & Somes, G. (1993). Gun ownership as a risk factor for homicide in the home. *New England Journal of Medicine*, 329, 1084-1091.

Kellerman, A.L., Rivara, F.P., Somes, G., Reay, D.T., Francisco, J., Banton, J.G., Prodinsky, J., Fligner, C., & Hackman, B.B. (1992). Suicide in the home in relation to gun ownership. *New England Journal of Medicine*, 327, 467-472.

Kindergartners suspended for playing "cops." (2000, April 7). *Los Angeles Times*, p. A15.

Kirk, M. Navsky, M., & O'Connor, K. (Producers). (2000, January 18). The killer at Thurston High. In *Frontline*, Alexandria, VA :PBS.

Korn. (1999). Falling away from me. On *Issues* [CD]. New York: Immortal.

Kraemer, G. (2000, September). *Preventing workplace violence: A 21st Century legal perspective*. Association of Threat Assessment Professionals Annual Training Conference. Anaheim, California.

Landa, M. (2000, June 2). Parents of threatening student sue complainant's parents. Los Angeles: KNX1070.

Leonard, J. (1998, June 23). Ex-teacher convicted of filing false police report. *Los Angeles Times*, p. B3.

Lunde, D.T. & Morgan, J. (1980). *The die song: A journey into the mind of a mass murderer*. New York: W.W. Norton.

Macdonald, J. (1968). *Homicidal threats*. Springfield, IL: Charles C. Thomas.

Meloy, J.R. (2000). *Violence risk and threat assessment*. San Diego: STS Publications.

Meloy, J.R. (Ed.) (1998). *The psychology of stalking: Clinical and forensic perspectives*. San Diego: Academic Press.

Meloy, J.R. & Gothard, S. (1995). Demographic and clinical comparison of obsessional followers and offenders with mental disorders. *American Journal of Psychiatry*, 152, 258-263.

Meloy, J.R., Hempel, A.G., Mohandie, K., Shiva, A, & Gray, T.B. (2001) Offender and offense characteristics of a nonrandom sample of adolescent mass murderers. *Journal of the American Academy of Child and Adolescent Psychiatry, 40, 719-728.*

Meloy, J.R. & Mohandie, K. (2001). Investigating the role of screen violence in homicide cases. *Journal of Forensic Sciences, 46, 1113-1118.*

Mitchell, J.T. & Resnik, H.L.P. (1986). *Emergency response to crisis.* Ellicott City, Maryland: Author.

Mohandie, K. & Hatcher, C. (1999). Suicide and violence risk in law enforcement: Practical guidelines for risk assessment, prevention, and intervention. *Behavioral Sciences and the Law*, 17, 357-376.

Mohandie, K., Hatcher, C., & Raymond, D. (1998). False victimization syndromes in stalking. In J.R. Meloy (Ed.), *The psychology of stalking: Clinical and forensic perspectives* (pp. 225-256). San Diego: Academic Press.

Mohandie, K. & Meloy, J.R. (2000). Clinical and forensic indicators of suicide-by-cop. *Journal of Forensic Sciences*, 45, 390-395.

Monahan, J. (1992). Mental disorder and violent behavior: Perceptions and evidence. *American Psychologist*, 47, 511-521.

Monahan, J. & Steadman, H.J.(1996). Violent storms and violent people: How meteorology can inform risk communication in mental health law. *American Psychologist*, 51, 931-938.

Mullen, P.E., Pathe, M., & Purcell, R. (2000). *Stalkers and their victims.* London: Cambridge University Press.

National Center for Education Statistics (1998). *Executive summary: Violence and Discipline problems in U.S. public schools: 1996-97* [On-line]. Available: http://nces.ed.gov/pubs98/98030001.html.

Naughton, K. & Thomas, E. (2000, March 13). Murder in the first grade. *Newsweek*, 24-29.

New Jersey v. TLO, 469 U.S. 325 (1985).

Ohio boy, 12, holds class at gunpoint; no one hurt. (2000, March 24). *Los Angeles Times*, pp. A24, A22.

O'Toole, M.E. (2000, August). *The school shooter: A threat assessment perspective.* Association of Threat Assessment Professionals Annual Convention. Anaheim, California. [On-line]. Available: www.fbi.gov.

Parents of slain student settle suit against school. (2000, July 15). *Los Angeles Times*, p. B4.

Payne, P. (2000, February 11). *Mississippi shooter's friend sentenced.* Associated Press [On-line]. Available: www.associatedpress.com.

Pearl Jam. (1991). Jeremy. On *Ten* [CD]. New York: Epic Associated.

Rosenblatt, R. (2000, March 23). The killing of Kayla. *Time*, 26-29.

Reza, H.G. & Willon, P. (1998, November 24). Father said 'I came here today to get myself killed'. *Los Angeles Times*, pp. B1,B3.

Schneidman, E.S. (1996). *The suicidal mind.* New York: Oxford University Press.

Shooter's friend gets 5 years in jail. (2000, February 12). *Los Angeles Times*, p. A13.

Snyder, H.N. & Sickmund, M. (1999). *Juvenile offenders and victims: 1999 annual Report.* Washington, D.C.: U.S. Department of Justice.

Stephens, R.D. (1999). *The National School Safety Center's report on school-associated violent deaths* [On-line]. Available: www.nssc1.org.

Sullivan v. River Valley School District, 197 F3d 804 (6th Cir 1999), cert denied, 120 S. Ct. 527 (1999).

Teen pleads guilty to e-mail threat. (2000, February 10). *Los Angeles Times*, p. A23.

Tomes, H. (1999, December). Preventing suicide: A call to action. *APA Monitor*, 39.

U.S. Department of Education. (1999). *1998 annual report on school safety.* Washington, D.C.: U.S. Department of Justice.

Vossekuil, B., Reddy, M., Fein, R., Borum, R., & Modzeleski, W. (2000). *U.S.S.S. Safe school initiative: An interim report on the prevention of targeted violence in schools.* Washington, D.C.: U.S. Secret Service, National Threat Assessment Center.

Wright, R.K. & Davis, J.H. (1977). Studies in the epidemiology of murder. *Journal of Forensic Sciences*, 22, 464-470.

Zona, M., Sharma, K., & Lane, J. (1993). A comparative study of erotomanic and obsessional subjects in a forensic sample. *Journal of Forensic Sciences*, 38, 894-903.

Recommended Resources

Additional Readings:

Borum, R. (2000). *Assessing violence risk among youth.* Journal of Clinical Psychology, 56, 1263-1288.

Ewing, C.P. (1990). *Kids who kill.* New York: Avon.

Goldstein, A.P. & Conoley, J.C. (Eds.) (1997). *School violence intervention.* New York: Guilford.

Gordon, D.A., Jurkovik, G., & Arbuthnot, J. (1998). Treatment of the juvenile offender. In R.M. Wettstein (Ed.), *Treatment of offenders with mental disorders* (pp. 365-428). New York: Guilford.

Grossman, D. & DeGaetano, G. (1999). *Stop teaching our kids to kill: A call to action against TV, movie, & video game violence.* New York: Crown.

Hatcher, C. (1994, 1995, 1996) Workplace Violence: A Risk Assessment Model. In G. Mathiason, S. Avila, et al. (Eds.), *Terror and Violence in the Workplace.* H. Littler, Mendelson: San Francisco.(1st, 2nd, & 3rd Editions).

IACP (1999). *Guide for preventing and responding to school violence.* U.S.: Bureau of Justice Assistance.

Johnson, K. (2000). *School crisis management: A hands-on guide to training crisis response teams.* Alameda, CA: Hunter House.

Meloy, J.R. (2000). *Violence risk and threat assessment.* San Diego: STS Publications.

Mitchell, J.T. & Resnik, H.L.P. (1986). *Emergency response to crisis.* Ellicott City, Maryland: Author.

Sells, S. P. (1998). *Treating the tough adolescent: A family-based, step by-step guide.* New York: Guilford.

Vossekuil, B., Reddy, M., Fein, R., Borum, R., & Modzeleski, W. (2000). *USSS Safe school initiative: An interim report on the prevention of targeted violence in schools.* Washington, D.C.: U.S. Secret Service, National Threat Assessment Center.

Legal Consultation:
Caplan & Earnest — 303-443-8010
Curiale Dellaverson Hirschfeld Kelly & Kraemer — 310-712-3082
Littler Mendelson — 415-433-1940
Takehara & Stuart — 310-260-6970

Crisis Management
Public Safety and Media Consulting — 661-287-3291
School Emergency Management Consultants — 303-771-6960

Security Consultation:
Advance Tech Security — 323-468-3767
Discreet Interventions — 818-865-0103
Kroll Associates — 213-687-2600
School Safety Consulting — 626-797-5101
wmitchel1@earthlink.net

Threat Assessment Consultation:
International Assessment Services — 415-512-1299

Training Resources:
Association of Threat Assessment Professionals — 213-473-7844
Specialized Training Services — 800-848-1226

Videos:
Youth Violence. Available to police. — 916-227-4892
Workplace Violence: The First Line of Defense. — 415-433-1940
The Killer at Thurston High. Available PBS. — 800-424-7963

Websites:
www.iacp.org
  IACP website to download school violence prevention guidelines.
www.forensis.org
  Contemporary research on targeted violence risk.
www.nssc1.org
  National School Safety Center website.
www.treas.gov/usss/ntac
  U.S.S.S. Safe School Initiative Research Document